POLITICAL TRIALS IN
ANCIENT GREECE

POLITICAL TRIALS IN ANCIENT GREECE

Richard A. Bauman

London and New York

First published 1990
by Routledge
11 New Fetter Lane, London EC4P 4EE

Simultaneously published in the USA and Canada
by Routledge
a division of Routledge, Chapman and Hall, Inc.
29 West 35th Street, New York, NY 10001

Set in 10/12pt Palatino by
Mews Photosetting, Beckenham, Kent
Printed in Great Britain by
Biddles Ltd, Guildford and King's Lynn

British Library Cataloguing in Publication Data
Bauman, Richard A.
Political trials in Ancient Greece.
1. Athenian empire. Law
I. Title
343.8'5

ISBN 0-415-00932-4

Library of Congress Cataloging in Publication Data
Bauman, Richard A.
Political trials in ancient Greece / Richard A. Bauman.
p.   cm.
Includes bibliographical references.
1. Trials (Political crimes and offenses) — Greece — Athens.
2. Trials (Political crimes and offenses) — Macedonia. I. Title.
LAW
345.38'0231–dc20   89-24203
[343.805231]
ISBN 0-415-00932-4

To Sheila

CONTENTS

CONTENTS

CONTENTS

PREFACE

This book sees the realization of a project long nurtured, an investigation in a Greek context of the theme of law and politics on which the writer has laboured for many years in a Roman context. The original plan was for a comparative study of Greek and Roman trials, but that did not prove to be practicable. Roman parallels do, however, play a part of some importance in the work. A number of striking similarities have been uncovered, one of which has prompted an amplification of the writer's theories concerning the origins of the *crimen maiestatis*. Also, the search for the origins of Hellenistic *asebeia* is a response to the extreme paucity of information on that subject encountered when working on the Roman equivalent some time ago. Roman parallels also bear significantly on the search for Greek *iuris consulti*, the domestication of international law, the evidence of slaves, posthumous trials, and the Macedonian *hostis* declaration.

The originality of the work resides in the first place in the overall scope. It is the first work to combine Athenian trials with those of another Greek state – a combination which is, if only because of the *asebeia* component, much more than a mere juxtaposition. It is also the first full-length work to make trials as a whole, rather than the law attested by trials, the main focus of attention. Hansen's case-book on illegal proposals covers the same period for Athens but is confined to the one category of charges; similar remarks apply to Roberts's book on accountability. Von Wedel's long article on Athenian trials

covers various categories of charges, but only for the fifth
century. A wealth of case material is supplied by such writers
as Thonissen, Bonner and Smith, Derenne, MacDowell, and
Ostwald, but the primary objective is the isolation of legal
rules; nor does the scope extend beyond Athens. Lipsius' case-
law is the weakest part of his book. Other works from which
I have benefited, such as those of Calhoun, Harrison, Jones,
Quass, Rhodes, Sealey, Sinclair, and Szegedy-Maszak, are
pointed towards principles rather than cases by their particular objectives. The trials of Alexander and his successors
are usually explored in articles covering particular trials,
but something more comprehensive is provided, within the
context of studies of the history of the period, by Berve,
Briant, Ferguson, Hammond, Hammond and Griffith, and
Schachermeyr.

On a more specific level the present work can claim originality for a number of new solutions to old problems, and also
for solutions to some problems that have not previously been
addressed at all. The solutions offered cover not only cases but
also institutions, such as the jurisdiction of the Areopagus, trials
by *synedria*, trials of communities, joint trials, and the personal
jurisdiction of the Macedonian king.

The book has been written with two classes of reader in mind
– the specialist in ancient history or law and the non-specialist.
In the interests of the latter technical discussion is kept, if not
down to a minimum, at least within reasonable bounds. Greek
names are uniformly Latinized; Thucydides the historian and
Thoukydides son of Melesias are a hazard to the uninitiated, and
even the trained observer pauses at Aiskhylos. The vexed question of whether to give Greek passages in the Greek alphabet or to
transliterate them has been solved by a compromise. Short technical phrases of up to four words are transliterated. Longer
passages are given for the most part in English, but in a few cases
where the Greek is indispenable to the argument the Greek
alphabet is used.

I wish to express my thanks to the anonymous reader who
read the manuscript for the publishers and commented ex-
tensively on the first six chapters; and to Dr J.L. O'Neil of the
University of Sydney, who read and commented on the chapters
on Macedon. A number of their suggestions have been incorporated. My thanks are also due to Mr Richard Stoneman, Senior

Editor at Routledge, for his unfailing courtesy and assistance throughout.

R.A.B.
Sydney,
June 1989

I

INTRODUCTION

1 THE SCOPE OF THE INVESTIGATION

Political trials are an important part of the history of any society, providing illumination in many areas besides the purely historical; its constitution, law, politics, foreign policy, and ethos can all be given a deeper perspective in the light of the information supplied by the criminal courts. Two matters need to be clarified at the outset. What do we mean by 'Greece', and what do we mean by 'political trials'?

For the fifth, and much of the fourth century BC, 'Greece' is primarily Athens; but for the last third of the fourth century the field broadens out to include Macedon. That is the scope of the present work. A few trials in other Greek cities will be included in the discussion, but lack of evidence precludes any broader canvas than Athens and Macedon. Even Sparta, whose law has recently been examined in some detail (MacDowell 1986), yields abstract law rather than concrete cases for the most part.

The present study divides broadly into three notional sections – fifth-century Athens, fourth-century Athens, and Macedon from Alexander to the end of the fourth century. The method of treatment differs for each of these sections. Fifth-century Athens lends itself quite naturally to a straight chronological coverage from the beginning of the century to the end, running in tandem with the whole history of the Athenian empire from the bright promise of its birth to the agony of its collapse. For a large part of the period the discussion focuses on the great empire-

1

builders, all of whom brushed against the criminal law at some stage of their careers: Miltiades, Themistocles, Cimon, Pericles – the trial-list reads like a roll of honour, for some of the cardinal features of the Athenian imperial idea were tested and debated in the courts. But until about the last third of the century the process was a fairly haphazard one, and it was not until Cleon that the political trial became a regular weapon in the politician's armoury. Unfortunately the weapon rapidly became a two-edged sword, and over the last fifteen years of the century the seemingly wild swings of the Demos in its judicial aspect contributed significantly to the final catastrophe.

Fourth-century Athens calls for a different approach. The essential feature of the period is no longer charisma; it is technique, professionalism. Special machinery had been installed in the hope of checking the excesses of the immediate past, and its use in political trials can best be illustrated by a thematic rather than a chronological approach. Four themes have been selected for this purpose. The first ushers in the fourth century by way of a survey of law reform at the turn of the fifth century. The second theme covers the calling to account of those who occupy public office, the third describes the trials of those who make illegal proposals, and the fourth discusses the *asebeia*, or impiety, trials over the period. The last-mentioned is part of a theme that runs across all three sections. Indeed, if any aspect of the work can be described as the major theme it is the elevation of crimes against the gods to the status of crimes against the state.

The third section reverts to a chronological approach, covering the trials of Alexander in Asia and the trials of the first successors down to Demetrius Poliorcetes. The section has two objectives: first, to cover the main political trials of the period; and second, within that coverage to examine some of the evidence for the initial phase in the evolution of Hellenistic *asebeia*. In the hands of the Hellenistic kings the crime of impiety underwent an important change in direction and emphasis; what had been an offence against the gods became an offence against the god-king. The change was only just beginning in our period, but some of the co-ordinates of the new dispensation are already visible.

Our next question, the meaning of 'political trials', does not

admit of an exact answer. Our situation is not unlike that of the philosophers, who cannot define their discipline 'but know when they
are doing it'. We are concerned with criminal trials and criminal
law, expressions which do not have exact Greek equivalents but are
useful signposts for what an Athenian might have defined as
wrongs affecting the community as a whole rather than particular
individuals. Even that is only a partial equivalent, since some acts
that we would regard as wrongs affecting the community, such as
homicide, were not so regarded in Athens, but the convenience of
the modern terminology outweighs the lack of exact equivalence, as
a number of writers have realized. In general, then, it can be said
that criminal process was employed to keep things on an even keel
to ward off threats to the security of the state. A society's perception
of what constitutes a threat to its security changes with the passage
of time, and some of the acts stigmatized as treason in antiquity
would be viewed with puzzlement, and even with Gilbertian
amusement, today. Nevertheless, to define political trials as trials
concerned with the security of the state sufficiently describes part
of the institution. But it is not a complete description, for it is also
true to say that political process was employed as a political
weapon, as an integral part of the game of politics. Very often an
accuser's main purpose was to bring down a public figure who in-
convenienced the accuser and his friends. If the charge was capital
the victim would be definitively removed from the arena, either by
being put to death or by being driven into exile. Even where the
penalty was sub-capital the prosecution could serve political ends
perfectly well: character-assassination was just as effective through
the medium of public court hearings as it is through the printed
and electronic media today. As for the type of offence brought up
in political trials, crimes against the state formed the bulk of the
material but were not the only criterion, for charges which were not
usually regarded as treason even in antiquity were freely used
against political opponents: corruption was one admirable surro-
gate, and the grey area between offences against the gods and
offences against the state was another.

2 THE LAW APPLICABLE TO POLITICAL TRIALS

At this point it is appropriate to make a preliminary survey of
as much of the criminal law of Athens as bears on political
trials.[1] Early Athenian law categorized crimes procedurally

rather than substantively: defining the crime was less important than identifying the court or procedure by which offenders were brought to book. This opened the way to many anomalies, such as the fact that an offence could often be charged under different procedures carrying different penalties, so that two men guilty of the same crime might atone for it in vastly different ways. Anomalies like this, and the extraordinary resistance of Athenian procedure to all modern attempts to give it coherence and clarity, have caused one assiduous investigator to declare that the result of modern research 'is to a certain extent a muddled account but I fear that a clear one would be a wrong one'.[2] We might well prefer to keep procedure down to a minimum, to concentrate on what an offender did rather than on how he was punished for it, but some understanding of the procedure is essential.

The problem is partly historical, in that institutions surviving from ancient times continued to operate in the fifth-century democracy alongside new procedures. Thus the council of ex-archons known as the Areopagus continued until the mid-fifth century to exercise a function which Aristotle describes as watching over the laws, controlling the major concerns of the community, and punishing and fining offenders of all kinds. As a result of Ephialtes' reforms it is said to have lost its guardianship of the constitution and other powers, but to have retained jurisdiction in homicide cases.[3] Another jurisdiction that remained active in the fifth century was that of the *thesmothetae* who presided over a large volume of cases and were one of the most important criminal jurisdictions. Mention should also be made of the *basileus*, the successor to the religious functions of the old kings, and as such vested with jurisdiction (concurrently with other jurisdictions) over impiety and homicide.[4]

The great watershed in criminal justice was believed by later generations to have been the reforms of Solon at the turn of the seventh century. He was credited with laying the foundations for criminal law proper by substituting public prosecution for private vengeance; this he did by allowing a *graphē*, or public lawsuit, to be launched by any citizen, whether or not he had been personally injured by the wrong. But in Aristotle's opinion Solon's most important reform was the right of appeal (*ephesis*) 'to the law-court' – *eis to dikastērion* (*AP* 9.1). The 'law-court' was probably the Heliaea, which appears to have been the name applied to the Assembly known as the Ecclesia (and also com-

4

monly referred to as 'the Demos') when it sat as a court. The 'appeal' was either an appeal proper against the judgment of a magistrate sitting as a court of first instance, or a remittal to the Demos of any case in which a penalty in excess of the magistrate's competence was sought. In order to entrench his reforms Solon reputedly prescribed a penalty of *atimia* (roughly 'infamy') for any attempt to repeal or amend his laws.[5]

The most important advance on the Solonic system was the creation of *dikastēria*, jury-courts manned by jurors drawn from a panel of 6,000 citizens, which was chosen annually by lot.[6] But the Heliaea appears not have ceased to function as a court despite the new institution of the *dikastēria*. Cases falling under the jurisdiction of the *thesmothetae* seem to have come either before the full Heliaea or before a jury two or three times as large as usual; expressions like 'the Heliaea of the *thesmothetae*' and 'the *dikastērion* of the *thesmothetae*' occur.[7] Judicial powers were also exercised by the Boule, or Council of Five Hundred, established by Cleisthenes. Aristotle says that it once had the power to punish by fines, imprisonment, or death, but subsequently it was restricted to fines up to 500 drachmae, and anything above that limit had to be brought before the *dikastērion* by the *thesmothetae* (*AP* 45.1).

It becomes relevant at this point to say something about the remedy known as ostracism. It was not a trial, but when the Demos met, with a quorum of at least 6,000 citizens, to vote the banishment for ten years of a citizen deemed to be threatening the stability of the state, it was imposing a quasi-judicial punishment on him. But the principles of natural justice were flouted, because the proposed exile was not heard in his defence, nor was there any debatement of charges to guide the Demos to a just decision. The attack on Alcibiades attributed to Andocides includes a scathing denunciation of ostracism (Andoc. 4.3–6). The dislike of the institution to which that passage testifies is perfectly understandable. If a death sentence imposed by the Boule in 403 could be stigmatized as *akritos* because it was not ratified (*AP* 40.2), then *a fortiori* a process in which there was no trial at all was open to attack. Nevertheless ostracism is so closely linked to the fifth-century trials that some of the cases will be incorporated in our discussion.

We may now address the substantive criminal law. Political trials were based largely, though not exclusively, on charges of treason, but it is not easy to plot the parameters of that crime

5

in Athenian law. The Romans devised a single, unified concept, the crime of diminishing the *maiestas*, or 'greaterness', of the Roman people, and they subsumed under that broad umbrella all acts which endangered the state in both its external and its internal aspects.[8] The Athenians had no comparable umbrella. They had a general word, *prodosia*, which covered external treason in various forms, such as treachery and betrayal of one's country. But for internal treason, in the shape of acts subversive of the state or of its system of government, there was a different set of laws with different labels. Solon empowered the Areopagus to try anyone who sought to deprive the people of their sovereign rights; the crime was known as *katalysis tou dēmou*. There was a late sixth-century law sanctioning any attempt to set up a tyranny, and the constitution was also protected by laws punishing anyone who proposed a law which was contrary to an existing law, or misled the Demos, or improperly aroused its expectations.[9] There was also a law cast in very general terms penalizing anyone who wronged the Athenian people; if Xenophon (*Hell.* 1.7.20) correctly reflects the text of that law it ranks as a broader umbrella than anything that Rome devised.[10] Laws against impiety also belong here; they were used in political trials at Athens long before they became the criterion for Hellenistic treason.

Of the various forms of criminal process, the first calling for mention is *eisangelia*, 'laying an information' or 'impeaching'. An information was laid before the Boule or the Ecclesia, which either tried the case or remitted it to a jury-court (*dikastērion*). The informant usually acted as prosecutor at the trial. One of the interesting features of *eisangelia* is that the preliminary hearing by the Boule or Ecclesia gave the informant a first, and uncontradicted, bite at the cherry. Another process, *mēnysis*, was also initiated by laying an information, but the informant did not prosecute at the trial; the process was thus favoured by accomplices seeking immunity, non-citizens, and women. The most common type of public process was the *graphē*, an action before a jury-court which it was open to any citizen to bring; something like fifty different types of *graphē* were known, including the *graphē paranomōn* against the proposer of a law which ran counter to an existing law. Other processes will be noticed in due course, but mention may be made here of *euthynai*, the scrutiny of an official's administration at the end of his term of office; it could, and often did, generate a criminal trial.[11]

A wide range of punishments was known. The penalty was

sometimes laid down by the relevant *nomos*,[12] as in the law of *prodosia* (Xen. *Hell.* 1.7.22), but at other times the court had a discretion which it exercised after hearing proposals from the accuser and the accused. The most severe penalty was death. Next came *atimia*, originally a decree of outlawry, but by the late fifth century entailing only the loss of civic rights. Exile could be imposed as a specific sentence but also served as a voluntary means of avoiding trial; similarly imprisonment was both a sentence and a means of securing the accused's attendance. These penalties, all somatic,[13] were supplemented by ancillary punishments – confiscation of property, denial of burial rights in Attica, loss of civic rights by descendants. The most common penalty of all was the non-somatic fine; it was sometimes so heavy as to be comparable to confiscation, and was available as a substitute for a somatic penalty in some cases.

3 LAWYERS, LEGAL SCIENCE, AND POLITICAL TRIALS

Two questions arise, the second of which has received very little attention in the literature. Who appeared in court to argue cases, and how was the law applicable to a case ascertained? The answer to the first question is that as a general rule both the accuser and the accused had to speak for themselves; no legal ban on representation is known,[14] but custom frowned on it. A party did, however, have access to two types of assistance. He might arrange for a speech to be written for him by a *logographos*, which he himself would then deliver at the trial; the first speech-writer was probably Antiphon in the second half of the fifth century. Or he might call on supporting speakers (*synēgoroi*) who would use the unexpired time on his water-clock;[15] the *synēgoros* would deliver either a short epilogue or, in important cases, an exposition of points raised by his principal in the main speech.[16] There were two cases in which official appointments of speakers were made. In an *eisangelia* process the Assembly might name joint accusers up to ten, though this practice ceased at some time in the fourth century when a definitive *eisangelia* statute was enacted;[17] and when a retiring magistrate's accounts were found to be unsatisfactory the ten auditors (*logistai*) might be assisted by ten *synēgoroi* in bringing the defaulter to trial.[18]

Our second question, as to how the law applicable to a case

was ascertained, is partly answered by the generally accepted statement that statutes had to be proved just as much as facts; both were treated as evidence, hence the frequent injunctions to the registrar in court speeches: 'Read me the law.' In the fourth century (if not before) the speech-writers were notorious for misquotations and citations of irrelevant and sometimes invented laws which propped up a client's case. That much is common cause. But what needs to be considered is the interpretation of the laws. The speech-writer (or the speaker where, as quite often, a Demosthenes or an Aeschines appeared personally as a party to the case) needed to include a particular interpretation in the speech, and the question is whether he had to rely purely on the rhetorical canons of interpretation known to his craft or whether there was a body of legal science, of jurisprudence, assembled by legal experts rather than by orators. In other words, did the Athenians have an equivalent to the Roman *iuris consultus* who practised public consultation and gave *responsa* which ranked as a source of law?[19]

Most scholars would give a negative answer,[20] and for much of our period they would be right. Greek law cannot boast of anything like the *Corpus Iuris* that Rome bequeathed to the world. There is a relative abundance of literary material – epic poems, plays, histories, court speeches, philosophical discourses – a few local codes and, for Ptolemaic Egypt, a wealth of papyri, but that is as far as it goes. It is true that the orators in particular are a fertile source of information, and one recalls that reconstructions of the law in the Roman Republic rely heavily on Cicero,[21] but the Justinianic compilations are always there to supplement and clarify what Cicero says. There is no similar check for Demosthenes. It is generally concluded that Greece did not possess anything to compare with the legal science evolved by Rome, and the reason is taken to be the absence of a legal profession, meaning trained lawyers as distinct from orators who happened to have acquired a store of practical knowledge.[22] The orators did develop a comprehensive set of rhetorical canons for interpreting statutes, such as analogy and intention versus literal meaning,[23] but that does not qualify as a legal science. One of the reasons is that the orators argued one way today and the diametrically opposite way tomorrow, quoting (or misquoting) the laws that favoured the particular point being made at the time and throwing consistency to the winds. This technique of arguing *in utramque partem* was quite inconsistent with jurisprudence; it produced victories in court, not legal norms. The Roman orators inherited the Greek rhetorical canons, but precisely because of the jurisconsults there was a brake on their enthusiasms. Can we hope to find a braking mechanism in Greece?

The assumption that one would like to validate is that in a society as sophisticated as fifth- and fourth-century Athens there must have been *someone* who regarded the law as a serious discipline rather than as a game of musical chairs. One possibility is the *thesmothetae*, who were not only straightforward jurisdictional magistrates. They had another function as well, though opinions differ as to what it was. According to Aristotle they publicly recorded *thesmia* and preserved them for the trials of litigants (*AP* 3.4). *Thesmia* have been taken to mean either customary law, or decisions of the thesmothetes or others in individual cases (law reports?).[24] It is also thought that in the fourth century they searched annually for contradictions in the law and initiated procedures to iron out anomalies, but that seems to encroach on the preserves of the *nomothetae*.[25] In any case the thesmothetes were annually elected magistrates, while the nomothetes were not even that, being selected by lot for a tenure of only one day at a time. What we are looking for is a free-wheeling professional cadre which was permanently in place.[26]

The best guess is a particular line of philosophers starting with Theophrastus, who succeeded Aristotle as head of the Peripatetic School in 322. Works such as Plato's *Laws* belong to legal philosophy rather than to 'lawyers' law', and the latter is what is needed for the formation of any legal science.[27] It has been surmised that the work written by Theophrastus under the title of *Nomoi* combined philosophical ideas about what the law should be with a practical exposition of what it actually was,[28] and the fragments bear this out.[29] There is one striking illustration of Theophrastus' approach in the field of criminal law. According to the *Lexicon Rhetoricum Cantabrigiense*, Caecilius, a rhetorician in the first century BC, said that the *eisangelia* process was used for new crimes for which no law existed (*kainoi kai agraphoi*), but in the fourth book of his *Nomoi* Theophrastus gave a precise and comprehensive statement of the scope of *eisangelia*; he included therein undermining the Demos, taking bribes to make proposals to the assembly not in the best interests of the Demos, betraying forts, and naval and land forces, communicating with the enemy

9

without the authority of the Demos, and living amongst the enemy or serving with him as a mercenary.[30] The difference between the two approaches is unmistakable. Caecilius the rhetorician did not feel any need for precise norms; the vaguer the concept was, the more scope there was for free interpretation. But Theophrastus the jurist could not tolerate the idea of legal rules being in free fall. He may or may not have been reciting the actual text of the troublesome *eisangelia* statute of the mid-fourth century,[31] but he was certainly able to bring internal and external treason under one roof, a combination that had hitherto eluded the Athenians. The new, streamlined legal approach that had made its appearance in the last decade of the fifth century[32] continued to gain momentum in the fourth, and Theophrastus was able to capitalize on it in his writings. He also showed the way to others, for when his friend and pupil Demetrius of Phalerum carried out a comprehensive programme of law reform over 317–307 he incorporated many of Theophrastus' ideas in his reforms.[33] When these two friends of Macedon were joined by the Macedonian Craterus, compiler of a collection of Athenian *psēphismata* in at least nine books,[34] something of a special interest in legal science began to take shape.[35] It was not for nothing that Demetrius, the most politically prominent of the three, was recognized as the third lawgiver of Athens after Dracon and Solon (Syncellus 521).

The basis, then, on which we go forward is that for most of our period the law applicable to political trials was in the hands of amateurs, some of them better informed and more honest than others, but none of them ranking as professional lawyers. In so far as there was any restraint on them it was imposed by the thesmothetes, but we can do little more than note that possibility; concrete examples are not available. Even more shadowy are the restraints imposed on forensic oratory by the transfer of the legislative function from the Ecclesia to the nomothetes at some time in the fourth century. In any event none of this amounts to a legal science. It was only right at the end of our period that something like such a science began to emerge, and even then its effect on political trials is hypothetical: Theophrastus himself was paralysed with fright when he was charged with impiety. Probably the most important influence on future developments, including those in the area of Hellenistic *asebeia*, was exerted by Demetrius of Phalerum. After his expulsion from Athens he

10

compiled a law code for Ptolemy Soter, later Ptolemy I of Egypt,[36] and Ptolemy played a crucial role in the evolution of Hellenistic *asebeia*.

II

FIFTH-CENTURY ATHENS: EARLY EMPIRE-BUILDERS AND THE COURTS

1 PRELIMINARY

Fifth-century Athenian trials ought to run without interruption from the beginning of the century to the end, from the eve of Marathon, through the rise of the empire and down to the long agony of the war and defeat. But there is reason to subdivide the period into three parts. There is a hiatus of some two decades between the first phase in the Athenian perception of empire, when the trials of Phrynichus, Miltiades, Themistocles, and Cimon were held, and the second phase, which is ushered in, forensically speaking, by the reform of the Areopagus, and continues down to the death of Cleon. The hiatus may be no more than an accident of transmission, but it does correspond to a broad dividing-line between the end of haphazard amateurism and the start of systematic imperialism. The third subdivision, from 415 to the end of the century, also follows a hiatus in political trials; but the cases from 415 more than make up for that, supplying a micro-cosm of the whole tragedy of the decline and collapse.

2 PHRYNICHUS AND ORDER IN THE MARKET-PLACE

We open our account with the case of the tragic poet Phrynichus. The fall of Miletus in 494 BC marked the end of the Ionian revolt against Persia and the deferment of the idea of a Grand Alliance of Ionians led by Athens. Phrynichus, a possible rival to Thespis

12

as the inventor of tragedy, produced a play entitled *Milētou Halōsis*, 'The Sack of Miletus', at the Dionysia of 493; it may have been the first drama to draw its theme from contemporary history instead of mythology. The piece so moved the audience with its graphic portrayal of the disaster that had befallen Miletus – the men put to death, the women and children enslaved and the sanctuary at Didyma destroyed – that the whole theatre burst into tears (Hdt. 6.19.3, 21.2). According to the scholiast on Aristophanes (*Wasps* 1490), Phrynichus was greeted with a torrent of abuse and slunk off the stage like a frightened rooster. He was fined 1,000 drachmae for reminding the people of their misfortunes, and the further production of the play was banned forever (Hdt. 6.21.2). It has been surmised that the ban did not merely relate to theatrical performances but was some sort of *memoriae damnatio* precluding further dissemination of any kind.[1]

It has been argued, with every justification, that the case was politically motivated. It is seen as the pro-Persian faction's reply to Themistocles, who is said to have urged Phrynichus to write the piece in order to stir up anti-Persian sentiment and to promote Themistocles' naval policy.[2] That attitudes towards Persia were prominent in the politics of the 490s is clear enough, and that Themistocles was in a position to commission the piece is probable: he was Phrynichus' friend and would be the *chorēgus* of a winning play of his in 476 (Plut. *Them.* 5.4). But Phrynichus may have gone further than Themistocles intended, for a late source says that what mainly upset the audience was the fact that the playwright's motive was not consolation but reproach for Athens' failure to stand by her former colony (Ammian. 28.1.4).

What was the legal basis of the charge? It has been argued that the disturbance caused by the play profaned the festival of Dionysus at which it was being performed and thus amounted to impiety/*asebeia*.[3] But that needs careful consideration, for this is one of the cases in which identification of the process employed is of paramount importance in identifying the charge. It is said that the process known as *probolē* ('a putting forward') was used,[4] but there are hidden shoals in that hypothesis. *Probolē* was used in three types of case – profanation of festivals, unfulfilled promises to the people, and sycophancy; it generated a preliminary hearing by the Ecclesia, but for a definitive verdict there had to be a trial in the court of the *thesmothetae*.[5] Specifically on profanation

13

cases, Demosthenes notes four examples of the use of *probolē*, including the assault on him when he was a *chorēgus* at the Dionysia, and in all those cases the wrong is perpetrated against an individual, not against the Demos (Dem. 21.175–80). A law cited by Demosthenes restricts *probolē* based on profanation to the injured party (ibid., 10). But Phrynichus' offence concerned the whole Demos, and we therefore need a process which was less restricted as far as the right of prosecution was concerned. A question that has not been asked before may guide us to a solution: Who were the accusers in Phrynichus' case?

The answer that I propose is to be found in the prosaic confines of a particular magistracy, the *agoranomoi*. This is suggested by the first case of *maiestas minuta* at Rome, for if that momentous innovation owed anything to Athens the debt will have been owing specifically to the *agoranomoi*. It will be appropriate to glance briefly at the Roman parallel before discussing the *agoranomoi*. In 246 BC Claudia was jostled by the crowd when leaving the theatre. She ill-temperedly regretted that her brother was not there to reduce the rabble, as he had done when losing a fleet at Drepana three years before. She was prosecuted by the plebeian aediles (not, as one might have expected, by the tribunes) and was sentenced to a heavy fine.[6] The aediles were market-masters and Claudia had reminded the people of their misfortunes in much the same way as Phrynichus had done.

We may now address the *agoranomoi*. They were responsible for the maintenance of honest standards in the market-place, and their duties included the maintenance of order in the Agora. They had jurisdiction over crimes up to a maximum fine of, probably, fifty drachmae, and for anything over that limit they had to remit a proposal to the Demos.[7] This should be linked with the fact that the early dramas were performed in the Agora rather than in a theatre located somewhere else.[8] As Phrynichus was very close in time to the origins of tragic drama, we seem to have a situation in which the peace and quiet of the Agora was violently disturbed by the audience's reaction to *The Sack of Miletus*. The disturbance occurred within the area of jurisdiction of the *agoranomoi*, and they took action against Phrynichus. But the mass hysteria that had been provoked by the play called for a fine of considerably more than fifty drachmae, and the *agoranomoi* proposed a fine of 1,000 drachmae to the people. That figure may have been a mandatory amount laid down by law rather than an assessment by the market-masters. Demosthenes notes that if a *chorēgus* queries the citizenship of a rival *choreutēs* he is liable to a fine of fifty drachmae, but if he has the stranger expelled from the chorus the penalty is 1,000 drachmae (Dem. 21.56). And Plutarch cites a fourth-century *nomos* which prescribed a penalty of 1,000 for having a foreigner in the chorus (*Phoc.* 30.3). Although the *agoranomoi* were no longer responsible for law and order at dramatic performances in the fourth century, it is a fair guess that during their period of responsibility similar penalties of fifty and 1,000 drachmae, depending on the seriousness of the breach, had been in operation. It is also possible that the law[9] gave the *agoranomoi* a general mandate to maintain order in the Agora, in which case they may have acted independently of the Demos as far as banning further performances of Phrynichus' play was concerned. The ban will thus have been a purely administrative act, and might have included a refusal to allow copies of the play to be exposed for sale in the Agora.

Does the introduction of the *agoranomoi* into the equation affect our belief that the case was politically motivated? Did they bring a routine charge in the ordinary course of their duties, or were they moved by animosity towards Themistocles and his friends? A routine prosecution would appeal to von Wedel, who argues that the Demos adhered rigidly to existing laws even though it meant imposing punishments which ran counter to its own convictions.[10] Von Wedel does not offer any suggestions as to the nature of the proceedings or the content of the law, but on our terms it would be a case of the people approving of the strict performance of their duties by officials, regardless of personalities. Whether that is in fact what happened it is not possible to say, for we do not have any controls by which to determine the usual practice of the *agoranomoi*. But two things are clear: Phrynichus was a friend of Themistocles, and he knew exactly what he was doing when he injected such a strong note of pathos into his play. He knew that the worst that could happen was a fine of exactly 1,000 drachmae, which was far from exorbitant, judging by Demades who cheerfully paid the fines for 100 foreigners whom he had included in his chorus, at the rate of 1,000 drachmae for each foreigner (Plut. *Phoc.* 30). By comparison, Phrynichus' fine was a small price to pay. Something had to be done to counteract the medising of the Peisistratid, Hipparchus, as archon in 496–5, and indeed a return on Phrynichus' investment was not long in coming. Themistocles was elected archon later in the same year, and Phrynichus himself was subsequently chosen as a *stratēgos*, perhaps at the time of his victory in the dramatic competition of 476; Aelian (*Var. Hist.* 3.8) does not date Phrynichus' election as *stratēgos*, but he does say that he was chosen because of the warlike songs and dances in his plays, and 476 marks the start of the intense military fervour that followed Athens' appointment as leader of the Delian League.

Our conclusion is that not only did *The Sack of Miletus* probably have a political motivation, so did the prosecution of its author; it was a political riposte rather than a routine enforcement of law and order. One is tempted to suggest that there was a similar riposte in the dramatic sphere, for if the play which brought Phrynichus victory in 476 was his *Phoenician Women*, and if that play dealt with the same theme of Persia's defeat as Aeschylus' *Persians*,[11] there may have been a sharp contrast between the rabid chauvinism of Phrynichus' piece and the more thoughtful portrayal of the Persians by Aeschylus. This may imply an ideological difference between the imperialist firebrand ('Old Blood 'n Guts') and the traditionalist whose enthusiasm for democracy was more restrained. But this is only a conjecture.[12]

3 THE TWO TRIALS OF MILTIADES

The year of Phrynichus' trial also saw the first of the two trials of Miltiades, that flamboyant buccaneer so reminiscent of the Elizabethan corsairs at a comparable stage of their country's history. In the late sixth century the Peisistratids sent Miltiades to the Thracian Chersonese (the modern Gallipoli) to watch over Athenian interests, and according to some accounts to found a colony. Miltiades gave his mandate a liberal interpretation, imprisoning local Greek dignitaries, surrounding himself with a bodyguard of 500 mercenaries, marrying a Thracian princess, and virtually playing the independent ruler (Hdt. 6.39). On the credit side he is said to have settled large numbers of Athenians in the Chersonese and to have wrested Lemnos from Persia and handed it over to Athens. But by 493 the collapse of the Ionian revolt made his situation untenable, and after a series of hair-raising adventures he managed to reach Athens. Arriving soon after Phrynichus' trial, he was attacked by his enemies and put on trial on a charge of 'tyranny in the Chersonese'. But the court (the

Areopagus rather than the Heliaea)[13] acquitted him and he was elected *stratēgos* (Hdt. 6.104.2). Three years later he repulsed the first Persian invasion at Marathon.

The charge of tyranny raises some interesting questions. At some point in his chequered career Miltiades had become a vassal of the Persian king and had taken part in the Scythian campaign,[14] but his accusers were apparently unable to base a charge of *prodosia* on that.[15] Yet it may have been brought up at the trial in order to create prejudice against Miltiades, and when we are told that he advised the Greeks to destroy the Danube bridge[16] we may well think that this was a submission by Miltiades himself at the trial, by which he hoped to counteract the adverse inference sought by the accusers. More to the point, how could Miltiades' actions in Thrace have been seen as a threat to the *Athenian* constitution? Opinions are divided on this question. Some see the legal anomaly as so insuperable that they argue that there was no trial, but only a routine examination (*dokimasia*) prior to Miltiades' assumption of office as *stratēgos*, and it was at that examination that the Chersonese tyranny was raised in order to show that he was not a fit and proper person for the office of general.[17] Others argue that his 'subjects' in Thrace consisted partly of Athenian citizens and partly of non-Athenians, and it was in respect of the former that tyranny was charged.[18] In favour of this theory is the fact that personality of law – one set of laws for locals and another for Greeks – was well known in Ptolemaic Egypt, for example, and could have had an Athenian predecessor. But in the last resort the two theories may lead to much the same result. This is because the *dokimasia* of archons-elect included what Aristotle describes as 'referral to the court' (*ephesis eis to dikastērion*) in the course of which witnesses were called, charges were framed and the defence was given a hearing (*AP* 55.2–4). A similar examination can be postulated for *stratēgoi*, in which case Herodotus 6.104.2 could be referring to a *dokimasia*, and that would have been tantamount to a trial anyway.

Was Miltiades' acquittal the result of legal interpretation or political pressure? If the former, the court will have anticipated the question that worries modern investigators, it will simply have held that tyrannical acts in Thrace were not breaches of Athenian law. To the second question, the role of political pressure, the short answer is that we have no direct evidence as to the identity of Miltiades' accuser. But Xanthippus, an Alcmaeonid connection and father of Pericles, was the accuser at Miltiades' second trial and may have discharged the same function at the first; personal rivalry between the Alcmaeonids and the Philaid clan to which Miltiades belonged was real enough.[19] Miltiades' supporters may have included Themistocles; though well to the left of Miltiades on the political spectrum, he may have shared his vigorous anti-Persian sentiments.[20] The alliance, if such there was, helped Themistocles to secure an archonship soon after the case.

Miltiades' second trial is better documented than his first, but that is by no means an unmixed blessing. We possess two accounts of the case, by Herodotus and Nepos; the latter is largely a reflection of Ephorus.[21] Herodotus says that after Marathon Miltiades asked the Athenians for seventy ships, an army, and money; he did not disclose his destination but said that he would lead them to a land rich in gold. He was given his armada and sailed against Paros in the Cyclades, alleging that the Parians had helped the Persians at Marathon; but in reality he had a private grudge against a Parian. When Paros refused to pay an indemnity of 100 talents he laid siege to the city. At this point Herodotus says that he is switching from a Panhellenic to a Parian source. On the advice of a captured Parian priestess Miltiades made his way into the sanctuary of the temple of Demeter, but he took fright and ran out again, and was injured while making his escape. After twenty-six days he raised the siege and returned to Athens with neither treasure nor Paros to show for his pains. Xanthippus charged him before the people with deceiving the Athenians and demanded the death penalty. Miltiades was present in court, lying on a stretcher, but he could not speak because his wound had turned gangrenous. His friends spoke for him and made much of Marathon and Lemnos. The people 'stood by him by rejecting the death penalty', but fined him fifty talents. He died of his injuries and the fine was paid by his son Cimon.

The Ephorus–Nepos version seems at first sight to refer to quite a different case. Miltiades is given the armada in order to punish islands that had helped Persia; there is no mention of a land rich in gold. Some islands are reduced, but Paros holds out. The siege goes well until a grove catches fire on nearby Myconos; Miltiades takes this as a signal to the defenders from the Persians, breaks off the siege and returns to Athens. He is charged with *prodosia* on the grounds that he was bribed by the Persians. The account of the actual trial agrees partly with Herodotus, but Nepos has the injured Miltiades defended by his brother who was in fact already dead, he makes the fifty talents the cost of the seventy ships,[22] and he has Miltiades die in prison; there is no mention of Cimon paying the fine. Nepos adds that the Chersonese tyranny was brought up at the trial and this, rather than Paros, was responsible for the verdict, though Nepos denies that Miltiades had acted tyranically.

Plato introduces another problem. According to him the people in fact voted a death sentence but the presiding *prytanis* overruled them (*Gorgias* 516D–E). But Demosthenes cites an ancient law: 'If anyone deceives the people by promising them something he is to be tried, and if convicted is to be sentenced to death' (Dem. 20.135). *Prima facie*, then, if this or a similar law was in force as early as 489 the death sentence was mandatory and there was no room for a counter-proposal sounding in money.

The conflict between Herodotus and Ephorus–Nepos has produced much expenditure of ink but no consensus. It is clear that if Miltiades promised to lead them to a land rich in gold he did not mean Paros; that island was noted (later) for its marble, but not for gold. Thasos possessed gold-mines in Thrace, but Miltiades did not lead them to Thasos. Thus the inducement, if made, was a deception. But it has been argued that gold was not the objective at all; Athens is said to have had ambitions in the Cyclades, either to straddle the route of the expected second Persian invasion or to continue the expansionist policy initiated at Lemnos, and Miltiades was a general acting in an official capacity and preserving secrecy in the interests of his mandate. A variant of this view denies that he acted in an official capacity: he made a contract with the Demos to enrich them in return for an armada with which he hoped to set up a personal tyranny on Paros.[23] It can be conceded that if Athens did not have ambitions in the Cyclades a commercial bargain is possible, but an official interest in the region is more likely. It is affirmed unequivocally by Ephorus–Nepos, and despite his Alcmaeonid bias even Herodotus says (though he considers it a pretext) that Miltiades claimed to be bringing a mediser to heel. Herodotus also observes that he brought back neither treasure nor Paros; clearly either would have sufficed.

It is probable, then, that Miltiades led an official expedition to the Cyclades in 489, but for security reasons he concealed this from the people and obtained their authority by a promise of enrichment. The expedition may well have been a replica in miniature of the future Delian League – primarily strategic but potentially expansionist. To this extent Ephorus–Nepos do better than Herodotus, but on the actual trial the latter's version rings true. There is no reason to doubt his description of the charge; no source would have invented a crime of misleading the Athenians. But does this mean that the charge of *prodosia* in Ephorus–Nepos[24] has to be dismissed as a falsification or was there in fact more than one charge?

Bearing in mind that this was the earliest known trial before the Heliaea,[25] let us review the possible course of events after Miltiades' return to Athens. Xanthippus charges 'misleading the Athenians' and claims that the false inducement caused the people to vote the armada. Thus fraudulent misrepresentation was elevated to the status of a crime against the state (as it would be at Rome).[26] But the accusers were not certain of the legal effect of the fraud, for Pompeius Trogus, writing in Augustus' reign, is said to have described the charge as *peculatus*, theft of state property (Justin 2.15). Presumably Trogus found *klopē dēmosiōn* in his source. We also have it from Nepos that the fifty talents represented the cost of the ships, and if the crime was seen as theft by false pretences we have a penalty which amounted, in effect, to returning the stolen property.[27]

If the legal implications of the fraudulent promise were so uncertain, it is possible that the crime of misleading the people was not yet on the statute-book and was charged for the first time at Miltiades' trial. Bonner and Smith so argue, taking as their starting-point the *psēphisma* of Cannonus, which is described by Xenophon as an extremely harsh decree whereunder anyone who wrongs the people is to plead his case in chains, and if condemned is to be thrown into 'the Pit' (*barathron*) and to have his property confiscated.[28] The date of the decree is not later than 489.[29]

Two points can be adduced in support of Bonner and Smith. First, the law's prescription of 'the Pit' is echoed in Plato's reference to the case (*Gorgias* 516D–E). Second, Miltiades' death in prison can well mean that the family fortune was no longer available, having been confiscated under Cannonus' *psēphisma*, leaving it to Cimon to retrieve the family's honour by funds obtained elsewhere.[30] But how, it will be asked, could a law concerning 'doing wrong to the people' have generated a charge of 'misleading the people'? This is explained by Bonner and Smith, who argue that the *psēphisma* dealt generally with *adikia*, 'wrongdoing', leaving particular cases to be interpreted into that category as the occasion arose; 'misleading the Athenians' was one of those cases. We accordingly conclude that the law on misleading the people known to Demosthenes (Dem. 20.135) is not the law under which Miltiades was charged; the Demosthenic law came later. It applied not only to misleading the Demos but also to misleading the Boule or a *dikastērion* (ibid., 20.100), from which we may infer that the concept of *apatē tou dēmou* ('misleading the people') was detached from the *adikia* law at some time subsequent to Miltiades' trial, and put on a broader basis in order to restrain the excesses of orators in a variety of circumstances.[31] The *ad hoc* weapon against Miltiades became a general rule of conduct.

There remains the charge of *prodosia*. Where did Ephorus get the idea that there had been such a charge? The answer can only be that *prodosia* was brought up as a separate count in the indictment. It may even have been the original charge with which *adikia/apatē* was joined when the weakness of the case for betrayal became apparent. (Nepos virtually admits that the *prodosia/proditio* charge failed.) An intelligent member of the prosecuting team cast around for a second string to his bow and found the right answer in fraud.

The two trials of Miltiades are one of the most important events of the first half of the fifth century. Two legal innovations, extraterritoriality and treasonable fraud, were canvassed in quick succession, and the political currents were equally strong. The basic message, as Ephorus-Nepos knew but Herodotus did not, was that though the aristocratic clans still retained a grip on power, the gap between democratic theory and reality was shrinking. It was not only to gratify the Alcmaeonids that the Demos turned on the hero of Marathon. The accusers needed some strong medicine to counteract the people's memory of the battle, and they found it in the fear of tyranny, as Nepos realized. By reminding their audience of the Chersonese they played on an ancient phobia and got a strong reaction. Even Marathon itself fuelled fears of tyranny: Themistocles is said to have declared that Miltiades' fame kept him awake at nights (Plut. *Them.* 3.4). So strong was the popular feeling against tall poppies that it was, if Plato is to be believed, only the mysterious intervention of the

21

prytanis that saved Miltiades from a death sentence voted by the people.[32]

Miltiades' case was not an isolated reaction against tyranny, for it was followed about a year later (488-7) by the first known use of ostracism, when Hipparchus, archon in 496-5 and the leading Peisistratid of the day, was banished (*AP* 22.3-4). Ostracism solved the problem of how to deal with Hipparchus, 'the man who had done no harm during the troubles' and had been exempted from the banishment imposed on most of Peisistratus' family.[33] There being nothing more susbstantial than suspicion against him, and no windfall like Miltiades' deception being on offer, no formal criminal charge could hope to succeed. But ostracism, involving as it did neither charges nor defence, was an admirable substitute. It is only fair to say, however, that sidestepping the burden of proof was not the only purpose of the new institution,[34] for it allowed the exile to retain his property and his civic rights. In any event the sponsors of Hipparchus' ostracism were vindicated eight years later when he refused to respond to the amnesty offered to exiles and joined Xerxes. He was impeached by *eisangelia* and tried *in absentia* (probably by the Areopagus) on a charge of *prodosia*. He was sentenced to death, but as he was not available for execution they melted down his statue on the Acropolis and turned it into a plaque on which the names of traitors were inscribed.[35]

4 THEMISTOCLES: THE DOMESTICATION OF INTERNATIONAL LAW

Ostracism is part of the forensic history of Themistocles. The broad lines of the story emerging from a hopelessly confused tradition are that he was ostracised in 472-1[36] and took up residence in Argos; thereafter, perhaps a year or two later, he was tried *in absentia* for *prodosia* connected with the activities of the Spartan Pausanias. His punishment was either death or perpetual banishment for both himself and his family, and he also suffered confiscation and denial of burial rights in Attica. He failed to find asylum in any Greek state but managed to reach Persian territory and was well treated by the king, Artaxerxes.[37]

The sources are sometimes helpful, more often frustrating. But separating the wheat from the chaff is not impossible. It will help to state in advance the theory – new, though of course building on many valuable findings in the literature – which it is proposed to develop. It is that Themistocles' shift from an anti-Persian to an anti-Spartan stance earned him three reprisals at the hands of the pro-Spartan and anti-Persian lobby in Athens. They began by securing his ostracism. Then they collaborated with the Spartans in an attempt to have him tried by the *koinon synedrion*, the common council of the Hellenic League. The charge was to be that he had done things 'which were not good for Greece'. Themistocles' flight put an end to this manoeuvre, but his enemies then took the most momentous step of all. They charged him (*in absentia*) before the Areopagus on an indictment which alleged *prodosia*, but they managed to give a most subtle twist to that word. The facts on which the charge was based were the same as those on which they had hoped to charge him before the common council, doing things 'which were not good for Greece', but now they subsumed that concept under the domestic Athenian crime of *prodosia* and submitted it to the adjudication of an Athenian court. They thus established the notion that wrongs against the Hellenes as a whole were cognizable by Athenian courts. Nothing could have contributed more dramatically to the burgeoning Athenian dream of empire.

We begin our survey of the sources with Thucydides. After a lengthy account of Pausanias' trafficking with the Persians and his intrigues with the helots, (1.128.3–134), he turns to Themistocles. The Spartans send envoys to Athens to accuse Themistocles of complicity in Pausanias' medism; the envoys cite evidence (not disclosed by Thucydides) which had come to light during the investigation of Pausanias, and demand that he be punished in the same way as Pausanias; the Athenians agree and send men to arrest Themistocles (1.135). Thucydides then gives a long account of Themistocles' flight (1.136–8). There is no immediate reference to the trial *in absentia*, but at the very end of his account Thucydides notes the clandestine burial of Themistocles in Attica by relatives, 'although it was not lawful to bury in Attica one who had been banished for *prodosia*' (1.138.6).

Plutarch notes the ostracism without giving the reasons – probably because his source, Theophrastus,[38] did not give reasons – but he is more expansive on the trial. He names the accuser, the Alcmaeonid Leobotes, and the charge, *prodosia* (*Them.* 23.1); he is here following either Theophrastus or Craterus, whose collection of *psēphismata* included Leobotes' *eisangelia* against Themistocles (*FGrH* C.342 F 11). Switching to Ephorus,[39] Plutarch records the failure of Pausanias' overtures but says that Themistocles erred in not disclosing Pausanias' plans to anyone; documents incriminating Themistocles were found after Pausanias' death; the Spartans denounced him with the support of some Athenians; the absent Themistocles sent a written reply based on his defence to an earlier charge; the Demos decided to send men to arrest him in order to put him on trial 'before the Hellenes' (*Them.* 23.1–4). Diodorus, who also goes back to Ephorus,[40] has Themistocles tried and acquitted, and then ostracized; a Spartan delegation again accuses him of complicity in Pausanias' *prodosia* and claims that as the crime affects the whole of Greece, it should be judged not by an Athenian court but by the common council (*koinon synedrion*) of the Hellenes, which is due to hold its regular meeting soon; the Athenians agree, but Themistocles remembers the common council's bias on the awards for valour after Salamis and decides on flight.[41]

Our first question arising out of this information is a fairly straightforward one: Why did Ephorus (Plutarch/Diodorus) attest two trials? The answer can only be that the first trial is fictitious; it provides the basis for an insinuation that ostracism was resorted to in order to accomplish without trial what it had not been possible to accomplish by fair trial. There was always an undercurrent of dislike of ostracism, as we know from Ps.-Andocides (Andoc. 4.3–6), and Plutarch comments critically on the institution when noting its use against Themistocles (*Them.* 22.3). Plutarch may here reflect Theophrastus' strictures on the ajudicial remedy.

The proposed trial 'by the Hellenes' is less amenable to a simple answer, because not everyone is prepared to believe that such a proposal was made. Kahrstedt, for example, thinks it is an invention of Ephorus, who wanted to relieve Athens of the guilt of having condemned her greatest patriot; he will therefore have foisted the blame on to the Peloponnesian *synedrion*, using as his model the trial of Ismenias by the Peloponnesian League in the early fourth century.[42] On the other hand Frost accepts the evidence. He cites the poet Timocreon's bitter attack on Themistocles for 'restoring some exiles unjustly, driving others away and killing some' (Plut. *Them.* 21.2–5). In Frost's opinion this indicates a quasi-legal process after the war similar to the 'war crimes' trials after World War II; the fact that Timocreon himself was exiled for medising and that Themistocles joined in voting his condemnation confirms the existence of an international tribunal.[43]

Some features of the Ephorus account might be considered unsatisfactory. In particular, Diodorus' reference to 'a regular meeting'[44] of the almost defunct Hellenic league might be questioned. Also, the Spartan envoys' demand that Themistocles be punished 'in the same way as Pausanias' (Thuc. 1.135.2) does not help our case; whatever the ephors did to Pausanias after starving him out (Thuc. 1.134), they did not refer him to the *koinon synedrion*. But in the last resort it is a question of what we can make of the trial of Ismenias (Xen. *Hell.* 5.2.25–36), which Kahrstedt thinks inspired Ephorus' account.

Two Theban polemarchs, Ismenias and Leontiades, were at odds in 382. Leontiades got the upper hand, betrayed the city to the Spartans, and proceeded to settle accounts with Ismenias. Acting under a law which authorized a polemarch to arrest anyone who committed a capital crime, he arrested Ismenias 'as a warmonger'. The Spartans despatched three Spartan judges and one from each of the allied states to Thebes. But it was not until the court (*dikastērion*) began sitting that charges were framed against Ismenias. He was charged with acts of collaboration with Persia which were 'not good for Greece' (ἐπ' οὐδένι ἀγάθω της Ἑλλάδος); he was also held responsible, jointly with Androcleidas, for all the disorder in Greece (ibid., 5.2.35). He made an effective defence to all the charges, but was condemned and executed (cf. Themistocles' fear of bias).

It is significant that when Leontiades arrests Ismenias he does so on the authority of a Theban *nomos*. At that stage only Theban law was involved. But 'warmongering', which meant heading the anti-Spartan faction, was not the eventual charge. The international court replaced that domestic Theban charge by supra-national charges – acts which were 'not good for Greece' – before the first Greek word. This is on all fours with 'the crimes against all the Greeks' that Diodorus (11.55.4) has the Spartans allege against Themistocles in support of their demand for his referral to the *koinon synedrion*. The domestic jurisdiction merely acted as a trigger to get things started; in modern terms, domestic law supplied the *prima facie* case on which a warrant of arrest was issued. Ismenias was arrested by the Thebans on a domestic charge, although subsequently called on to plead to a supranational charge, and it is a fair guess that something similar would have happened to Themistocles if he had not sought safety in flight. It has been suggested by von Wedel that the charge on which Themistocles was ultimately condemned (in the *in absentia* proceedings) was *klopē dēmosiōn*, theft of public moneys,[45] and though I cannot agree that this was the ultimate charge, it may well have served as a trigger at the outset, given the vast increase in Themistocles' patrimony after his entry into public life (Plut. *Them.* 25.3). *Klopē dēmosiōn* may again have played the honest workhorse, as in Miltiades' case.

There is one more argument in support of the probability that trial by the *koinon synedrion* was indeed proposed in Themistocles' case. If Ephorus invented that proposal, using Ismenias' trial as a model, why did he not go all the way by having an international court assemble at Athens for the known trial *in absentia*? Even more important, why did he invent a court consisting of the general council of the League instead of a number of specially appointed judges, as at Thebes? The answer is that Ephorus did not invent anything on the basis of Ismenias' case. He accurately reported an attempt that had been made to have Themistocles tried by the *koinon synedrion* of the Hellenic League.[46]

Our next question relates to the Athenian trial at which Themistocles was condemned *in absentia*. By which court was he tried – the Areopagus, like Hipparchus before him, or the Heliaea? This depends on the extraordinary story retailed by Aristotle about how Themistocles helped Ephialtes to strip the Areopagus of its powers. Themistocles, about to be tried by the Areopagus for medism, tells Ephialtes what is afoot; but he also tells his fellow-Areopagites that he can point out men who are plotting against the constitution; he leads them to Ephialtes, who seeks sanctuary at an altar; thereafter Ephialtes and Themistocles repeatedly denounce the Areopagus and deprive it of its powers (*AP* 25.3–4). The only sense that can be got out of this story is that the Areopagus tried Themistocles. The rest is not only absurd but also chronologically impossible. In order to have Themistocles in Athens at the time of Ephialtes' reform of the Areopagus in 462–1 we must either give his trial an impossibly late date or we must accept Cicero's statement that he was exiled but returned;[47] but that means rejecting his perpetual exile and his clandestine burial in Attica. The whole thing is a fabrication,[48] no doubt inspired by resentment at the Areopagus' condemnation of the hero of Salamis. The Areopagus, not the Demos, tried Themistocles.[49]

What was the crime for which Themistocles and his family paid so dearly? We know it was *prodosia*, but what form did it take? The sources agree that it was medism, but they perversely concentrate on what was done by Pausanias before his death and by Themistocles after his flight, paying scant attention to the crucial question of how he was implicated in Pausanias' crime. One suspects that they simply did not know the gravamen of the charge. Can it be supposed that trials by the Areopagus were just as shielded from the glare of publicity as those in the Roman senate would be? The idea is intriguing but probably cannot be pressed. In Aeschylus' *Eumenides*, trial by the Areopagus is very public indeed.

The silence of the sources invites conjecture. Kahrstedt holds that Pausanias' real crime was his cultivation of the helots, and by keeping his knowledge of that to himself Themistocles failed in his duty as a citizen of a state which was a member of the Peloponnesian League; medism was mere window-dressing for the benefit of the Demos.[50] Curiously enough this would strengthen the case for a proposed *koinon synedrion* trial, which Kahrstedt flatly rejects, but one cannot brush medism under the carpet as easily as that. It is time to ask what is meant by medism, and here a persuasive case has been made by Cawkwell, who argues that it was a flexible notion, which here means Themistocles' new policy that discounted the danger of another Persian invasion and identified Sparta as the main threat. Themistocles was proved wrong when news of Persian preparations for a third attempt filtered through in about 471.[51]

One of the interesting aspects of Cawkwell's theory is that it puts Themistocles in opposition to Cimon, who is known to have been one of his accusers (Plut. *Arist.* 25.7). Our initial suprise at Themistocles' change of direction subsides when we recall not only that he is not mentioned in connection with the formation of the Delian League, but also that he frustrated Spartan attempts to deprive medising cities of Amphictyonic membership (Plut. *Them.* 20.3–4). We may suppose, then, that when his new direction became apparent, Cimon and his friends[52] opened their attack by securing a vote for ostracism. Sparta did not intervene at that stage, since the Persian issue as such was not of primary concern to her, but when Themistocles got in touch with Pausanias from his exile in Argos the threat of an upsurge of radical sentiment in the Peloponnese[53] was seen by Sparta as a similar destabilization of Greece to that for which she would one day condemn Ismenias. It was then that she made her *démarche* at Athens, and was received with an attentive ear by those like Cimon whose natural sympathy with Sparta was allied to an urgent desire to come to grips with Persia in the Aegean. The result was the unsuccessful attempt to organise a *koinon synedrion* trial, followed by the trial *in absentia* at Athens.

The trial at Athens conferred Athenian citizenship on the supra-national charges. The Athenians made wrongs against all the Greeks wrongs against Athens, and subsumed them under the domestic crime of *prodosia*. Exactly the same wrongs, medism and destabilization, would be charged against Ismenias. But in the international forum they could not be designated as *prodosia*; they were simply 'things which were not good for Greece'. But Athens was able to use her domestic terminology, thus achieving a forensic 'first' of great significance: wrongs against all the Greeks were cognizable by Athenian courts. Cimon and his friends could not have asked for a better pendant to their drive for empire.

5 CIMON AND CORRUPTION

Cimon was charged in 463-2, at the end of his third term as *stratēgos* and as part of his *euthynai*, with having been bribed by Alexander of Macedon not to invade his country, although it was at Cimon's mercy following the suppression of the revolt of Thasos. The people appointed the young Pericles as one of the accusers, thus, it is said, giving him his chance to make his mark as a populist leader, though it is not clear how much good it did him, for Cimon was acquitted.[54]

The acquittal has some extraordinary features. Demosthenes (23.205) has Cimon escape death by only three votes and incur a fine of fifty talents for attempting to alter the constitution of either Athens or Paros, depending on whether one reads *patrion* or *Pariōn* in Demosthenes' text. The latter is more likely, and some would reject the notice as a doublet of Miltiades' case.[55] But there may have been another trial at some time, for a fragment of Theopompus attacks Cimon's integrity, calling him a thief who was convicted of corruption more than once and taught Athenian generals the secrets of bribery.[56] There is no visible connection between the charge attested by Demosthenes and the charge concerning Alexander, but the Demosthenic case may be one of the other corruption charges hinted at by Theopompus and blown up into a constitutional issue by time or circumstance.[57] But let us proceed with the known trial of Cimon.

It is said that to the democratic leaders Cimon's acquittal was the last straw, it was the final proof that the curtailment of the Areopagus could be delayed no longer.[58] This presupposes that Cimon was tried by the Areopagus, but that is in contention.[59] On the one hand we are told that when Cimon returned to Athens after the curtailment he denounced the move and tried to restore the *status quo* (Plut. *Cim.* 15.2), which suggests that he had reason to be grateful to the Areopagus. On the other hand Pericles' appointment as an accuser was made by the people (Plut. *Per.* 10.5). But Plutarch's assertion (*Cim.* 14.3) that he made his defence 'before the judges' (*dikastas*) does not necessarily imply a popular court rather than the Areopagus; the Areopagite judges in Aeschylus' *Eumenides* are dicasts. On balance the Areopagus is likely. If the Demos would shortly be legislating that council out of the constitutional sphere altogether, it could have regulated its procedures in the meantime, *inter alia* by appointing accusers.

The great crux is the apparent conflict between the death sentence demanded by Cimon's accusers (Plut. *Per.* 10.5) and the fine of ten times the amount of the bribe that seems to have been the usual penalty for corruption. The penalties are described by Deinarchus: 'The laws lay down two penalties for bribery – either death, so that the punishment of the guilty may benefit others, or a fine of ten times the amount received, so that greed may not profit' (Deinarch. 1.60). Scholars are aware of the anomaly but tend to focus on the fourth-century scandal of Harpalus rather than on Cimon. Deinarchus, who was taught by Theophrastus, wrote his three extant speeches for the use of accusers in the Harpalus affair, and because he mentions a special *psēphisma* prescribing the death penalty for those who had received money from Harpalus (3.5), it is claimed that there was no general law authorizing the death penalty. But what seems to have been overlooked is that the alternatives of death or a fine were known in the fifth century, for the indefatigable Plutarch learnt from Craterus that Aristides had been fined fifty *minae* for accepting money from the Ionians when assessing the tribute (*Arist*. 26.1–3). Plutarch dislikes the information, complaining that Craterus has not furnished his usual documentary proof, and pointing out that there is no reference to such a case in any other compendium of trials, but the point is that Craterus knew that the allocation of such a penalty to Aristides' day was *not* an anachronism. Plutarch has no doubts about the proposal of the death penalty in Cimon's case. Someone did not like to think that Aristides the Just had had feet of clay.

There is an explanation for the alternative penalties. Thonissen was aware of part of it,[60] but it does not appear to have surfaced since then. It is that when corruption caused prejudice to the state of sufficient gravity to be classified as an offence against the state, it was in effect elevated to treason.[61] Cimon's real crime was his neglect of an opportunity to extend Athens' sway in the region. But as the Demos had not specifically told him to invade Macedonia[62] he could not be charged with disobeying orders. A substitute was found in aggravated bribery. The charge might have been framed under the flexible *adikia* law that had served Pericles' father so well in his vendetta against Cimon's father. Later on there may have been a special law formalizing the aggravated case – Deinarchus speaks of *nomoi*. But in that case why was a special *psēphisma* needed in the Harpalus affair? The answer is that the latter was a procedural device relieving the accusers of the onerous task of proving aggravating circumstances: *all* who had received money from Harpalus were deemed to have injured the state.

Cimon's trial was a *cause célèbre*. His enemies formed a coalition against him (Plut. *Cim*. 14.2), and it was because of the large number of accusers that the Demos made the special arrangements which included Pericles. Plutarch learnt from Craterus that after the fall of Themistocles professional accusers (sycophants) had proliferated, subjecting the great and the powerful to the jealousy of the masses (*Arist*. 26.1). The heyday of the sycophants was the fourth century, but the germ – and perhaps more than the germ – of the institution was there in the fifth, and the young Pericles, whose kinship with Cimon was outweighed by inherited enmity, was cultivated by the professionals as a useful figurehead. He was probably not much more than that, for after being solicited by Cimon's sister, Elpinice, he made only one speech against Cimon and did him the least harm of all the accusers (Plut. *Cim*. 14.4, *Per*. 10.5).

The charge of aggravated bribery helps to identify the court which tried Cimon. The Areopagus, as the guardian of the constitution, is the most likely forum for a case in which the interests of the state were so heavily involved. But the pressures for its curtailment were increasing, and the Demos' decree appointing the accusers might have been seen as a warning shot across the Areopagus' bows.[63] The message was not received, but the conservative council could hardly have reacted in any other way to the issue which lay at the heart of the case: Was the Demos to be supreme in jurisdiction, which was the cornerstone of its sovereignty,[64] and if so, should judicial power be used as a weapon in the drive for empire? The question had been asked at Phrynichus' trial, and it had been asked with increasing urgency at the trials of Miltiades and Themistocles. It received a negative answer in Cimon's case, leaving Ephialtes and Pericles with no recourse except direct action against the Areopagus.

III

FIFTH-CENTURY ATHENS: THE JUDICIAL SOVEREIGNTY OF THE DEMOS

1 THE TRIAL OF ORESTES

In the second half of the fifth century the first political process of which we have certain knowledge is the ostracism of Thucydides, son of Melesias, in 443. But some time before that, in 458, Aeschylus produced his Oresteian trilogy, the third piece of which, *Eumenides*, portrays a trial with contemporary relevance despite being set in the legendary past.

When Aeschylus produced his trilogy the reform of the Areopagus was still recent and controversial, for it was only in 462–1 that Ephialtes had deprived that council of 'the added powers which made it the guardian of the constitution' (*AP* 25.2). Ephialtes had first weakened the council by a series of trials of Areopagites[1] and had then stripped it of most of its functions, leaving only its jurisdiction over homicide and related matters untouched.[2] The democratic forces had followed this up with a decree of ostracism against Cimon, a decree made possible by the latter's failed pro-Spartan policy, but coming most opportunely at a time when Cimon was trying to restore the Areopagus' 'ancient function' – more precisely, its function as a brake on the radicalization of the democracy over the years since the Persian wars.[3] But Ephialtes had paid for his zeal by falling victim to a murder which was never solved (because the Areopagus was the investigator?).[4] The most explosive issue of the day was whether the Demos could tolerate judicial power in any hands except its own, and *Eumenides* shows that feelings still ran high in 458. Aeschylus, a Eupatrid who had fought with Miltiades at Marathon, may now have sided with Miltiades' son; or he may have supported the radicals despite his background; or he may have acquiesced in the change without enthusiasm.[5]

The legend encapsulated in *Eumenides* is well known. Orestes kills his mother Clytemnestra in order to avenge his father Agamemnon. He is pursued by the Furies (*Erinyes*) but solicits the aid of Athena, who agrees to help him and takes steps to substitute legal process for private vengeance. Orestes is defended by Apollo and the prosecution is conducted by the Furies. Orestes admits that he killed his mother but claims that the act was justified. The judges divide evenly, whereupon Athena gives a casting vote for acquittal.[6]

The charge is specifically one that remained within the Areopagus' competence after Ephialtes, and the question is whether Aeschylus accepts that the reduced jurisdiction was always the council's main *raison d'être*, thus presenting as a supporter of Ephialtes, or whether he is trying to get a larger message across, namely that an orderly society depends on judicial process and that such process can only be effective if kept in the hands of an elitist body like the Areopagus.

The answer is an ambivalent one, for both possibilities are covered in Athena's proclamation establishing the court of the Areopagus. Much of the goddess's language implies a *general* jurisdiction for the 'new' court, a jurisdiction corresponding to the guardianship of the laws ascribed to it by Aristotle.[7] Thus Athena:

> Awe and Fear shall check my citizens from all wrong-doing while they keep my laws unchanged. Do not pollute pure laws with new expediency. Let no man serve tyrants or disobey the law. Stand in just awe of the law's majesty and you will have such a bulwark and safeguard of your land and constitution as no man has ever had before. I hereby establish an incorruptible court, holy, quick to punish, keeping faithful watch that men may sleep.[8]

But at the start of the proclamation the goddess says that this is the first trial for homicide and *this* court will last for ever. Elsewhere she says that she will choose judges of homicide (*phonōn dikastas*) and will establish a court to endure for all time (*Eum.* 681–4, 483–4).

Aeschylus' position is ambiguous. He steadfastly defines the jurisdiction in terms of the post-Ephialtes format, but at the same time he gives it a stabilizing function which had in fact been transferred to the Boule and the Demos by Ephialtes, for treason and related crimes were now supposed to be the exclusive preserve of the democratic tribunals. But Aeschylus may have his tongue in his cheek in so far as he implies that homicide had *always* been the only area of Areopagite jurisdiction. Everyone in the audience would know that this was not the case, and by deliberately floating the broader, though vague, outlines of the general jurisdiction Aeschylus showed that he agreed with them. One of the most significant passages is that in which Athena says that she will choose as judges 'the best citizens', who will swear to give no judgment 'contrary to justice' (*Eum.* 487–9). That oath is in sharp contrast to the oath sworn by dicasts in the democratic courts, for they pledged themselves to judge 'according to the laws and decrees of the Athenians' (Dem. 24.149). To judge 'according to justice' was exactly the sort of vague formula with which the Areopagus had motivated its gradual assumption of judicial powers over the centuries. There was a higher legality than *nomoi* and *psēphismata* and it was still alive and well in spite of Ephialtes' reforms. Aeschylus has woven an intricate tapestry in which the elitist values of the Areopagus are indispensable to the stability of the city, hence to the constitution. He may have accepted Ephialtes' arrangements in a spirit of compromise, but at heart he remained a conservative. His faith in the permanence of the elitist values would be borne out by the Areopagus' gradual reassertion of a constitutional guardianship over the ensuing decades.[9]

Another matter of juristic interest in the play is worth a glance. Apollo is seen to discharge his duties as defence counsel (*Eum.* 614–751) in the manner of a dishonest lawyer;[10] he prevaricates, gives conflicting testimony, and tells Orestes that he will pack the court and win by trickery: 'I will find judges for your case and beguiling words to release you totally from your distress' (*Eum.* 81–3). There is a certain irony in Orestes' reply: 'Lord Apollo, you do not know how to be unjust' (*Eum.* 85). This is a reference to Apollo's function as the Interpreter of Zeus; Apollo was the god whom the Romans would recognize as the first jurisconsult,[11] and he advised Orestes on the law in addition to appearing for him in court (*ibid.*, 609–13). Aeschylus seems to be

34

drawing a contrast between his probity in his capacity as a jurist and his chicanery as a court practitioner. One wonders whether Aeschylus here reflects contemporary hostility between legal theorists and court pleaders, between the forerunners of Theophrastus and Demosthenes.

2 PERICLES AND THE ELDER THUCYDIDES

Pericles' minor role in the prosecution of Cimon may have been followed by a supporting role of similarly modest proportions in Ephialtes' attack on the Areopagus,[12] but the main thrust of his forensic history starts with the enmity between Thucydides, son of Melesias, and himself, then moves forward to a series of trials of Pericles' friends, and culminates in the trial of Pericles himself.

The enmity between Pericles and Thucydides dominates the 440s. Enmity crystallized around Pericles' plan to use reserve funds of the Delian League to rebuild temples that had been destroyed by the Persians. The opposition to this plan was spearheaded by Thucydides, a relative of Cimon and possibly the grandfather of the historian, to whom the conservatives looked for leadership after Cimon's death.[13] Thucydides may have forged the nucleus of a political party, or at any rate of a political machine, in the modern sense, for according to Plutarch he gathered the 'True Blues' (*kaloi k'agathoi*) into one body instead of leaving them scattered amongst the people, and his rivalry with Pericles polarized the distinction between 'the People' and 'the Few' into an ideological differentiation (Plut. *Per.* 11.1–3).

Despite their cohesion, however, the 'True Blues' do not appear to have made much use of the trial weapon in their campaign against Pericles. They put out scurrilous stories of how Pheidias, the genius behind the rebuilding programme, had pandered to Pericles' interest in women (ibid., 13.9–12), but none of this generated trials. Plutarch says that Thucydides and his party ('the rhetors around Thucydides') kept on shouting against Pericles for squandering public money, but the people acquiesced in the expenditure when he told them that if they thought he had spent too much he would dedicate the new temples in his own name (ibid., 14). Unlike sex scandals, misuse of public funds could certainly have acted as a forensic trigger, and Thucydides' rhetors could have been pleaders shouting in trial or *euthynai* situations. But Plutarch places everything in a deliberative rather than a judicial setting, and it must be supposed that Pericles got his accounts ratified before his opponents were ready to move. Attempts have been made to date the charge of impiety against Anaxagoras to this period, but that case was much later.[14] A better prospect is the charge of bribery against Callias, author of the much-debated Peace of Callias; the case can be discussed more appropriately at a later stage.[15] We also note Pyrilampes, whom Pericles charged with murder before the Areopagus, only to find him being successfully defended by Thucydides;[16] but here the forensic initiative was taken by Pericles, not by the opposition. Although Plutarch describes Thucydides' group as a *hetaireia* (*Per.* 14.2), it does not seem to have anticipated the (equally oligarchic) *hetaireiae*, which are said to have assisted Peisander not only in elections but also in trials (Thuc. 8.54.4).[17]

Thucydides' negative impact in the forensic sphere might have to be revised if the heavy forensic attack on Pericles in the late 430s could be credited to Thucydides, but that will be shown not to be the case.[18] It is possible that in the 440s the polarization of the courts deprived Thucydides of an effective trial weapon. He might hope to succeed in the Areopagus, but unless Pericles committed murder there was not much point in prosecuting him; no joy could be expected from the people's courts manned by dicasts who had Pericles to thank for the pay that they received for their services.[19] The radical democrats knew what they were doing when they clipped the wings of the Areopagus.

By contrast to trials proper, ostracism was prominent in the confrontation between Pericles and Thucydides. The latter was ostracized in 443;[20] Plutarch observes that after suffering many attacks Pericles 'finally ventured to undergo a contest of ostracism with Thucydides', the result of which was that Thucydides was banished and his *hetaireia* was dissolved (*Per.* 14.2). (One assumes that the dissolution was not a formal act by the people; there is no reason to think of the group as a legal *persona*, and Plutarch is merely saying that with the departure of the leader things fell apart.) That Thucydides had used ostracism against Pericles is proved by the case of Damon, Pericles' music-teacher and political adviser, who was ostracized for being 'a great operator' and a friend of tyranny (ibid., 4.1–2). If he was responsible for advising Pericles to institute pay for jury service he will have been most unpopular with the Thucydidean group, and that counts in favour of the 440s as the time of his banishment.[21]

3 PERICLES' FRIENDS: THE FIRST IMPIETY TRIALS

Plutarch, who we know had access to collections of cases (*Arist.* 26.3), supplies us with a mini-casebook of his own in which he records charges against both Pericles' friends and Pericles himself (*Per.* 31–2). The list includes the sculptor Pheidias and Pericles' mistress Aspasia, a *psēphisma* against impiety which was aimed at the natural philosopher Anaxagoras, and a *psēphisma* against Pericles. Plutarch makes all these matters broadly contemporaneous and locates them on the eve of the Peloponnesian War. Later on, when the war is already under way, he notices the trial of Pericles (ibid., 35.4). Hardly a word of all this is free of controversy. The following are some of the crucial questions: Were all the items on the list more or less contemporaneous, as Plutarch says? If so, do they date to the eve of the war or to some five or six years earlier? And regardless of the date, did the trials in question actually take place? Our position is that the trials did indeed take place and date to the eve of the war, in *c.* 433–2 (except for Pericles' own trial, which was later). It is also proposed to incorporate in the discussion something even more important than the date, namely the extent to which the concept of *asebeia*, impiety, figured in the trials.

Plutarch says of Pheidias' case that when Pericles refused to lift economic sanctions against Megara, his enemies decided to charge Pheidias as a trial run for charges against Pericles himself. Pheidias' assistant, Menon, sat at the altar of the gods in the Agora[22] and was granted an indemnity; he reported to the Ecclesia that Pheidias had stolen the gold that had been used on the statue of Athena Parthenos.[23] The charge failed because it was possible to remove and weigh the gold, but Pheidias was imprisoned because he had included likenesses of Pericles and himself in the battle against the Amazons portrayed on the goddess's shield; this was the element of *asebeia* in the case. Pheidias died in prison and the informer, Menon, was rewarded.[24] Ephorus' version (*ap.* Diod. 12.39.1–5) shows how the case was ultimately aimed at Pericles: he holds an official appointment as supervisor (*epistatēs*) of the work on the statue; Pheidias' assistants give information about Pheidias having, with Pericles' connivance, embezzled sacred funds (not gold); the Ecclesia orders Pheidias to be arrested, and the accusers charge Pericles with theft of sacred property (*hierosylia*, a religion-oriented crime); Pericles refuses to withdraw the Megarian decree.

The next case on Plutarch's list, Aspasia, expressly involves impiety. She is said to have been charged with *asebeia* by the comic poet Hermippus, who also alleged that she had acted as a procurer for Pericles' assignments with freeborn women (*Per.* 32.1). Pericles wept copiously at the trial and persuaded the dicasts to acquit her (32.3). Some would dismiss the case as a scene in one of Hermippus' plays or a grammarian's comment thereon.[25] The lachrymose Pericles is admittedly rather comic, and pandering to his amours was something of a stock theme (cf. Plut. *Per.* 13.9); also, Aspasia was one of the favourite targets of the comic poets.[26] But the charge of *asebeia* was not well suited to the comic vein, and the fact that every item on the list has a religious connotation lends it credence. Plutarch does not give details of her impiety, but it is probable that as a courtesan and pander she defiled temples by her presence.[27] We should be slow to reject any item on Plutarch's list lest we end up with no attack on Pericles at all,[28] and we may safely give our vote to those who believe that Aspasia was tried.[29]

Plutarch's third case, Anaxagoras of Clazomenae, is the first case of *asebeia* in the special form of attacks on philosophers. A certain Diopeithes moved a *psēphisma* applying the *eisangelia* process to those who did not believe in the gods or taught doctrines concerning the heavens.[30] The purpose, adds Plutarch, was to arouse suspicion against Pericles through Anaxagoras, who was the most influential of Pericles' preceptors. When the *psēphisma* was passed, Pericles feared for his friend's safety and sent him away (*Per.* 32.1, 3). Plutarch does not attest an actual trial here, but he possibly does so in his biography of Nicias, when he notes the general dislike of natural philosophers and observes that Anaxagoras was rescued from imprisonment by Pericles (*Nic.* 23.3).

The picture is a complex one, partly because of the conflicting versions of the case known to Diogenes Laertius (2.12–14). Of his two main sources,[31] Sotion informed him that Anaxagoras was prosecuted by Cleon on a charge of *asebeia*, the factual basis of which was that he had declared the sun to be a mass of red-hot metal and the moon an inhabited world, and he had attacked the popular belief in Zeus' thunderbolts.[32] He was defended by Pericles but was fined five talents and exiled. But Diogenes learnt from Satyrus that the accuser was Thucydides, son of Melesias, and that the charges included medism as well as *asebeia*; Anaxagoras was sentenced to death *in absentia*. Our other source, Diodorus, is mercifully brief; he notes only that Anaxagoras was falsely accused of impiety against the gods (Diod.12.29.2).

The instability of the sources has caused some to doubt the genuineness of the case,[33] but that should be more than compensated for by the specific documentary evidence of Diopeithes' *psēphisma*. Yet not even that has escaped the excisionist's axe, for it has recently been castigated by Dover as 'an irresponsible fiction based on fulminations attributed to Diopeithes in a comedy'.[34] Dover's first point is that the *psēphisma* is not mentioned in passages that ought to have noticed it, namely the Ephorus/Diodorus account and the *scholia* on Aristophanes' portrait of Diopeithes. But the Ephorus/Diodorus notice is extremely brief, little more than a footnote to the account of Pheidias' case, and it is tendentious (*esykophantoun*); the last thing that Ephorus' source wanted was a 'respectable' statutory basis for the charge. As for the *scholia*, Aristophanes' barbs against Diopeithes have nothing to do with legislation, hence there was nothing to draw the scholiast's attention to the *psēphisma*.[35] Dover also argues that Plutarch does not use the right language in his account of the *psēphisma*; his rendering of 'the heavens' as *ta metarsia* will be an anachronism, since the usual expression in Attic prose before Theophrastus was *ta meteōra*. The choice of Theophrastus as the criterion is unfortunate, for if he was Plutarch's source he will hardly have misquoted the text of a law. The same holds good if Craterus was the source;[36] his collection of *psēphismata* did not contain anachronisms. In any case, if Plutarch had in fact got his information from fifth-century comedy, why would he have wanted to replace *ta meteōra* by *ta metarsia*?

We may safely align ourselves with those who accept the Diopeithes decree.[37] We turn now to its wording as recorded by Plutarch: εἰσαγγέλλεσθαι τοὺς τὰ θεια μὴ νομίζοντας ἢ λόγους περὶ τῶν μεταρσίων διδάσκοντας. Two things are penalized: not believing in the gods, and teaching about the heavens. A twofold prohibition also underlay the charge against Socrates in 399; that is why his accusers attached great importance to Anaxagoras' case (Plato *Apol.* 26D). But in both cases the two heads are simply different species of the same genus: teaching astronomy is not criminal *per se*, but only in so far as it encourages disbelief in the

39

gods. By teaching, for example, that the sun was a mass of red-hot metal Anaxagoras denied the divine nature of the heavenly bodies and thus demonstrated, and encouraged his pupils (including Pericles) to demonstrate, disbelief in the gods.[38]

The next matter needing to be resolved is the conflict between Sotion and Satyrus, as noted by Diogenes Laertius. Diogenes shows his preference by citing Sotion first, and with good reason. Sotion was more of a scholar than Satyrus,[39] and the latter's inclusion of a charge of medism against a friend of Pericles renders him suspect. Provisionally, then, Cleon rather than Thucydides, son of Melesias, was Anaxagoras' accuser; there is more to be said below about Cleon's role in the whole series of anti-Periclean trials. It also follows from our acceptance of Sotion that a fine of five talents is the most likely penalty, but Pericles probably helped Anaxagoras to escape into exile to avoid paying the fine.

The key to the chronology of all the trials is the date of Pheidias' case. Plutarch and Diodorus locate it on the eve of the war, and that would be a firm date were it not for a conflict between Aristophanes' *Peace* 605–11 and the *scholia* thereon. The passage itself confirms Plutarch and Diodorus: Hermes says that Peace's troubles began with the troubles of Pheidias; Pericles, fearing lest he share Pheidias' fate, imposed sanctions on Megara and war followed. But the *scholia* appear to refute Aristophanes' date. As usually understood, they assert that in his *Atthis* Philochorus dated the trial to the archonship of Theodorus, that is, to 438–7; Philochorus will also have said that the charge concerned the theft of ivory, not gold, from the statue. Accordingly the scholiast argues that the Megarian question arose some six years after the trial.[40]

Scholarly opinion on this question is sharply divided. Derenne and Kienast support the eve of the war (specifically 433–2) and have Thucydides, son of Melesias, return from exile in c.433 and resume the struggle against Pericles by organizing the trials, though with limited success, since Thucydides himself was prosecuted and was again exiled.[41] Thus those scholars prefer Satyrus to Sotion, in addition to preferring Aristophanes to the scholiast. But currently there is something of a consensus in favour of the scholiast; its adherents include Frost, Mansfeld and Ostwald.[42]

Mansfeld bases himself on the length of Anaxagoras' stay in Athens after arriving there in 456–5 and holds that twenty years is closer to the mark than thirty. The most detailed case is made by Frost, who not only dates Pheidias' trial to 438-7 but also dates Aspasia's case to 438, on the grounds that in that year there were many complaints about the Samian War, and the Milesian Aspasia was blamed for Pericles' decision to assist her city; Anaxagoras' trial will not have taken place at all, though the Diopeithes *psēphisma* was passed and dates to 438-7; the master-mind behind the attacks was Cleon or an earlier demagogue rather than Thucydides, for the latter was still in exile.

One of Frost's conclusions can be endorsed without any more ado. The guiding hand behind the trials was not Thucydides. It was specifically Cleon rather than an earlier demagogue; that will be confirmed by our ultimate conclusions after discussing Pericles' own trial. But Frost's rejection of Anaxagoras' trial must be ruled out with equal despatch. If any confirmation of what we have already said is needed, it is supplied by a passage in Plato (*Apol.*26D). Socrates' accuser, Meletus, has said that Socrates does not believe in gods at all. The interrogation continues as follows:

> [Socrates] Why do you say this? Do I not recognize the sun and the moon as gods?
> [Meletus] No, by Zeus, judges, for he declares that the sun is a stone and the moon is earth.
> [Socrates] Do you suppose that you are accusing Anaxagoras, my dear Meletus?

This cannot be dismissed as confusion on Meletus' part. That astute individual cited Anaxagoras' case for two reasons: it was directly in point and it had actually happened.

The point about hostility to Aspasia having started at the time of the Samian War is likely enough, but it by no means follows that the trial took place at that time. Athenian public opinion was quite capable of storing up grievances for future use, as we know from the resuscitation of the seventh-century sacrilege of Megacles for use against Pericles (Thuc. 1.126). As for the date attested by Philochorus, Lendle argues with some plausibility that on a proper construction of the *scholia* Philochorus in fact gave 432-1 as the date.[43] But even without that we need an explanation as to why Aristophanes, who was alive and well at the time, should have been out on the date by five or six years. Would anyone have believed – or even have found it funny – that

41

Pericles wanted the war in order to divert a forensic attack that had come and gone some years before? Finally it comes down to probabilities, and we require something more than a second-hand version of what Philochorus said before we decide to abandon the plain statement of Aristophanes. We therefore take our stand firmly on c.433–2 as the date of Pheidias' trial, and consequently of the trials of Aspasia and Anaxagoras as well.

4 PERICLES ON TRIAL

Pericles' case is included in Plutarch's mini-casebook, inasmuch as the last item on Plutarch's list is a *psēphisma* which was passed on the motion of Dracontides, to the effect that Pericles lodge his accounts of public moneys with the *prytaneis*,[44] and that the jurors judge his case with ballots sanctified by being placed on Athena's altar on the Acropolis. But Hagnon moved that this provision be deleted and that the case be tried by 1,500 jurors in the ordinary way, irrespective of whether the charge thrown up by the audit was theft, bribery or malfeasance – *klopē, dōra, adikion* (Plut. *Per.* 32.2). Plutarch adds that Pericles, having clashed with the Demos in Pheidias' case, was so afraid of the *dikastērion* proposed for his own case that he stoked the fires of war (ibid., 32.3) – just as Aristophanes says. Later on, after the war has started, he notices Pericles' actual trial (ibid., 35.4).

It is now a question of trying to allocate the legislation against Pericles to its proper place in his personal forensic history. His earliest brush with the law was at the time of Pheidias' case, when the arrest of Pheidias was accompanied by the lodgement of a charge of *hierosylia* (temple-theft) against Pericles (Diod. 12.39.2). This is not exactly a conflation of the trial attested by Plutarch (which took place in 430), but it has a close, though often unsuspected, connection with that trial, as will be shown presently.[45] Pericles' next involvement is on the eve of the war, when the Spartans call on the Athenians to drive out the Cylonian pollution (Plut. *Per.* 33.1). The Spartans were hoping to see Pericles indicted (vicariously) for murder in respect of the sacrilegious killing of Cylon's followers by Pericles' ancestor, Megacles, in the seventh century, when both the killers and their descendants were pronounced guilty and accursed

(Thuc. 1.126–8). Given the nature of the charge, it is clear that the Spartans were looking to the Areopagus, but nothing came of it.

The actual trial of 430 is preceded, in Plutarch, by Cleon's attacks on Pericles' negative reaction to the invasion of Attica (*Per.* 33.7). The outbreak of plague was the last straw, and despite Pericles' oratory the Athenians took control of the situation, seized ballots of condemnation, deposed him from his generalship and punished him with a fine, the amount of which varied between fifteen and fifty talents according to various sources consulted by Plutarch (Per. 35.3–4). Diodorus says it was eighty talents; Thucydides does not state an amount.[46]

Plutarch was not sure who the accuser was. He found Cleon's name in Idomeneus, Simmias' name in Theophrastus, and Lacratides' name in Heracleides Ponticus (*Per.* 35.4). By citing Idomeneus' version first, Plutarch expresses something of a preference for it. It is possible that all three joined in the accusation, but in any case Cleon has a good claim; he is Anaxagoras' accuser in Diogenes Laertius' preferred version, and it has been surmised that he may have instigated Diopeithes' *psēphisma*.[47] Apropos of that, there is a curious aptness, whether accidental or not, about the passage in Aristophanes in which Philocleon ('Friend of Cleon') is advised to fill his heart with Diopeithes in order to teach Bdelycleon ('Enemy of Cleon') to respect the *psēphismata* of the gods (*Wasps* 377–80). We are also told that Cleon's attacks on Pericles were quoted with approval by Aspasia's accuser, Hermippus (Plut. *Per.* 33.7).

What charge was brought against Pericles? The sources are singularly coy about this; only Plato ventures to give it a name – theft (*Gorg.* 576A). That was one of the charges for which Hagnon's amendment of Dracontides' *psēphisma* had stipulated a court of 1,500 dicasts. This brings us to a question that has not been fully explored, the connection between the Dracontides/ Hagnon legislation and the trial. We recall that there were two phases in the legislation – the Dracontides phase, which sought to put Pericles' *euthynai* on a religious footing, and the Hagnon phase, which restored the normal secular basis. The crisp question now is, was the Hagnon amendment contemporaneous with the original decree, or was there an appreciable interval between the two? In other words, did Hagnon move a rider, which would probably have been contemporaneous, or an independent decree, which need not have been? Plutarch's account does not enable us to say whether Hagnon used the phrase that was typical of a rider, 'Let the rest be as proposed by AA'.[48] Plutarch merely says that the people accepted Diopeithes' decree with alacrity, 'and while they were in this mood a decree was passed on the motion of Dracontides' (*Per.* 32.2). Plutarch goes on to say, 'But[49] Hagnon deleted this part of the decree[50] and moved that. . . ' One's impression is that there had to be a change of climate in the Assembly before Hagnon's proposal could receive a sympathetic hearing; it had to be a time when the people were no longer in a mood of Diopeithic fervour. It is therefore possible that the Dracontides decree was never used in its original form; it lay dormant until 430, when Pericles was again vulnerable in the wake of the plague. Cleon may have tried to use (or reinstate) Dracontides' decree, but Hagnon, a friend of Pericles and obviously hostile to the ultra-religious approach, put a spoke in Cleon's wheel.

One question remains: In respect of which of Pericles' offices was the *euthynai*-generated trial of 430 held? The usual answer is the generalship from which, as Plutarch and Diodorus say in their accounts of the trial,[51] Pericles was deposed. But although we have no quarrel with the statement that he was deposed from his current generalship (*apocheirotonia*, or removal from office, was a necessary prelude to a prosecution), the *euthynai* cannot have related to that tenure. Dracontides' decree still regulated the *euthynai* apart from the changes introduced by Hagnon, and it cannot be supposed that Dracontides legislated for the *stratēgia* of 430. To so hold would mean that the people entered on that year still in a mood of Diopeithic fervour surviving from 433–2, and gave Dracontides his *psēphisma* only to have their enthusiasm suddenly dampened by Hagnon later in the same year. The dampening process should rather be a gradual one over several years, and the *euthynai* of 430 is not connected with Pericles' then current *stratēgia* at all. It is connected with that half-submerged strand in the tradition, his office as *epistatēs* of the Athena Parthenos project, when he had connived with Pheidias to steal something (whether gold or ivory, or both)[52] from the statue. The crime attracted the religious charge of *hierosylia*, and Dracontides proposed a special religious *euthynai*. The external crisis enabled Pericles to stave off the audit for the time being, but

44

Cleon and his friends did not forget, and two or three years later they dragged the skeleton out of the cupboard – subject to a slight rearrangement of the articulation by Hagnon, who managed to replace *hierosylia* by secular charges which were to be dealt with by the normal secular procedure.

5 RELIGION AND THE CRIMINAL LAW

All the cases in Plutarch's mini-casebook belong in one way or another to the sphere of religious crimes, but the significance of this concerted drive to give the gods the protection of the secular law needs more searching analysis than it has hitherto received.[53] Does it represent a sudden upsurge of religious fervour in the late 430s of such proportions that the popular conscience would tolerate nothing less than a criminal sanction for violations of its beliefs? Or was it something quite different, namely an attempt to reinforce the Demos' judicial authority, to cut down still further on the jurisdiction retained by the Areopagus after Ephialtes' reform?

We know that the Areopagus retained jurisdiction over one religion-oriented offence, cutting down sacred olive trees (Lysias 7), but were there others? It has been surmised that the Areopagus retained a general power of supervision in all religious matters,[54] but the question is whether something more substantial was involved, in the shape of an indirect reassertion of the conservative council's guardianship of the constitution. An inspection of some of the cases is indicated at this point.

If any trial for religious crime preceded those of the Pericleans it will have been the charge of *asebeia* said to have been preferred against Aeschylus for disclosing Eleusinian secrets in one of his plays, to which he successfully pleaded that he was not an initiate and had not known that he was revealing a cult secret; an alternative tradition credits his acquittal to the bravery of a brother at Marathon, or of another brother at Salamis.[55] Large sections of the evidence have recently been rejected by Ostwald,[56] but it is proposed to show that in fact the sources fit together suprisingly well and tell a most interesting story. It will be argued that the sequence of events was as follows: In one of his plays produced at the Dionysia Aeschylus inadvertently disclosed Eleusinian secrets. The audience was enraged, started an even more violent riot than the spectators had done at the production of Phrynichus'

45

Sack of Miletus, and advanced on Aeschylus with the intention of stoning him to death. The poet took refuge at the altar of Dionysus. Members of the Areopagus prevailed on Aeschylus to abandon his sanctuary, promising him safe conduct and an orderly, judicial disposal of the case. The trial was held before the Areopagus and Aeschylus was acquitted.

Our first clue is provided by Aelian (*Var. Hist.* 5.19). He is the only source to name the charge as *asebeia;* the others only give the facts. Aelian goes on to say that the Athenians were about to stone Aeschylus when his brother secured his acquittal by showing the judges how he had been maimed at Salamis. The attempted stoning speaks well for Aelian's credibility. Lapidation had been a recognized penalty in early Greece, but it was not a recognized trial penalty in developed Athenian law,[57] and thus Aelian has chosen the *difficilior lectio,* so to speak. The populace was about to take the law into its own hands; under the influence of intense emotion it was about to administer lynch-justice.[58] This case, then, appears to support the people's perception of impiety as a threat to its deepest religious convictions.

Heracleides Ponticus fills in some important details. In his version, when Aeschylus realized what he had done he took refuge at the altar of Dionysus; members of the Areopagus persuaded him to stand trial; he was acquitted by the *dikastērion* because of the bravery of his brother and himself at Marathon (fr. 170 Wehrli). The question that arises is evident: Against what danger did Aeschylus seek refuge? The answer can only be, a mob of enraged citizens who wanted to stone him. His choice of the altar of Dionysus needs no explanation: it was the obvious refuge from a riot which had broken out during the production of his play at the Dionysia. Heracleides' attestation of trial by *dikastērion* is said to conflict with Clement of Alexandria's statement that Aeschylus was tried and absolved by the Areopagus (*Strom.* 2.14, 60.3), but there is no real conflict. When the Areopagites urge Aeschylus to stand trial in Heracleides, they obviously do so in an attempt to persuade him to abandon his sanctuary, and by implication they guarantee due and proper trial. But they could not have given that assurance if another jurisdiction was going to conduct the trial, therefore they are referring to their own court. It has been argued that the Areopagus played no part in impiety cases before the late fourth century,[59] but there is no substance in the argument.[60]

The part played by the Areopagus in Aeschylus' survival raises a question as to whether that has anything to do with Aeschylus' favourable picture of the council in *Eumenides*.[61] We do not have the date of his trial, but it was after Salamis (cf. Aelian, ibid.) and before Ephialtes' reform. It was thus in the immediate post-war period, when the authority of the Areopagus was at its peak. We have no direct evidence of Aeschylus' involvement in politics over that period, but if he followed a moderate line in *Persians* compared with a strong imperialist line by Phrynichus in *Phoenician Women*,[62] and if that put him on the opposite side of the fence to Phrynichus' friend Themistocles on, amongst other things, the Areopagus question,[63] it is conceivable that political interests used his accidental revelation of mysteries to stir up the spectators against him: in which case the eruption of outraged religious feelings might not have been so spontaneous.

Another possible example of Areopagite jurisdiction is Euripides. According to Satyrus, Cleon prosecuted him for impiety (*Vit. Eur.* fr. 39 Arrigh.). A late list of rhetorical exercises includes the following: 'Euripides having represented Heracles as mad in a play at the Dionysia, is on trial for impiety' (*P. Oxy.* 2400). And Aristotle notes that during an exchange between Euripides and an adversary there was talk of a charge of impiety arising out of the poet having said that 'my tongue swears but my mind is unsworn' (*Rhet.* 3.15, 1216A 28).

Some see the evidence as so tenuous that they reject the trial completely, though freely conceding the atheistic character of Euripides' thinking as a whole.[64] The rhetorical exercise is admittedly questionable, for if the play was *Hercules Furens*[65] it might not have come down to us if it had been condemned as impious. But we still have Satyrus and Aristotle, and thus a prosecution by Cleon for denigrating the value of an oath. And there is a piece of evidence that counsels reflection before rejection. According to Plutarch, Euripides was unwilling to state openly whether or not he believed in the gods because he was afraid of the Areopagus (*De Plac. Philos.* 7.2). In Plato's *Apology* Socrates refrains from dealing specifically with the charge of atheism, perhaps because he, too, is afraid of a reaction from the Areopagus if he is acquitted in the present trial.[66] We also know that Cleon had a special aversion to dramatists.[67] It might be hazardous to revert to the attack on Heracles and to suggest that

47

POLITICAL TRIALS IN ANCIENT GREECE

the demigod's key role at Marathon (Pausan. 1.15.4) aroused an imperialist like Cleon to special protective action, but the idea is intriguing. All in all, Euripides' case cannot be ruled out entirely.

The most clear-cut example is also the briefest. Cicero states unequivocally that Sophocles informed the Areopagus of a dream in which Hercules named the thief who had stolen a gold dish from his temple, whereupon the Areopagus put the culprit on trial (*Div.* 1.54). This case broadens the scope of the jurisdiction, for it is here *hierosylia* rather than *asebeia*.

Three cases are too many for summary dismissal, and we may reasonably postulate some sort of Areopagite jurisdiction over religious crimes as a whole in the fifth century. This enables us to describe the Periclean trials of the late 430s as the first step towards the democratization of religious crimes. Laws were passed giving some acts in the religious sphere statutory definition[68] and conferring jurisdiction on popular courts. That is why *eisangelia*, by now a completely popular process in which the Areopagus no longer had a part,[69] was expressly laid down as the procedure in Diopeithes' *psēphisma*. In the hands of the Areopagus religious jurisdiction had never been defined;[70] it formed part of the 'added powers' (*ta epitheta*), some of which had been added by statute,[71] but others of which had simply arisen by being exercised, such as the power to try religious crimes. Expansion of the religious jurisdiction by extensive interpretation had been relatively easy because of the pollution aspect of homicide, and we may suppose that by the late 430s the Areopagus' infiltration into areas that had been closed off by Ephialtes had reached considerable proportions. A fourth-century example illustrates the point. A litigant for whom Lysias wrote a speech in *c.* 384-3 makes the following statement: 'I am charged with murdering my father – I who took it upon myself as soon as I was of age to indict the Thirty before the Areopagus' (Lys. 10.31). If we can assume that the repeal of Ephialtes' restrictions by the Thirty (*AP* 35.2) had been ephemeral,[72] the Areopagus of 384-3 was again in the position of having to extend its powers through the back door. But it did so with remarkable success, for while investigating the murder alleged against Lysias' client it took the opportunity to enquire into the whole question of the legitimacy of the Thirty, so that in effect it was once more watching over the constitution.

We conclude, then, that by the late 430s the Areopagus was

48

once again a major threat to the judicial sovereignty of the Demos. Cleon and his friends set out to counter that threat, since they did not see good prospects for their attack on Pericles' monarchical aspirations[73] in proceedings before the elitist council, which would favour Pericles' more restrained enthusiasm for democracy. Cleon therefore democratized an area in which Anaxagoras, who had been selected as one of the main guinea-pigs for the attack on Pericles, was prominent, namely natural philosophy and its effect on religious beliefs. Hence the Diopeithes *psēphisma*. Why Diopeithes, a hot gospeller whose involvement in politics was minor at best,[74] was chosen for this momentous task remains a mystery.[75] Perhaps it was *because* he was a hot gospeller that they chose him; some strong medicine was needed to counteract conservative influence. We again recall the admonition to 'fill your heart with Diopeithes in order to inculcate respect for the *psēphismata* of the gods' (Ar. *Wasps* 377–80). We also recall Cleon's reputation as the man who dealt heavily in oracles and exploited the superstitions of the Demos (Ar. *Knights* 997–1100).

The successful outcome of the charge against Anaxagoras encouraged Cleon to use the same weapon against Pericles himself. Hence the Dracontides *psēphisma* giving Pericles' *euthynai* as supervisor of the Athena Parthenos statue a religious ambience. Time and circumstance blunted that particular weapon, but the democratization of religious crimes was only at the beginning of its career. It was basically a dangerous innovation. Originally designed as a weapon against Pericles, it would be used with devastating effect in 415, and again in 399, and thereafter at regular intervals. What had originated as a protection for the democracy against real or imaginary dangers would become a millstone around that same democracy's neck.

6 THE JUDICIAL REIGN OF CLEON

The dominant figure in the politics of the 420s, until his death in action in 422, was Cleon, the new man from the commercial classes who found a new way to the top. His 'new technology of political power'[76] included the systematic use of the trial weapon, the first fruits of which we have already gathered over 433–30. The main thrust came in the 420s, when Cleon made trials an integral part of his equipment, assembled a special team to assist him in his forensic endeavours, and put innovations like the idea of an Athenian imperial court on a firm footing.[77]

In the late 430s Cleon's litigious target had been an internal one, but his cases in the 420s – the Mytilenians, Aristophanes, Laches, the historian Thucydides – were all connected with imperial affairs, thus returning political trials to their origins, as exemplified by the cases of Phrynichus, Miltiades, Themistocles, and Cimon.

Cleon's involvement in external affairs began in 427 in connection with the suppression of the Mytilenian revolt. As we learn from Thucydides, the Athenian commander on the spot, Paches, rounded up suspects on Lesbos and sent them to Athens, where the Assembly discussed their fate. On the proposal of Cleon it was decided to put them to death; that sentence was also decreed for all men of military age at Mytilene, and the women and children were to be enslaved. The Demos was incensed at Spartan support for the revolt, and also took a serious view of the fact that Mytilene had revolted without being a subject of the empire.[78] The verdict was despatched to Paches, but on second thoughts it was decided to take another vote. The result was the well-known debate between Cleon and Diodotus, respectively defending and attacking the resolution of the day before. By a narrow margin the Demos responded to Diodotus' plea for leniency and remitted the sentences on the Mytilenian populace, expropriating some of the best land for Athenian cleruchies instead. But the death sentences on the Lesbians held in Athens were confirmed; Thucydides says there were more than a thousand of them (3.51), though the figure has been doubted. The episode ends with the dramatic despatch of a second trireme carrying the reprieve to Paches.

The Mytilenian debate is one of the pressure points of Thucydidean scholarship, but there is a question not usually asked: Were the proceedings a trial or merely a deliberation?[79] Thucydides, never at his best where anything to do with the law is concerned, makes no exception here, and evidence must be sought elsewhere. We are looking for an Athenian precedent for the Roman practice of putting whole communities on trial,[80] and we begin by recalling the attempt to have Themistocles tried by the *koinon synedrion* of the Hellenic League; that would not have been a trial of a community, but one of the strands of inter-state jurisdiction is there. The *synedrion* of the Delian League cannot, however, be cited as another precedent, for there is no trace of its employment of a judicial mode in addition to the deliberative.[81] Athenian jurisdiction over Lesbians should therefore be seen as part – albeit an unusual part – of the jurisdiction over allies assumed by Athens independently of the Delian League and its *synedrion*.

The close link between sovereignty and jurisdiction in Greek states meant that when one state became subordinate to another the impairment of its autonomy was reflected in a diminution of its judicial powers in favour of the dominant state.[82] On the Athenian scene this applies in the first place to Delian League allies classified as subject allies; they suffered restrictions on jurisdiction, more particularly in respect of hostile acts against the Athenian Demos.[83] Athens' special interest in exercising, or controlling,[84] jurisdiction in such cases was the logical end-result of something which had begun with the trial of Themistocles, when acts which were 'not good for Greece' were charged as *prodosia* under domestic Athenian law. But Thucydides specially notes that Mytilene was reproached for having defected although it was not a subject ally like the others (3.36.2). This may well be a reflection of something that the Demos inserted in its decree, but not in the ambiguous form in which Thucydides records it. What we have here is the subordination of an ally who had not previously been subordinated as the result of a revolt, but was being subordinated then and there; instead of imposing Athenian jurisdiction by means of a dictated treaty, it was being imposed by merely exercising it. That is why Thucydides goes on to say that 'the anger of the Demos was increased by the support given to the revolt by the Peloponnesian fleet, for that proved long premeditation' (ibid.). In other words, special aggravating circumstances were cited in support of the immediate assumption of jurisdiction. But the validity of the innovation was immediately challenged, at the second day's hearing. A number of statements in Cleon's speech make it clear that a legal issue was being discussed:

> The worst thing is to pass measures and then not to abide by them, for bad laws which remain stable are better than good laws which lack authority. No city has ever done you as much harm as Mytilene, they have not merely revolted, but have mounted a conspiracy and an insurrection. We

should long ago have treated them like the rest, so let them receive the punishment that their crime deserves. Resolve to inflict on them the penalty that has already been voted.[85]

Diodotus' speech includes one statement that seems to go against our hypothesis. He appears at first sight to help our case by saying that their bitterness towards the Mytilenians may make them amenable to Cleon's argument because it is based on the more legal aspects of the case (3.44.4). But he then proceeds to say, 'We are not going to law with them, but are considering how to make them useful to us.' On a proper construction, however, Diodotus is not so much denying that there is a legal argument as playing it down. Nowhere in his speech does he impugn the death sentence which was imposed on the ringleaders held in Athens; he speaks only for the populace at Mytilene. Does this mean that the Demos' right to try the ringleaders was settled law, or had it, too, been raised for the first time the day before? To this there is only one answer. It could not have been settled law unless there had previously been a dictated treaty, and that is not the case: Mytilene is still not a subject ally, though Cleon regrets that they have not been treated like the others. Cleon had proposed two innovations: an assumption of jurisdiction over Mytilenians and its use against both the ringleaders and the populace as a whole. The important point is that the proceedings against the latter must have been *eiusdem generis* with the proceedings against the ringleaders; there can be no question of Procedure A against the ringleaders and Procedure B against the populace. Therefore if the ringleaders were dealt with by way of trial, so was the populace. Indeed a passage in Cleon's speech confirms that he advocates putting the whole community on trial:

> Punish them as their crime deserves and do not, while putting the blame on the Few, absolve the People. All alike attacked you, though they could have come over to us and be now back in control of their city. But they thought it safer to join the oligarchs in their revolt. (3.39.6)

This was the part that failed to stand up when the verdict was reviewed.

The doctrine that an entire community could be tried for *prodosia* against Athens was not repealed on the second day, however. All that happened was that the Mytilenians were reprieved on political grounds. The doctrine surfaced again in 416-5, for I suggest that the Melian Dialogue (Thuc. 5.84-116) is simply Thucydides' elaboration of a trial conducted by the Athenian generals on the spot. Hence the dramatized portrayal of the Melians putting their defence. Hence, too, the statement that the Melians did not bring the Athenians before the people but told them to address the magistrates and the few (5.84.4). Thucydides has the Athenians attribute this to the force of their case (5.85.1), but could it not have been because the Melians had heard how Cleon had implicated the Mytilenian populace and hoped to avoid a similar fate? If so the strategy did not succeed, for the outcome was an identical sentence to that which had been proposed by Cleon for Mytilene (5.116).

Cleon soon made another foray into the area of allied relations, when he attacked Aristophanes in 426. The gravamen of the charge was that the poet's second comedy, *Babylonians*, which was produced in the name of Callistratus at the Dionysia of 426, had criticized Athens' treatment of her allies and had done so in the presence of strangers who were attending the festival. The evidence for the case is supplied by Aristophanes' *Acharnians*, which was staged in 425. Dicaeopolis, speaking as the mouthpiece of Aristophanes (not of Callistratus),[86] says, 'I know what I suffered at Cleon's hands for last year's comedy; he dragged me to the Boule, slandered me and abused me, until I nearly drowned in his muckraking' (377-82). Later on Dicaeopolis says that he will be talking politics, 'and this time Cleon cannot complain that I am slandering the city in the presence of strangers, for this is the Lenaea at which strangers are not yet present' (496-506). The scholiast remarks that in *Babylonians* the poet made fun of magistrates, both elected and chosen by lot, and of Cleon. Cleon brought a *graphē adikias* against him for having inflicted *hybris* on the Demos and the Boule; he also lodged a *graphē xenias* and brought the poet to trial (Schol. ad 378).

The *graphē xenias* was a charge of falsely assuming citizenship.[87] But where does it fit in? Does it imply a second prosecution later on, or was it simply a second count added by Cleon in 426 to bolster his case? In *Wasps* we are told how Aristophanes had been abused and harassed by Cleon and had been forced by lack of public sympathy to make his peace with his tormentor; but the peace was a sham, for eventually 'the stake deceived the vine' (1284–91). In other words, Aristophanes broke the truce.[88] But when did he do so? On one view it was in 424 when he attacked Cleon in *Knights*, to which Cleon responded with the *graphē xenias*; that charge will be the rough treatment referred to in the *Wasps* passage.[89] But in the latter passage the stake deceived the vine *after* the harassment and truce, thus *Wasps* itself may have been the truce-breaker. A third possibility is that the citizenship charge was a second string to Cleon's bow in the *Babylonians* case, in which event that case will have been his one and only forensic confrontation with Aristophanes; the latter will have reopened hostilities in *Knights*, but without any further retaliation by Cleon. But these are only possibilities; there is no sure way through this particular morass.

We now address the *graphē adikias*. The scholiast's attachment of that label to the charge has aroused misgivings because of *ekōmōidēsen* – '*he made fun of* the magistrates and Cleon'. It is said that the *psēphisma* against 'comedising' (*peri tou mē kōmōidein*) attested by the *scholion* to *Acharnians* 67 had no sequel after its short life as an emergency measure during the Samian War of 440–*c*.437; nor, it is said, does the Old Oligarch's assertion that 'they do not *allow* comedising or speaking ill of the people' (Ps.–Xen. *Ath. Pol.* 2.18) mean anything more than social disapproval; nor, again, is Syracosius' *psēphisma* of *c*.414 prohibiting stage attacks on officials by name (Schol. ad *Birds* 1297) allowed to have a predecessor in the 420s.[90] It is accordingly argued that since there was no statute there could not have been a *graphē*, and Aristophanes must have been brought before the Boule for 'an unwritten crime' by way of *eisangelia*.[91]

There is one feature to which not enough attention has been given, and that is that both in 440 and in *c*.414 the prohibition was enacted by *psēphisma* rather than by *nomos*. It was thus an interpretation,[92] a particular example drawn from the general reservoir known as *adikia*.[93] But the scholiast speaks of a special category of *adikia*, namely *adikia eis tous politas* ('wrongdoing against citizens'), and it has been argued that this is equivalent to the Roman *laesa maiestas*.[94] That is however an overstatement, because Aristophanes was alleged to be guilty of *hybris* towards the Demos and the Boule, and in Roman law *hybris* was primarily the concern of *iniuria* in the private law (Just. *Inst.* 4.4 pr.). There is a general notional equivalence with *laesa maiestas*, but the equivalence is not a technical one.[95]

Cleon's approach to the Boule against Aristophanes may have been preceded, then, by a *psēphisma* defining the new recruit to the ranks of *adikia eis tous politas*. This brings us back to the scholiast's assertion that the poet made fun not only of magistrates but also of Cleon. Is Cleon mentioned as a magistrate or in spite of not being a magistrate? He is said to have been chosen as a Hellenotamias in 427-6,[96] but he is better known as a member of the Boule,[97] and that may give his mention by the scholiast special significance. Cleon may have managed to extend a category which had previously only covered *hybris* towards the Demos by adding 'or the Boule'; purely private individuals certainly had no remedy.[98] As for the outcome of the case, that is not attested, but an acquittal, or a dismissal without a formal hearing, is likely.[99]

How did Aristophanes present his theme in *Babylonians*? The play has not come down to us, but an intelligent reconstruction was compiled by Croiset,[100] according to which the Mytilenian affair alerted the Athenians to the grievances of the allies, and the politicians, as the driving force behind trials of allied citizens, were blamed for the dissatisfaction, with the major share of the blame being laid at Cleon's door. Aristophanes will have capitalized on this in *Babylonians*. As he tells us in *Acharnians* (630–42), in *Babylonians* he warned his countrymen not to be misled by the rosy picture of Athenian imperialism painted by allied envoys, and showed them what democracy really meant to allied cities; for this he was charged with making fun of the city and insulting the Demos, and to that charge he *now* wishes to make his defence.[101] The magistrates who felt the sting of his attack will have been the generals who dealt with the allies, and the Archon Polemarch who had a special jurisdiction over foreigners. The 'Babylonians' forming the chorus were slaves forced to work a treadmill. The treadmill was Athens and the manager who ran it for the people was Cleon; the farmers who had to hand over part of their produce were the allies. Cleon was a tyrannical manager who squeezed the farmers but also robbed his master. The Great Dionysia at which the play was performed was when the allies brought in their tribute; thus the satire struck a responsive chord amongst the strangers in the audience.

Cleon's third possible prosecution in the 420s depends on a single source, Aristophanes' *Wasps*.[102] In that great satire on Athenian trials the Dog of Cydathenaion accuses another dog,

Labes of Aexone, of having stolen a Sicilian cheese and eaten it alone; the proposed penalty is a figwood collar (895–8). After a speech for the prosecution by the Dog of Cydathenaion (907–30) the reply for the defence is made by Bdelycleon ('Enemy of Cleon') on behalf of Labes, who either has nothing to say or is tongue-tied (949–81). Bdelycleon calls a cheese-grater to say that it had grated the spoils amongst the soldiers, thus rebutting the charge of having eaten the cheese alone; Bdelycleon also tries a plea *ad misericordiam* by producing Labes' whimpering cubs. The trial takes place before Philocleon ('Friend of Cleon'), an inveterate juryman who, however, tries Labes by a private trial at his house. Philocleon intends to convict Labes, but is induced by a trick played on him by Bdelycleon to vote for an acquittal.

The trial is generally held to be a parody of a charge of embezzlement of state moneys brought by Cleon against Laches, a friend of Nicias who served in Sicily as a general with a roving commission in 427–6 and perhaps in 426–5.[103] But MacDowell is doubtful, because *Wasps* was only staged in 422. This will be too late for Laches' *euthnyai*, which must have been completed by 425–4, and the Chorus' statement that 'Laches [*not* Labes here] *will be* for it today' (240) proves that Laches had not been tried when *Wasps* was produced; he may never have been tried, and the poet may simply be making fun of the fact that Cleon, who often prosecuted those undergoing *euthynai*, had recently been saying that Laches had made money out of his generalship; the satire persuaded Cleon not to prosecute.[104]

The first answer to MacDowell's objections is that if Cleon had been able to prosecute Pericles some time after his defalcations in the Pheidias affair there is no reason why the lapse of time should have been an impediment here. If it was an impediment to anything, it was to the belated *non-forensic* attack on Laches. What was the point in going about some three years after an uneventful *euthynai* muttering about what should have been done? Why had Cleon not done it? And how could he be persuaded to abandon his planned prosecution by the play if it was already too late in any case? Moreover, why should it be supposed that respect for chronology rather than a humorous re-enactment of a well-known case motivated Aristophanes? Furthermore, calling the cheese-grater as a witness is a clumsy and almost unintelligible device if it was invented by the poet, but it makes sense – both to us and to the audience – if it reflects the real-life testimony given by Catania in Sicily on behalf of Laches.[105] Notice must also be taken of the *scholion* on v.240, according to which Laches was recalled from Sicily to stand trial. Thucydides (3.115.2) does not say that the recall was for the purpose of trial, but before being carried away by his silence[106] we should ask ourselves whether a recall from active service could ever have had an innocent explanation. Finally, we must be careful not to make Cleon a man who enjoyed a considerable reputation as a prosecutor but never prosecuted. It is probable that Cleon charged Laches with embezzlement of state funds in c.425, but Laches was acquitted, either on the evidence of the Catanians or on compassionate grounds.

Cleon's last possible prosecution ought to be the most dramatic of all, for it involved the historian Thucydides. As is well known, Thucydides was one of the generals in the Thracian sector in the winter of 424-3, when the key city of Amphipolis on the River Strymon fell to the Spartan commander, Brasidas. Thucydides was held responsible for the disaster. He was banished and spent the next twenty years travelling in the Greek world, returning to Athens in 404-3 after the defeat. These are the undisputed facts. The rest depends on what can be made of the historian's own, carefully edited account of the affair (4.103-7, 5.26.5), supplemented by a late biography by Marcellinus and its derivatives. Three questions are of special interest. Was Thucydides responsible for the fall of Amphipolis? Was his exile the result of a trial verdict, or did he avoid trial by not returning to Athens? If he did stand trial, who was the prosecutor and what was the charge?

The basic facts may be summarized as follows:[107] In the winter of 424-3 Brasidas forced the Strymon bridge at Amphipolis late at night and occupied the area outside the city walls. He pitched camp, expecting the gates to be opened by his collaborators inside. The pro-Athenian faction prevented that, and next day Eucles, co-general with Thucydides in Thrace, sent a call for help to Thucydides, who was with a squadron of triremes at Thasos. Brasidas then offered moderate terms of surrender, which were accepted. Late in the afternoon Thucydides reached Eion at the mouth of the Strymon, three miles from Amphipolis, only to learn that Amphipolis had just surrendered to Brasidas. Thucydides secured Eion but could do nothing about Amphipolis.

Any attempt to uncover the truth must be tentative, because Thucydides is to all intents and purposes an accused making his defence. One possible reconstruction[108] runs as follows: Eucles' part in the joint command was that of a civil administrator; the military side was in Thucydides' hands. A system of signals enabled Eucles to alert Thucydides at Thasos when Brasidas captured the bridge. The defenders were confident of being able to hold the city until Thucydides arrived, but the latter's assessment convinced him that the fall of the bridge had sealed the city's fate. He therefore signalled that he planned only to secure Eion. This left Amphipolis with no alternative but to accept Brasidas' terms. Thucydides miscalculated badly, because the surrender preceded his arrival at Eion by a very narrow margin, and if the defenders had not been disheartened by his signal they would have been able to hold out.

On the above terms Thucydides was guilty of a serious error of judgement, but nothing more. That would no doubt have sufficed for a charge of maladministration, *adikion*, but Marcellinus says he was charged with *prodosia* (*Vit.Thuc.* 55). Could such a charge have been brought? One answer is that there might have been other factors besides negligence. Why was Thucydides at Thasos, a good half-day's sailing from Eion, and not at Eion itself? Thasos was in no immediate danger, for Brasidas had no fleet. Thucydides might have gone to Thasos for private reasons, and that might have led the Demos to ask some awkward questions.[110] The other possibility is that *prodosia* might have been based on Thucydides' miscalculation after all. The standard definitions of *prodosia* do not include *bona fide* miscalculation, but if Athenian law knew anything like the Roman maxim *magna culpa dolus est* (*Dig.* 50.16.226) an inference of *mala fides* might have been possible.

To the question as to whether Thucydides was actually charged there can only be one answer. He may not have returned to Athens after the disaster, but the idea that by going into voluntary exile he avoided a criminal verdict altogether is misconceived. Thucydides says, 'It befell me to be an exile from my country (*pheugein*) for twenty years after my *stratēgia* at Amphipolis'; he adds that because of that he was well placed to find out what was going on, especially amongst the Peloponnesians (5.26.5). Those who would place him in voluntary exile without trial[112] would say that *pheugein* can mean 'to run away' as well as to be technically exiled, and here, in the 'Second Introduction', Thucydides is focusing on his access to information for his

History, not on his personal life. But this does not stand up. First, because his notice of the Amphipolitan command is not just a date but also a cause: 'After my generalship at Amphipolis' = *post hoc ergo propter hoc.*[113] Second, because there is evidence apart from Thucydides which makes a trial highly likely. According to Pausanias (1.23.9) Thucydides was recalled from exile by a *psēphisma* moved by Oenobius; the latter was a general in 410–9 and may have been a son of Thucydides' colleague Eucles.[114] Pausanias rather blots his copybook by adding that Thucydides was murdered on his way home, because if that fate did befall him it did so after 404–3, which is the date of the general amnesty under which he is usually assumed to have returned.[115] But before rejecting Pausanias there is a question that needs to be asked: If the moderate oligarchy of the Five Thousand was, to Thucydides, the best government that Athens had had in his time (8.97.2), why was he not recalled then? Or to put it another way, was it the best government because it *did* recall him, as Pausanias says? Did Oenobius secure a decree for his recall, only to find that threats of violence had forced Thucydides to postpone his return? And did the strong tradition for his ultimate murder confuse Pausanias? The one thing against this is Thucydides' assertion that the Four Hundred did not recall the exiles because of Alcibiades (8.70.1). But this is not necessarily fatal, since Oenobius' decree was a *privilegium* for the benefit of only one man; also, what the Four Hundred did is not binding on the Five Thousand. On the whole Thucydides' formal exile is sufficiently certain, and we conclude that he was put on trial.[116]

Did Thucydides return to Athens to stand trial or was he arraigned *in absentia*? Aristophanes once more comes to our assistance. In *Wasps* (288–90) the Chorus of jurors declares, 'Here comes a rich fellow, one of those who betrayed the Thraceward region. Let's finish him off.' Gomme thinks this may refer to a trial of Thucydides which was still recent when *Wasps* was produced early in 422.[117] The time-lag has been raised against this,[118] but although treachery was Brasidas' staunchest ally in Thrace, no hint of any other trial has surfaced. The time factor need not be fatal if this particular trial was very much in men's minds, even though it was a year or so in the past; they still remembered it, possibly with murderous intent, twenty years later. There is another passage in *Wasps*, one in which a Thucydides is expressly named: Labes being unable to speak,

59

Bdelycleon says, 'I think he has been struck dumb, as Thucydides once was when he stood trial' (946-7). This is said to be Thucydides, son of Melesias, because of *Acharnians* 703-12,[119] but it should be observed that Labes/Laches is, like Thucydides the historian, a general who was prosecuted for what he had done on active sevice, which is not the case with the son of Melesias.[120] However, the evidence is not conclusive for the inference that 'the rich fellow[121] who betrayed the Thraceward region' is Thucydides returning to Athens to stand trial. Accordingly trial *in absentia* remains equally possible.

Finally, who was Thucydides' accuser? Mercifully the only candidate is Cleon. Marcellinus is quite explicit: 'He was exiled by the Athenians, Cleon being the accuser' (*Vit. Thuc.* 46). The notice has been criticized as a mere guess,[122] but the argument is circular. The biographer could have deduced Cleon's name from Thucydides' notorious hatred of the demagogue,[123] but, equally, Thucydides could have hated Cleon for what he had done to him. It is an interesting thought that Cleon could have been the unwitting instrument of Thucydides' access to unique opportunities for research. Like any good Socratic wasp, Cleon's sting was not all bad.

IV

FIFTH-CENTURY ATHENS: 'WHOM THE GODS WISH TO DESTROY'

1 PRELIMINARY

Cleon's systematic use of the trial weapon leads us to expect a similar strategy from Hyperbolus, who succeeded him as demagogic leader, but the only forensic fact known about Hyperbolus is that he was ostracized in 417 after trying unsuccessfully to secure the ostracism of Nicias or Alcibiades; the institution was discontinued after Hyperbolus because, says Plutarch, its use against such a disreputable character had debased it.[1]

It is not only Hyperbolus' personal dossier that is bereft of trials, for the period 421–16, the period of the uneasy truce known as the Peace of Nicias, is altogether devoid of evidence of judicial activity, and it is not until 415 that political trials reappear. But from then until the final catastrophe the trial lists are filled to overflowing. The main victim is, however, not so much the defendants as judicial integrity. The democratization of religious crimes had removed one of the major brakes on the judicial autonomy of the Demos, and the ending of the lull was marked, in 415, by the greatest witch-hunt in Athenian history. From the legal point of view the most interesting feature of the exercise was the forging of a definitive link between impiety and treason, thus taking to its logical conclusion the process that had begun with Diopeithes. After 415 it was downhill all the way. Philosophers were rounded up, dead men were put on trial, and – the ultimate madness – brilliantly successful commanders were executed. Yet through it all legal ingenuity was hard at work,

61

finding a legal plaster for every sore. For that reason, if for no other, the period is of absorbing interest.

2 MUTILATIONS, MYSTERIES, AND ALCIBIADES

On a June night in 415, shortly before the Sicilian expedition was due to set sail, someone carried out a mass mutilation of the Hermae, stone busts of the god Hermes standing in both public and private places all over the city. As coherent an account as possible of Thucydides' far from orderly narrative[2] will be given.

An investigation was set on foot, rewards were offered for information, and immunity was also offered to anyone, be he citizen, stranger, or slave, who gave information about any other acts of impiety. The matter was taken very seriously, not only because it was a bad omen for the expedition but also because it was seen as a pointer to a conspiracy aimed at the overthrow of the democracy (katalysis tou dēmou). Information (though not, it seems, about the Hermae) supplied by resident aliens and servants, who disclosed previous mutilations by inebriated young men and celebrations of Eleusinian Mysteries by mock ceremonies in private houses. Amongst those whom they incriminated was Alcibiades, that flamboyant kinsman of Pericles of whom Thucydides had previously expressed a favourable opinion (5.43).

The formal charges (ta mēnymata) were denied by Alcibiades, who offered to stand trial before setting sail with the Sicilian expedition, to the command of which he had been appointed jointly with an unwilling Nicias and Lamachus. Alcibiades' enemies did not accept his offer to stand trial immediately; they were afraid of his popularity and had the proceedings postponed, hoping to gather more evidence and to have him recalled later on (6.29). In due course Alcibiades was recalled from Sicily, and with him were recalled a number of soldiers, some to stand trial with him for profaning the Mysteries, others to be charged in connection with the Hermae (6.53). Thucydides says that by accepting the new evidence and linking the parody of the Mysteries with an attempt at tyranny the people showed themselves abnormally suspicious; in order to demonstrate the frailty of the evidence he adverts to the late sixth-century assassination of Hipparchus by Aristogiton and Harmodius, rejecting the heroic version of that episode and implying that

62

Alcibiades' enemies were using it to bolster up their case (6.54–9).

Having sketched the background, Thucydides turns to the witch-hunt. Many good men were in prison and arrests were being made every day.[3] One of the prisoners, reputed to be the most guilty, was persuaded by a fellow-prisoner to give information. The truth of his information has never been satisfactorily established, adds Thucydides, but he was urged to secure immunity for himself even if he was not guilty. He accordingly informed against himself and others in regard to the Hermae. The people were so delighted at having, as they thought, uncovered the conspirators that they released the informer and anyone whom he had not accused. Men whom he had incriminated were put on trial; those in custody were executed and those who had escaped were outlawed. Thucydides again expresses doubts as to their guilt, but concedes that the city as a whole benefited (6.60).

Thucydides does not name the informer, and for this he is criticized by Plutarch (*Alc.* 20.4). We know, however, that the informer was Andocides, and we also know that the fellow-prisoner who persuaded him was his cousin, Charmides (Andoc. 1.49–50). Plutarch names a different persuader, Timaeus, but he correctly names Andocides (*Alc.* 21). Thucydides stands alone in omitting the names. He is equally reticent about the names of the informers who gave the original information on which Andocides and others were arrested, such as Dioclides who recognized the mutilators 'by the light of the moon' (Plut. *Alc.* 20.4–5). Thucydides omits names deliberately rather than because of lack of information, and the reason may be that he wishes to focus our attention exclusively on Alcibiades, whom he considers innocent.

Returning to Alcibiades, Thucydides says that the people, having as they thought uncovered the truth about the Hermae, were more convinced than ever that Alcibiades' profanation of the Mysteries was part of the same plot against the democracy. They also suspected him of plotting to send a Spartan force against the city, and of conspiring to overthrow the democracy at Argos (6.61.1–3). The Demos decided to recall him from Sicily in order to try him and put him to death. But they ordered the captain of the state trireme, the *Salaminia*, which was sent to bring him back, not to arrest him, because that would alarm the troops in Sicily; he was simply to be summoned to return to make his defence. Alcibiades and others broke away from the *Salaminia* at

Thurii, the Panhellenic colony that Alcibiades' relative, Pericles, had founded in South Italy. Alcibiades, now an outlaw, made his way to the Peloponnese and was sentenced to death *in absentia* (6.61.4–7).

There is some doubt as to whether Alcibiades was the subject of only one, or of more than one impeachment. It has been suggested that Pythonicus impeached him prior to his departure, but the better view is that Pythonicus was merely one of those who gave information.[4] The eventual accuser was Cimon's son, Thessalus (Plut. *Alc.* 22.3), and the probable master-mind behind the attack, the demagogue Androcles, does not appear as an official accuser at all.[5] But his presence behind the scenes reinforces the democratic coloration that Cleon had given to the impiety trials of the late 430s.

The chronology of the trials has generated a lively debate,[6] but our more immediate concern is with the new, expanded use to which the charge of *asebeia* was now put. Two features stand out. The first arises out of the fact that in the case of both convivial mutilations and mock mysteries seclusion was of the essence; mutilations were planned by societies which met in secret[7] and mock mysteries were staged in private houses. The sort of act for which Anaxagoras had been punished was overt and manifest, but how did you prove what happened behind closed doors? The solution was, I suggest, to link the impious act with a treasonable purpose, in this case *katalysis tou dēmou*. One of the reasons for doing that was in order to gain access to the evidence of slaves. Servile evidence was indispensable in these cases; the slaves (*akolouthoi*) who described what had gone on in private houses (Thuc. 6.28.1) were in a unique position to know. They included Alcibiades' slave, Andromachus.[8] But normally the only way that a slave's evidence could be admitted was with the consent of both parties, obtained by the cumbersome process of challenge known as *proklēsis*.[9] Here the enormous number of persons being investigated[10] and the sense of urgency, almost of panic, that pervaded the proceedings demanded some more expeditious way of getting at the truth. It was found in the rule, probably of ancient vintage, whereby in cases of treason owners could be compelled to surrender their slaves for examination under torture.[11] That rule was now invoked by bringing *katalysis tou dēmou* into the picture and treating the mutilations and the mysteries as evidence of a conspiracy to overthrow the democracy.

The formal mechanism by which this link between impiety and treason was forged was probably a *psēphisma* giving the Boule special powers for the investigation.[12] Once the link with treason had provided the investigators with the necessary machinery to uncover the facts, the accusers were at large to frame detailed indictments for impiety. The *crimen maiestatis* would provide the Roman emperor with a similar fact-finding mechanism.[13]

The second noteworthy feature of *asebeia* as charged at this time is that it was not based on a statute. We are exceptionally well placed to consider the nature of the charges thanks to an actual copy of the *eisangelia* against Alcibiades supplied by Plutarch:

> Thessalus, son of Cimon, of the deme Laciadae, indicts Alcibiades, son of Cleinias, of the deme Scambonidae, for an offence against the Eleusinian goddesses, Demeter and Cora, in that he did mimic the mysteries and shew them to his companions in his own house, wearing a robe such as the High Priest wears when he shews the sacred objects, giving the title of High Priest to himself, that of Torch-bearer to Poulytion, and that of Herald to Theodorus, and hailing the rest of the company as Initiates and Watchers, *contrary to the laws and ordinances of the Eumolpidae, Kerykes and Priests of Eleusis*. (Plut. *Alc.* 22.3)

Plutarch does not say where he got the copy, but Craterus is likely; the document should increase our confidence in Plutarch, at least when he has access to such sources as Craterus and Theophrastus. His source also gave him other important information, for he tells us that judgment was given against Alcibiades by default, his property was confiscated, and it was decreed that his name be publicly cursed by all priests and priestesses. But, adds Plutarch, the decree aroused controversy, for Theano, daughter of Menon, refused to obey it, claiming that she was a praying priestess, not a cursing one. (Was there a technical difference between the two?)

The crucial part of the indictment is the statement that Alcibiades' acts were 'contrary to the laws and ordinances of the Eumolpidae, Kerykes and Priests of Eleusis' – παρὰ τὰ νόμιμα καὶ τὰ καθεστηκότα ὑπό τε Εὐμολπιδῶν καὶ Κηρύκων καὶ τῶν ἱερέων τῶν ἐξ Ἐλευσῖνος. The entire legal basis of the charge was provided by the laws and institutions of the priestly interpreters. The reason was that the case broke new ground. The

Mysteries had been parodied before this, but only the religious jurisdiction had dealt with the transgressors. Now for the first time the prescriptions of the religious authorities were given a secular sanction.[14] The democracy was moving quickly in the religious sphere. Not content with appropriating the religious jurisdiction of another secular court, the Areopagus, it now took over some of the jurisdiction of the priests themselves.

What were the political implications of the Hermae/Mysteries trials? Some things are clear. There was a mass judicial operation involving between fifty and a hundred persons, possibly more;[15] the Boule was given special powers of investigation; the traditional rules regarding the evidence of slaves were relaxed;[16] and a firm link between impiety and treason was forged. But much remains obscure. What possible part could Alcibiades, the man who was ready to sail, have had in mutilations which could only delay his departure? But if the Hermae and the Mysteries were in fact connected, can Alcibiades be divorced from the former on the grounds that he was only charged with the latter? And if the two were not connected, why did the Boule conduct an extraordinary investigation of both? Did either category pose a real threat to the democracy, or was that merely a fiction in order to overcome, first, the difficulties of proof, and second, the lack of a secular statute for the acts in question? Thucydides blames everything on the paranoia of the Demos, but despite our own unfavourable opinion of the Demos in court, can it be thought that the most massive series of trials in Athenian history had such a fragile foundation? And what about the key role assigned by Plutarch to Androcles the demagogue?[17] Are we to suppose that in order to gratify his hatred of Alcibiades the demagogue ruined a hundred of Alcibiades' friends? In effect that has been suggested,[18] but if Androcles was the successor to Cleon (and Hyperbolus) why would he have wanted to block the further expansion of the empire? And why does Thucydides postpone all mention of Androcles until he notices his murder in 411 (8.65.2)?

Some of these questions defy elucidation, at least by this investigator, but if anything should turn the scale it is the improbability of an all-out attack on imperial expansion by the demagogues. Common sense therefore requires the positing of some sort of devious deal between Alcibiades and the oligarchs. The fact that the deal included an assault on the democracy will not have troubled the flexible conscience of Alcibiades; it would, after all, be Critias of the Four Hundred and later the Thirty who would propose his recall in 411, though he would not actually return until 408.[19] If this is how it was, Androcles might have considered the jettisoning of Sicily a small price to pay for the preservation of the democracy. But this of course presupposes that *katalysis tou dēmou* was a genuine charge and not merely a subterfuge. On the evidence available that is something that cannot be fully determined one way or the other, although a genuine charge squares better with the probabilities.

3 THE DIOPEITHES PSEPHISMA AGAIN

The Hermae/Mysteries trials were in a certain sense outside the mainstream of secular *asebeia*, inasmuch as they had nothing to do with the Diopeithes *psēphisma* or with the restrictions on philosophers that it encompassed. But there were two trials in the same period as the Hermae/Mysteries series that do rank as attacks on philosophers in the Anaxagoras tradition. The one is the case of the philosopher Protagoras, who in *c.* 415 was accused of disseminating atheism, astronomy, and other pernicious doctrines in his book *On the Gods*; amongst other things he was alleged to have written that 'as for the gods, it is not possible to know whether they exist or not'. He was sentenced to either exile or death in *absentia* and his works were burnt in the Agora.[20] There was no need to worry about making the evidence of slaves available, for the facts were plain for all to see and raised no difficulties of proof. Therefore the Diopeithes *psēphisma* was used exactly as it had been against Anaxagoras. This does not mean, however, that the case did not have political overtones, and indeed it may have been more closely connected with Alcibiades' case than has hitherto been suspected. Protagoras was the lawgiver of Thurii[21] and had often debated law with Pericles (Plut. *Per.* 36.3). We also recall that Pericles' kinsman, Alcibiades, made his escape from the Athenian escort at Thurii. Protagoras may have been suspected of complicity in the escape, and that may have been the trigger that set the wheels in motion against him.

Another case probably dating to this time is that of the philosopher Diagoras of Melos. He was accused of atheism, but left Attica to avoid trial, and remained at large despite a decree offering rewards for his death or capture.[22] His case has something in common with the Hermae/Mysteries trials, for he is reported to have made a mockery of the Eleusinian Mysteries (Lys. 6.17). But whether he was in fact involved in the witch-hunt of 415 is a moot point. He is not listed in current balance-sheets of victims.[23] It is possible that he incurred odium for a reason peculiar to himself, for if he was attacked after the subjugation of Melos[24] a charge of *asebeia* may have been a convenient way of dealing with a prominent Melian who had spoken out for his city.

4 THE POSTHUMOUS TRIAL OF PHRYNICHUS

In 411 Phrynichus, a foundation member of the Four Hundred, was murdered. The assassins, Thrasybulus and Apollodorus, were arrested. But when the Four Hundred were replaced by the more moderate oligarchic regime known as the Five Thousand,[25] the people released them and decreed an investigation under torture. It was found that Phrynichus had betrayed the city and that their arrest was wrongful (Lyc. *Leocr.* 112). The finding was based on Phrynichus' actions as general in 412–11, when he was suspected of betraying Iasus to the enemy and of disclosing Athens' negotiations with Persia in which Alcibiades was the intermediary. Phrynichus had been deposed from his generalship but had not been prosecuted, though criminal charges usually followed deposition.[26]

The Demos not only released the murderers but passed a decree conferring Athenian citizenship on them (Lys. 13.70–6). Critias then moved that Phrynichus' corpse be charged with *prodosia*, and if found guilty be disinterred and cast out of Attica (Lyc. *Leocr.* 113). It was also decreed that in the event of a verdict of guilty those who appeared for the defence were to suffer a similar punishment, on the grounds that assisting a traitor was equivalent to *prodosia* (ibid., 114). The corpse was convicted and disinterred, Phrynichus' property was confiscated, his house was demolished, and two defence counsel were put to death.[27]

This is a nasty-looking case. Yet it is only fair to say that nearly every feature would be repeated in the Roman Principate, when posthumous treason trials and even the precarious situation of defence counsel were quite well known.[28] The recognition of Phrynichus' murder as lawful has numerous Roman parallels, notably the pronouncement of *iure caesum* in regard to the death of Tiberius Gracchus (Vell. Pat. 2.4.4). The only feature lacking a Roman parallel is the eviction of the bones, but even that is consonant with the ban on burial in Attica for those guilty of *prodosia*; it is even said that after Themistocles' clandestine interment his remains were hunted down and scattered, though Plutarch does not believe it (Plut. *Them.* 32.3). As for the political motives, it may well be that the moderate oligarchs[29] wanted to annihilate the memory of their extremist predecessor. In effect, therefore, casting out the bones was a cruder version of the Roman *memoriae damnatio*.[30]

5 ARGINUSAE: THE ULTIMATE MADNESS

Unpleasant as Phrynichus' case is, its observance of recognized legal norms, at least formally, qualifies our support for Thucydides' picture of an arbitrary and unpredictable Demos. But the acid test is supplied by the events of 406. In that year the naval battle at the Arginusae Islands brought Athens her last victory in the Peloponnesian War, but the sequel was more appropriate to a defeat than to a victory.

Serious reverses suffered by the Athenian fleet in the summer of 406 prompted a number of emergency measures, including unprecedented grants of citizenship to metics and slaves. A reorganized fleet was rapidly put in place under the command of eight of the ten generals, namely Diomedon, Lysias (rather than Leon), Pericles (son of the great leader and Aspasia), Erasinides, Aristocrates, Thrasyllus, Aristogenes, and Protomachus. Overcoming the enemy's superior seamanship, the Athenians scored a brilliant victory, sinking seventy-five Peloponnesian ships at a cost of thirteen of their own vessels sunk and twelve disabled. The generals despatched forty-seven ships under two trierarchs (ship's captains), Theramenes and Thrasybulus, to pick up survivors and the dead; the rest of the fleet sailed for nearby Mytilene in the hope of catching the remnants of the force that had blockaded Conon. But a gale sprang up and in the rough seas the rescuers were unable to save survivors or disabled ships, or to pick up the dead.[31]

The Athenians were presumably pleased with the victory (Diodorus 13.101.1 says so), but their elation is buried under an avalanche of accusations and counter-accusations. Xenophon's account (*Hell*. 1.7.1–35) runs as follows: The eight generals having been deposed *in absentia*, six returned to Athens but Protomachus and Aristogenes stayed away. Archedemus, currently the leading demagogue, accused Erasinides of embezzlement and dereliction of duty, whereupon the *dikastērion* ordered Erasinides to be imprisoned pending trial. The generals having reported to the Boule on the battle and the storm, the Boule ordered the imprisonment of the other five pending trial by the Demos. Theramenes, one of the ship's captains engaged in the abortive rescue operation, attacked the generals in the Assembly. They replied, but only briefly, because they were denied the full speaking-time prescribed by law. They blamed the ship's captains, to which Theramenes replied that he did not blame them because the storm was the deciding factor. (Everyone seems to have been thinking of Anytus, a general in 409–8 who had been charged with *prodosia* for failing to relieve Pylos but had been acquitted because a storm had blown up, though bribery of the jurors was suspected.)[32] A verdict in the generals' favour seemed imminent, but the Assembly was adjourned because it was by then too dark to see a show of hands, and it was left to the Boule to define the procedure by which they were to be tried. Theramenes put up Callixenus to propose to the Boule that, first, they be dealt with collectively 'for not picking up the men who had won the naval battle'; second, the vote be taken by tribes; and third, if found to have done wrong they be sentenced to death and confiscation, with one-tenth going to Athena (ibid., 1.7.9–10).

When the Ecclesia met to consider the three recommendations sent down by the Boule, a motion to indict Callixenus for making an unconstitutional proposal was moved by Euryptolemus, a kinsman of Pericles (ibid., 1.7.12); he aimed to delay the proceedings, because a *graphē paranomōn* suspended the suspect proposal pending trial.[33] Von Wedel thinks that Callixenus was guilty of a grave irregularity, in that he did not merely define the procedure but framed a charge and a penalty, thus going beyond the Boule's mandate;[34] but this remains to be seen. In any event Euryptolemus' *graphē* did not bring him much comfort, for when he moved it the people cried out that it was unconscionable for the Demos to be prevented from doing whatever it wanted to do. Thereupon Lysicus moved that the sponsors of the *graphē* be judged by the same vote as the generals unless they withdrew their motion. Euryptolemus gave in to the pressure, but some of the *prytaneis* refused to take a vote on Lysicus' proposal, which they judged to be unconstitutional. However, they changed their minds when Callixenus urged the same charge against them, except for Socrates, who refused to act contrary to law (ibid., 1.7.13–15).

The stage was now set for the last act. Euryptolemus called on the Demos to obey the law, religion and its own oaths instead of putting the accused to death unlawfully and without proper trial; let them observe both human and divine laws and not be false either to the gods or to themselves (ibid., 1.7.19, 25). He urged that they be tried separately and with a proper allocation of speaking-time, and that they be charged under either the *psēphisma* of Cannonus or the *prodosia* law (1.7.20–3). But when it came to framing his formal proposal, Euryptolemus abandoned the *prodosia* alternative and proposed that they be tried specifically under the Cannonus *psēphisma*, and that they be tried separately (1.7.34). He thus opted for an *eisangelia* before the Heliaea and, oddly enough, offered the Demos virtually the same package as that offered by Callixenus, for under the Cannonus *psēphisma* as cited by Euryptolemus the charge was doing wrong to the people (*adikia*) and the penalty was death, confiscation, and one-tenth to Athena (1.7.20), exactly as proposed by Callixenus. The latter's reference to 'failing to pick up the men who had won the naval battle' was simply a particular set of facts falling under *adikia*, and the only items on Callixenus' list not permitted by the Cannonus decree were the joinder of trials and the curtailment of speaking-time.[35] In effect, therefore, Callixenus had only overstepped the law in those two respects, and as they were both procedural matters they fell within the Boule's mandate 'to define the procedure by which they were to be tried'. Euryptolemus' *graphē paranomōn* was directed at the two procedural innovations. His case was that the mandate to the Boule was unconstitutional; it conflicted with laws guaranteeing separate trial and a full ration of speaking-time. He would have succeeded on that issue if improper pressure had not been exerted.

The rest of the story is soon told. A vote was taken on the trial procedures proposed respectively by Euryptolemus and Callixenus, and Euryptolemus' proposal was adopted on a show of hands. But Menecles gave notice under oath of his intention to attack that decision by *graphē paranomōn*, whereupon a second vote was taken and Callixenus' proposal was adopted (ibid.,

1.7.34). The legal reasoning behind Menecles' gambit is beyond the reach of conjecture, but they were down to the end-game and the possibilities were virtually unlimited. All eight generals were condemned in a single verdict, and the six held in Athens were put to death.

Diodorus (13.100–3) is largely to the same effect as Xenophon,[36] but he makes the failure to pick up the dead, rather than the failure to rescue the survivors, the main thrust of the accusation. The religious obligation to give the dead honourable burial was entrenched in Athenian society, as Sophocles reminds us in *Antigone*, but a link with secular crime had not previously been forged. Diodorus' source concentrated on the religious aspect, for when the generals are led away to execution Diodorus has Diomedon call on the people to honour the vows for victory that the generals had made to the gods. As we have seen, Euryptolemus warned the Demos not to violate its duty to the gods; he did not deny that burial was a religious obligation, but he emphasized that in giving it a secular sanction they should not ride roughshod over their own laws. His message was that they should not fight *asebeia* with *asebeia*. Despite succumbing to Menecles' ploy the people were left with a feeling of uneasiness, and we are not surprised to learn that after the executions they changed their minds and decreed *probolae* against those who had deceived them – including Callixenus, though he managed to escape (Xen. 1.7.35). He may have escaped after an adverse finding on the *probolē*, for Diodorus says that he was not allowed to speak in his defence (Diod. 13.103.2).

The case is seen by von Wedel as a confrontation between two opposing principles – the absolute sovereignty of the Demos contended for by Theramenes and Callixenus, as against the subordination of that sovereignty to the law as maintained by Euryptolemus and Socrates.[37] We can endorse this, but have reservations about von Wedel's further point, namely that Euryptolemus relied more on a general notion of justice than on formal laws. In fact he took his stand on a law, the Cannonus *psēphisma*, which we may suppose included procedural rules such as those concerning separate trials and speaking-time; Euryptolemus abandoned the alternative of the *prodosia* law because it probably did not deal with procedure. At all events, if his *graphē paranomōn* had not been underpinned by specific statutory evidence they would not have needed a bulldozer to get past it.

We conclude, then, that the case depended on choosing between two perfectly rational legal principles – the sovereignty of the Demos and the sovereignty of the law. But that does not alter the fact that the Athenian Demos was given to unpredictable changes of direction. Rational principles were not of much use when applied inconsistently. The Romans made no secret of what they thought:

> Ancient Greece fell because of one weakness, the freedom and irresponsibility of its assemblies. In Athens, at a time when she was pre-eminent in almost the whole world, ignoramuses sat in the assembly, undertaking useless wars, putting trouble-makers in charge, driving out deserving citizens. The position is no different today. Athenagoras was flogged. He came forward and, being a Greek amongst Greeks, he did not speak of his crime but complained of his punishment. They raised their hands and a *psēphisma* was born. Such decrees have no probative value; they are the ravings of a mob, the words of the capricious, the din of the ignorant, the excitable decisions of the unstable. (Cicero *Pro Flacco* 17, 19 – adapted)

Strong words, but Thucydides says much the same thing in his denunciations of the demagogues and in his contemptuous dismissal of the case against Alcibiades as a figment of the Demos' fevered imagination. Euryptolemus made the mistake of thinking that reasoned legal argument could prevail in the dying Athenian empire.

A number of questions about the Arginusae case remain. Why did someone decide precisely at this time to push popular sovereignty to the limit? Why were they so indifferent to public morale as to demote the greatest naval victory of the war to the level of a rescue operation? But in spite of the procedural irregularities, does the process qualify as a regular trial? The last question is the easiest. The Callixenus *probouleuma* laid down that votes (by tribes) were to be cast by placing ballots in urns (Xen. 1.7.9). In contrast to the non-judicial session at which it had been too dark to see a show of hands, this would be a trial session. As for the procedural rules, it is pertinent to recall that it was Hagnon, the father of Theramenes, who scrapped the procedural innovation that had been devised for use against Pericles. Hagnon's son did not show Pericles' son the same consideration, and the reason is that the younger Pericles was able to raise a special defence if given a separate trial. In this regard we recall Euryptolemus' assertion that the generals wanted to blame the ship's captains but were dissuaded by Pericles and Diomedon (Xen. 1.7.16–18). Is it a proper return for their civilized behaviour (*philanthrōpia*), asks Euryptolemus, to put them in danger of their lives? In other words, at separate trials their *philanthrōpia* might get them acquitted, but in a joint trial the accused would stand or fall together; the defence case was only as strong as its weakest link. The accusers were also relieved of the onerous task of proving criminal negligence against each and every accused; proof against one saddled the others with vicarious responsibility. By this means the one general who was himself shipwrecked and saved by chance (Xen. 1.7.32) would be held liable with the rest. The doctrine of common purpose has a long pedigree.

Finally, what were the political motives that prompted the launching of this insane enterprise at precisely this time? Two names stand out: Archedemus the demagogue and Theramenes the ship's captain.[38] Archedemus set the wheels in motion with his attack on Erasinides, but he charged embezzlement of money from the Hellespont; Xenophon says that 'he also accused him in connection with his *stratēgia*' but does not give details (1.7.2). Now, as *stratēgos* in 410 (with Thrasybulus) Theramenes was responsible for collecting badly needed money in the Hellespont region.[39] This gives Theramenes a clear interest in the Archedemus prosecution. The case may have started as a routine part of Erasinides' *euthynai*, which Archedemus, as the administrator of the Two-Obol Fund, was the logical person to undertake; hence his proposal of no more than a fine against Erasinides (Xen. 1.7.2). But in the course of the proceedings evidence pointing to something more serious came to light. The case was converted into an *eisangelia*. When the other generals reported to the Boule (1.7.3) signs of a serious difference of opinion became apparent, for Diomedon testified that he had urged his colleagues to make the rescue operation their top priority, whereas Erasinides wanted to set sail immediately for Mytilene; Thrasyllus had proposed a compromise (1.7.29–30). It was then that Theramenes thought up the idea of a joint trial which would dispense with the necessity of apportioning the blame to some while exonerating others.

Theramenes was well placed to devise this ingenious solution.

He was an expert on criminal law, having introduced the three penalties employed by the Four Hundred in 411, namely execution, imprisonment, and exile, which came to be known as *ta tria Theramenous*, the three penalties of Theramenes; the scholiast who credited him with having introduced them 'against those who committed illegalities' had a nice sense of humour.[40] He also had the necessary flexibility to turn a great patriotic occasion into a bloodbath; it was not for nothing that his rapid alternations between oligarchy and democracy earned him the nickname of 'Cothurnus' (Plut. *Nic.* 2.1, Xen. *Hell.* 2.3.30–1) – the actor's boot which could be worn on either foot. But his motives in the Arginusae affair are less easy to unravel. That he destroyed eight generals in order to save his own skin is unlikely; he already had Erasinides, who wanted to take the whole fleet to Mytilene, and separate trials would also have sufficed for convictions against one or two others. What of a political motive? The generals could hardly be seen as a threat to the democracy,[41] even if we could bring ourselves to accept Theramenes as its champion. Nor can it be thought that his basically oligarchic sympathies prompted the deliberate orchestration of an unbalanced performance by the Demos in order to undermine the system; destabilization is a modern invention.

One possibility remains. It is that Theramenes unscrupulously manipulated the Demos in order to secure re-election to the *stratēgia* which he had held over 410–7 but to which he had failed to be re-elected for 407–6. It is no accident that he won re-election for 405–4 in the wake of the trial, although rejected at the *dokimasia* for disloyalty to the democracy (Lys. 13.10). Diodorus furnishes a valuable clue when he says that the generals relied on their crews, who were numerous, to aid them at the trial, but they were unable to counteract the numbers of mourning relatives assembled by Theramenes (Diod. 13.101.5–7). During the family festival of the Apaturia, which was celebrated halfway through the affair, Theramenes drummed up support for his flagging initiative amongst the families of the fallen (Xen.1.7.8). In other words, Theramenes had assembled a constituency by playing on religious sentiment, and he had to give them their pound of flesh if he wanted their votes.[42]

The final catastrophe of the war at Aegospotami adds an interesting pendant to the Arginusae trial. Cleophon was indicted, ostensibly for desertion but in reality because of his opposition to the peace party. But the accusers were afraid of the influence of the last champion of the Demos on the jury and got Nicomachus, an expert on legislation, to 'find' a law authorizing the Boule to sit with the dicasts in the *dikastērion* which tried the case (Lys. 30.10–13). The law was a falsification, but the interesting part is that where Arginusae had brought demands for the absolute supremacy of the Demos even against its own laws, it was now enough to mention the word *nomos* to neutralize the Demos' power.[43] Thus the fifth-century trials ended with the ultimate absurdity: the Demos was able to crash through *nomoi* at will, but a non-*nomos* was able to stop it in its tracks.

V

FOURTH-CENTURY ATHENS: LAW REFORM, SCRUTINY, AND ILLEGALITY

1 TOWARDS THE FOURTH CENTURY

The unbridled sovereignty of the closing years of the Peloponnesian War was not an unmixed blessing. The Demos had
asserted its right to do whatever it liked, but at great cost; it
had hardly promoted its real interests by twice voting itself out
of power (in 411 and 404), not to mention the incalculable
damage that it had inflicted on the war effort by its displays of
judicial pyrotechnics. But there was a reaction against the abuse
of sovereign power even while it was taking place. A possible
scenario has the process of reform begin in 410, when *anagrapheis*
were appointed to inscribe the laws of Dracon and Solon.[1] This
restatement of the basic laws was admittedly more of a safeguard
against any renewal of the recently dislodged oligarchic regime
than against democratic excesses, and the law of Demophantus,
which renewed and amplified the ban on subverting the democracy in the same year,[2] was also aimed at the oligarchs. So, too,
was the law limiting the jurisdiction of the Boule, if it can be
dated to c.410 and seen as a sequel to the case of Lysimachus,
who was sentenced to death by the Boule but was rescued from
the executioner by Eumelides on the grounds that no citizen
should die without a verdict of a *dikastērion*; Lysimachus was
then tried and acquitted by a *dikastērion* and the Boule's verdicts
were made subject to ratification by jury-courts convened by the
thesmothetae.[3] But despite the anti-oligarchic posture of all these
measures they also acted as a brake on the Demos. The need

to rethink the parameters of sovereignty was beginning to be perceived, and once the Demos found it necessary to give those parameters greater statutory definition it was tacitly conceding the existence of an obligation on it to respect the parameters; it was moving towards the rule of law. The Arginusae débâcle was the last throw of the dice by those who believed that you could have it both ways. The people gave the first signs of a return to sanity when they tried to punish Callixenus and his friends, and after that they continued to tread the path of reform, though not without interruptions.

In 405 the Aegospotami disaster inspired Patrocleides' amnesty decree,[4] one of the provisions of which indemnified those whose conduct in public office had attracted an adverse finding by the auditors, but one which had not yet been translated into a criminal trial (Andoc. 1.78). This may be regarded as a reaction against the disastrous chain of events set in motion by Erasinides' *euthynai* in the Arginusae débâcle, but whether the indemnity ushered in a genuine improvement in the *euthynai* procedure remains to be seen.

The restatement of the laws of Dracon and Solon may have been close to completion by 404, but in that year law reform received a setback when Athens' defeat brought a suspension of the democratic constitution and the installation of the extreme oligarchy known as the Thirty. During that regime's first phase, when it is said to have acted moderately and in accordance with 'the ancestral constitution', it lifted the restrictions imposed on the Areopagus by Ephialtes, repealed such of Solon's laws as were uncertain, and abolished the sovereignty of the jurors.[5] This can only mean the total abolition of the jury-court system,[6] thus eliminating the radical jurisdiction in a manner reminiscent of a reform in the Roman Republic.[7] But what courts took the place of the *dikastēria*? In addition to the Areopagus one would expect the original version of the Heliaea, which was also part of the ancestral/Solonic system,[8] but the trials of the Thirty's 'good' period do not point to either of those courts. The trials divide broadly into two groups, those who had opposed Theramenes' peace initiative and were denounced by the devious machinations of Agoratus, and a motley collection of sycophants and embezzlers,[9] and both groups appear to have been tried by the Boule, presided over by the Thirty.[10] That the Thirty's judicial reforms included a law conferring capital jurisdiction on the Boule is likely despite Lysias' complaint that the anti-peace group were tried by the Boule, although the people had decreed that it be before a *dikastērion* of 2,000 (Lys. 13.35); that decree of the people will have preceded the advent of the Thirty, since the proceedings against the group had started under the democracy,[11] and it must be supposed that Lysias has suppressed the subsequent law sponsored by the Thirty. Another law, dating to the 'bad' period, forbade the execution of any member of the elite known as the Three Thousand without a vote of the Boule, but gave the Thirty an absolute discretion to execute anyone else.[12] Critias used the law to get rid of Theramenes; with a nice touch of irony he charged him with having failed to pick up survivors after Arginusae and with having accused, and thus caused the deaths of,[13] the unfortunate generals.[14] Under the same law the Thirty executed some 1,500 persons in order to eliminate enemies and seize their properties.[15]

The Thirty had nullified much of the progress that had been made with law reform since 410, but the democratic restoration brought a renewed attempt when, 'in the archonship of Eucleides' (403–2), the famous reconciliation (*dialyseis*) was enacted.[16] It included a revision of the homicide procedure and a general amnesty. Homicide was to be tried under the traditional procedure where someone killed with his own hand (*AP* 39.5). The meaning is not that direct murder was excluded from the amnesty,[17] but that the Areopagus' jurisdiction was limited to that form of the crime; it would no longer try cases of indirect murder, such as accusing someone and securing a death sentence against him.[18] As for the amnesty, it simply consigned past events to oblivion, but this did not apply to the Thirty or their agents, or to those who had governed Piraeus, unless they successfully underwent audit (*AP*. 39.6).[19]

Attention was then given to drafting a blueprint for the future. The *psēphisma* of Teisamenus made ancestral custom and the laws of Solon and Dracon the basic law of the land (what the Romans called the *ius civile*). This would be supplemented as required by laws inscribed and scrutinized by *nomothetae*;[20] citizens could inspect and comment on proposed laws, but formal approval was entrusted to the Boule and the 500 elected *nomothetae*, with the Assembly having no part therein; when laws had been enacted the Areopagus was to have a watching brief to ensure that magistrates applied the enacted laws.[21]

The last-mentioned provision is enigmatic. Did Teisamenus retain the Thirty's full restoration of the Areopagus' guardianship of the laws, or did he do something else? For the most part scholars either assume the former[22] or doubt it, because there is no evidence of the Areopagus having exercised such a power between 403–2 and the mid-fourth century.[23] As good a solution as any is that of Harrision, who thinks that the Areopagus was simply given custody of the new statute-book, from which it would be able to say whether a given ordinance was 'an enacted law'.[24] One of the arguments in favour of this view is that on our interpretation of the revised homicide procedure the Areopagus tended to be distanced from the political sphere, since it could no longer pronounce on indirect murder.[25] Another argument in favour can be deduced from the history of Nicomachus, one of the *anagrapheis* in the first phase of law reform who was reappointed, as a colleague of Teisamenus, in the post-Thirty phase.[26] In 399 he was accused by Lysias or his client (Lys. 30), mainly on a charge of refusing to render an account of his office, but other interesting facts emerge from the speech. Thus, he is said to have inserted or erased laws in return for payment, to have supplied parties to suits with opposing laws, to have refused to hand over laws when brought before a *dikastērion*, and to have concocted a law allowing the Boule to sit with the dicasts at Cleophon's trial (Lys. 30.2–3, 11–14).[27] All this (if true) shows that Areopagite custody of the new statute-book and verification of its contents would certainly have been needed. It can of course be asked how, in that case, Nicomachus was able to get away with his frauds, but that is sufficiently answered by another question: How did Lysias know of the frauds if there was not some sort of central registry?

Teisamenus' decree was followed by five supplementary measures, probably extending over 403–399.[28] The decrees listed by Andocides (1.85–9) include the following: no uninscribed law (*nomos agraphos*) to be enforced, which is said to have amounted to a tacit repeal of pre-403–2 rules unless incorporated in the code;[29] no *psēphisma* to override a *nomos*, thus subordinating *psēphismata*, which the Assembly was still at large to pass, to *nomoi*, which were the exclusive business of the new legislators;[30] no law applicable to a particular person rather than to the Athenians as a whole to be valid unless passed by a quorum

of 6,000 citizens by secret ballot;[31] laws passed since the archonship of Eucleides to be enforced.

As finally consolidated in the fourth century, *nomothesia*, or the
procedure for revising the laws,[32] displays the following
features: In the first prytany of every year the Assembly was
invited to consider the existing body of laws, which were grouped
in four categories.[33] The Assembly voted as to whether the *nomoi*
in each category were satisfactory. If any changes were thought
to be required, any citizen was at large to propose new laws. Five
men were appointed to defend the existing laws, and a board of
nomothetae drawn from those who had sworn the jury-court (or
heliastic) oath was constituted. The Assembly decided how much
time was to be allowed to the *nomothetae* to decide between the
existing law and the proposed amendment. The decision of the
nomothetae was final, so that once more the Assembly was
excluded from the legislative process. But this exclusion was only
partial, for the initiative for the review came from the Assembly,
leaving the power of decision with the *nomothetae*. But in the case
of *psēphismata* both initiative and decision remained with the
Assembly, as hitherto.

The role of the *anagrapheis*, and after them the *nomothetae*, raises
an interesting question: Have we at last got a clear-cut forerunner
to Theophrastus and Demetrius of Phalerum? Given the new professionalism that now informs lawmaking, given also that drafting
laws and codifying were amongst the functions of the Roman
jurisconsult,[34] the idea seems possible in principle. The very fact
that Lysias has to denigrate Nicomachus and Teisamenus as
'under-clerks' (*hypogrammateis*) not worthy to be doing the same
work as Solon, Themistocles and Pericles,[35] suggests that their
status was sufficiently elevated to worry him. Moreover, when
he enumerates Nicomachus' falsifications of laws, is he perhaps
disclosing something more subtle than fraud, namely interpretation? In particular, when Nicomachus is accused of supplying
opposing laws (*nomous enantious*) to the parties in a suit (30.3),
are we in fact looking at *opinions* given to litigants by Nicomachus
and falsely labelled *nomoi* by Lysias? That is no more than an
outside possibility, but the *nomothetae* (fourth-century version) are
on firmer ground, for they had to decide the juristic merits of
competing laws – the extant and the proposed. And in reaching
a decision they were, as persons who had sworn the jury-court
oath, obliged 'to judge according to the laws and decrees of the

Athenian people and the Boule, or *in a case not covered by any law, according to my opinion (gnomē) as to what is most just*, after listening to both sides' (Dem. 24.149–51). The power to supplement a *casus omissus* by, for example, analogy was at the very heart of a jurist's activity; it was his way of giving effect to principles of equity,[36] and that is exactly what the *nomothetae* were expected to do. The fact that a *nomothetēs* was in office for only one day[37] is something of a stumbling-block, but it is possible that certain persons with special expertise were chosen repeatedly. All in all, the architects of law reform over the late fifth and fourth centuries are of interest not only because of the stability that they may well have brought to the judicial and legislative scene, but also because of their qualifications.

2 OFFICIAL MISCONDUCT

There were three procedures by which a man's suitability for, or performance in, office could be scrutinized. First, *dokimasia*, a preliminary scrutiny by a jury-court before entering on an office; second, *apocheirotonia*, deposition from office followed by a trial (generally by way of *eisangelia*); third, *euthynai*, the mandatory audit which was held at the end of an official's term and could lead to his trial at the instance of any citizen.[38]

The battery of remedies by which the Demos asserted strict control of its officials applied not only to regular office-holders like generals, archons, and members of the Boule, but also to *ad hoc* appointees like envoys entrusted with diplomatic missions. In the fifth century the great bulk of cases concerned generals, as we know from the trials of Miltiades, Cimon, Pericles, Thucydides, and the Arginusae eight. The fourth-century records also disclose a preponderance of military leaders, but there are some important civilians as well.

A representative selection of cases under the first two heads, *dokimasia* and *apocheirotonia*, would include the following: Philo, whose candidacy for the Boule was challenged because by leaving Athens and turning to banditry he had failed to play an active part against the Thirty (Lys. 31); Leodamas, who failed his *dokimasia* for an archonship in 382, it is said on political rather than moral grounds,[39] though dressing the former up as the latter was easy enough, as Philo's case shows; Timotheus, whose brilliant military career was first interrupted and later terminated in the court-room rather than on the battlefield: in 373 he was deposed for failing to relieve Corcyra but was acquitted when tried by *eisangelia*, only to be brought down in 356-5 when his refusal to fight in the Hellespont because of the weather earned him a charge of *prodosia* and a heavy fine at the instance of Chares,[40] a fellow-general who preferred prosecuting his colleagues to co-operating with them;[41] Timomachus, who was charged with *prodosia* in 361-0, either for betraying the Chersonese to Cotys[42] or for illegally assisting the exiled Callistratus;[43] Cephisodotus, who was deposed and fined in 360-59 for concluding an unfavourable treaty with the mercenary Charidemus, which the Athenians refused to ratify, but bounced back to become archon in 358-7;[44] and Theocrines, the thesmothete whose co-option of his brother, a notorious sycophant, as an assessor in 344-3 raised such a storm that the Assembly would have deposed all the thesmothetes if the offender had not been dismissed.[45] The last-mentioned case is a striking example of how standards of judicial decorum had improved.

We now address impeachment after completion of a full term of office. Primarily this means the launching of a prosecution pursuant to the final audit, the *euthynai*, but it has recently been argued that comparatively little use was made of *euthynai*-generated impeachments of generals, most of whose misdeeds were brought home to them by deposition and trial during their terms of office.[46] It is admittedly curious that the only trials expressly attested as flowing from the *euthynai*, namely Cimon and Paches, date to the fifth century,[47] but unless we include a completely hypothetical change in the law in the revision of 403-399, it must be supposed that at least some of the post-office trials which are not expressly linked to *euthynai*[48] in fact belong under that head.

It is only in respect of generals that the apparent anomaly arises, for *euthynai*-generated trials of officials other than generals are as common in the fourth century as in the fifth.[49] Two of these, Andocides and Aeschines, will be included in our special discussion of the accountability of envoys.[50] At this point mention may be made of Melanopus, whose many trials for corruption included a charge of embezzlement following his *euthynai* as a member of the *synedrion* of the Second Athenian Alliance.[51] Also pertinent is the case of Timarchus, whose corruption as inspector of mercenaries earned him a trial in 348.[52]

If any trial merits special mention it is that of Lysicles, at Lycurgus' instance, in 338. The accused was held responsible for Athens' defeat by Philip at Chaeronea, and was condemned to death; but his co-commanders, Stratocles and the agile Chares, appear to have gone scot-free.[53] A fragment of Lycurgus' speech for the prosecution establishes this as a *euthynai*-generated trial of a general: 'You were in office as a general. [The disaster of Chaeronea] occurred under your command, yet you dare to live, to look upon the sun, and even to show yourself in the Agora' (Diod. 16.88.2). This is a picture of a man who is no longer in office but has not yet been called to account. Therefore his vacation of office was due not to premature deposition but to effluxion of time. It is possible, however, that Lysicles' misdeeds other than Chaeronea had been brought up earlier by way of an *apocheirotonia* which had fired a warning shot across his bows, if a Latin quotation in Rutilius Lupus is from the same speech of Lycurgus: 'For the moment I pass over his grave transgressions which were committed without authority, I pass over his false despatches to the Boule and the frequent warnings that you gave him, and I turn to the much more serious acts that he committed very recently.'[54]

One would also think that Ergocles, who was arraigned in 388 for *prodosia*, embezzlement and corruption during the Asia Minor expedition of 389 in which he had served with Thrasybulus, had completed his generalship prior to his receipt of a sentence of death and confiscation of property.[55] This impression is strengthened by the trial of Philocrates, purser on one of Ergocles' ships, for in a speech for the accuser Lysias says that Ergocles was recently condemned to death because his embezzlement had netted him more than thirty talents, but not a trace of the money could be found (Lys. 29.1–2). Clearly Ergocles' audit had been carried out immediately prior to his impeachment.

3 DIPLOMATIC MISSIONS

One particular aspect of the process of official scrutiny is of special interest, namely the scrutiny of envoys entrusted with diplomatic missions, which for the most part means peace negotiations. This scrutiny has one unique feature, in that it did not lend itself to the deposition option; your performance of your mission could hardly be assessed until you had completed your task.[56] It was thus essentially a matter for *euthynai* followed by, probably, *eisangelia*. There are two leading cases, Andocides and others, arising out of a peace mission during the Corinthian War, and Aeschines at the instance of Demosthenes, arising out of a peace mission to Philip of Macedon. But in order to put those cases in perspective it is appropriate to begin with a survey of some of the fifth-century trials that preceded Andocides' case.

The first case that comes to mind is Callias, who is said by Demosthenes to have been brought up at his *euthynai* for taking bribes on an embassy, for which he was fined fifty talents and narrowly escaped the death penalty (Dem. 19.273–5). Demosthenes adds that on that embassy Callias negotiated a peace treaty with the Persians. This is the famous (or notorious) Peace of Callias, the authenticity of which was put in issue by the historian Theopompus in the fourth century and has remained in contention ever since.[57] Without wishing to enter the debate, one is constrained to say that the use to which Demosthenes puts the treaty in his speech against Aeschines needs careful attention. He describes it as the most honourable ever made by Athens, but says that this did not help Callias, for the Athenians ascribed the peace to their city's standing, the bribes to the character of the envoy. They held that corruption was so damaging to the state that it could never be tolerated. This is an interesting proposition: an act wrongful *per se* was not condoned merely because it benefited the city. (We recall Thuc.6.60, condemning the witch-hunt but conceding that it benefited the city.) More often, however, damage to the city's interests was the test. Thus, when the generals Pythodorus, Sophocles, and Eurymedon approved of the treaty by which the cities of Sicily settled their differences in 424 in order to present a united front against Athens, the generals were indicted for bribery and Eurymedon was fined, while the other two were exiled (Thuc. 4.65.3).

The case of Antiphon, Onomacles and Archeptolemus in 411–10 is of special interest, for Pseudo-Plutarch has preserved the text of two legal documents transmitted by Caecilius and going back ultimately to Craterus' collection of decrees.[58] Antiphon and the others were part of a peace mission sent to Sparta by the Four Hundred. But no treaty was struck (Thuc. 8.91.1). It has been surmised, however, that they came to some sort of understanding with the Spartans.[59] Be that as it may, after the democratic restoration a prosecution was stirred up by

Theramenes. Pseudo-Plutarch quotes the *psēphisma* voted by the Boule:

> Regarding the men denounced by the generals for acting to the detriment of the city and the army[60] while serving as envoys to Lacedaemon, and for sailing on an enemy vessel and for passing by land through Deceleia, namely Archeptolemus, Onomacles and Antiphon, Andron moved that they be arrested and brought before the *dikastērion* for trial. The thesmothetes shall summon them tomorrow and on the return day shall propose that the appointed accusers, and the generals and anyone else who so desires, shall accuse them of *prodosia*. Whoever is convicted by the court shall be punished according to the law relating to traitors.

Pseudo-Plutarch also quotes the judgment in the case:

> Archeptolemus and Antiphon, both present, were convicted of *prodosia*. Their sentence was that they be handed over to the Eleven for execution, that their property be confiscated and ten per cent thereof be paid to the Goddess, that their houses be demolished and boundary-stones be set up with the inscription, 'Property of Archeptolemus and Antiphon, traitors'. The two demarchs shall make a declaration of their property. They shall not be buried at Athens or in Athenian territory, they shall be infamous [*atimous*], as shall their descendants both legitimate and illegitimate, as also shall anyone be who adopts any descendant of theirs. This decree shall be inscribed on a bronze tablet set up where the decrees relating to Phrynichus[61] are set.

Onomacles did not appear to stand trial. It has been conjectured that the Onomacles named by Xenophon (*Hell.* 2.3.2) as one of the Thirty is the same man.[62]

It is evident that the indictment comprised two separate heads – prejudicing the city and the army on the diplomatic mission, and committing treachery at home (cf. Thuc. 8.90–1). This raises a thorny question, for there is support for the view that the *nomos eisangeltikos* attested by Hyperides and defining three categories of treachery[63] was passed shortly after Antiphon's case.[64] Without debating that question fully, one is constrained to draw attention to something which not only supports a date in the vicinity of Antiphon's trial but suggests that the trial may actually have prompted the *nomos*. Thucydides says that Antiphon was often consulted on lawsuits, and when on trial made the best speech ever (Thuc. 8.68). Pseudo-Plutarch also expresses great admiration for the speech *Concerning eisangelia* which Antiphon composed in his defence (Plut. *Mor.* 833D). It is possible that Antiphon put up such a spirited defence, including a comprehensive review of *eisangelia*, that a consolidating ordinance was needed in order to close loopholes to which his speech had drawn attention.

The cases discussed so far do not greatly illuminate the nature of the charge of *parapresbeia*, which is the generic term for charges against envoys.[65] Callias' crime benefited Athens; the generals in Sicily acquiesced in someone else's treaty rather than struck one for Athens, and in any case they were regular commanders, not special envoys; and though *parapresbeia* was one of the charges against Antiphon, we are completely in the dark as to the facts on which the charge was based. The question now is whether our first fourth-century case, concerning the peace mission of the orator Andocides during the Corinthian War, is able to offer a higher magnitude of illumination.

In 392 two peace initiatives were launched in the hope of ending both the Corinthian War and Sparta's war with Persia. The first, for which Xenophon is our source, took the form of a mission to Sardis by the Spartan Antalcidas, who when his *démarche* became known was joined by a contingent from Athens and her allies; Antalcidas proposed a treaty under which the Great King would retain suzerainty over the islands and Greek cities of Asia Minor, but on condition of autonomy for those areas; Athens objected because this would deprive her of Lemnos, Imros and Scyros, and nothing came of the negotiations (Xen. *Hell.* 4.8.12–15). This initiative, as well as another which followed it, was also discussed by Philochorus, according to the account of Didymus. Philochorus said that the Athenians had stigmatized the treaty as an impious crime (*asebes paranomēma*) because it recognized the King's rights over the Greeks of Asia; Callistratus impeached the envoys who had come to terms at Sparta, namely Epicrates, Andocides, Cratinus, and Euboulides, and they were exiled *in absentia* (*FGrH* 3B 328 F149). The Argument to Andocides' speech *On the Peace* records another fragment of Philochorus. After noting that the Athenians sent envoys with plenary powers (*presbeis autokratores*) to Sparta, that the envoys were given forty days to submit the Spartan proposals to the people, and that Andocides' speech urged acceptance, the Argument goes on to say that according to Philochorus, Spartan envoys accompanied the delegation back to Athens but got nothing for their pains because Andocides was unable to persuade the people (ibid., F 149B).

It is generally concluded from these passages that after the abortive conference at Sardis, Athens sent ten envoys, still in 392, to Sparta, amongst them the four named by Philochorus.[66] It is also widely (but not universally) believed that the trial *in absentia* to which Philochorus refers was held after the mission to Sparta of 392, not after a subsequent mission in 386 which did produce peace.[67] The minority opinion which makes 386 the date of the trial[68] relies on a passage in Aristides, to the effect that the Athenians were the last of the Greeks to agree to the peace, and only did so when confronted with the prospect of fighting their own allies; and even then they did not accept it by a unanimous vote, and condemned those who had persuaded them, considering it contrary to their nature and improper for any of the Hellenes to negotiate with the King (Arist. 1.293 Behr). The scholiast takes 'condemned those who had persuaded them' to mean especially Epicrates, and the conclusion is reached that Aristides is referring to the peace of 386 and that Epicrates is the same man as Andocides' fellow-envoy; therefore the whole episode, including the trial, belongs to 386. But there are several answers to this. The most cogent is that Aristides does *not* identify the crime as *parapresbeia*. He says that they condemned 'those who had persuaded them', which can very well mean the rhetors whose eloquence had induced them to vote for the peace of 386, in which case the charge was a *graphē paranomōn* in its broadest sense, against a proposal which was contrary to the interests of the people.[69] If that is Aristides' meaning, the scholiast's identification of Epicrates is mistaken; indeed he merely says that Aristides is hinting at Epicrates, which is as good an indication as any that he is guessing. The dating of the trial to 392 must be allowed to stand.

It remains to consider the factual basis of the trial. What were the wrongful acts that caused the envoys to fall foul of the law? There is no point in running aimlessly through the possible types of *parapresbeia*[80] in the hope that one will fit, but there is a hitherto unsuspected category that may work. It is *asebeia*. The proof is Philochorus' assertion that the Athenians stigmatized recognition of the King's suzerainty over the Asia Minor Greeks as an impious crime (*asebes paranomēma*). That phrase, translated to the domestic criminal law, provided the juristic basis for an attack on the envoys; it was impious because trophies commemorating the victories over Darius and Xerxes had been dedicated to the gods and were inviolable.[71] It is true that Aristides (1.293 Behr) has the Athenians condemn the rhetors because the treaty of 386 was improper 'having regard to the trophies', but there is no reason why a principle established against the envoys in 392 should not have been used against the rhetors in 386. It has been noticed often enough that Andocides sidesteps sensitive questions in his speech,[72] and his silence is understandable. Whatever powers envoys plenipotentiary may have had,[73] they dared not flout the overriding veto represented by the religious barrier. The Spartans could propose the autonomy or subjection of the Asia Minor Greeks with a clear conscience, because the real thrust of Athenian thinking was towards the trophies of Marathon rather than those of the second Persian invasion. Andocides, who had already been in trouble with the gods on two occasions,[74] forgot his narrow escapes in 392, and this time the gods did not forgive.

Our next case is a fairly straightforward affair. In 367 missions from Greek states flocked to the Great King, who since the Peace of 386 had acquired something of the status of an international arbitrator. Sparta hoped to block the independence of Messene, Athens was trying to reassert her hold on Amphipolis, and Boeotia was bent on establishing the brief Theban hegemony over Greece. A symposium of six states was held at Susa, with Athens represented by Timagoras and Leon, and Thebes by Pelopidas and Ismenias. Pelopidas made a favourable impression on the King, reminding him of Thebes' pro-Persian attitude over the years. Timagoras confirmed the truth of everything that Pelopidas said, and that decided the issue in Pelopidas' favour. The King granted his request that Sparta and Athens recognize the independence of Messene and Amphipolis and that the Athenian fleet be beached. When the mission returned to Athens, Leon accused Timagoras of taking bribes to foster the interests of Thebes against those of Athens. Timagoras was sentenced to death.[75]

Our final case is Demosthenes' prosecution of Aeschines in 343. The bare facts are that in 348–7 the possibility of ending

Athens' war with Philip began to be mooted, and Philocrates proposed the initiation of peace talks. His reward was to be prosecuted for making an illegal proposal, but Demosthenes defended him and saved him from the enormous fine of 100 talents claimed by the accuser; the latter was punished for failing to secure one-fifth of the votes.[76] In 346 Philocrates proposed the despatch of ten envoys to Macedon. The party included Philocrates, Aeschines and Demosthenes. On their return they reported that Philip was interested in peace, but on the crucial issue of Athens' claim to Amphipolis he held out no hope of a compromise. Philocrates proposed an alliance with Philip to which Athens' allies would be admitted, with the exception of the Phocians and Halians. Aeschines and Demosthenes proposed that all allies be admitted, but next day Aeschines supported Philocrates' motion, except that the exclusionary clause was deleted, thus leaving the question open as to what 'allies' meant. A decree in this form was passed after Aeschines had assured the Assembly that Philip would respect its wishes in regard to the Phocians even though they would not be expressly safe-guarded in the treaty (Dem. 19.321–2). The same ten envoys were appointed to take the oaths of Philip and his allies and to discuss 'other questions' (Aesch. 2.103–4). Despite Demosthenes' protests the envoys moved slowly, and instead of taking each Macedonian ally's oath in its own city took the oaths of all of them at Pherae. The delay gave Philip time to strengthen his position in Thrace by making Cersobleptes a vassal (Dem. 19.150–81). When Philip appeared at Pella after keeping the mission waiting for some three weeks he made no concessions in regard to the Phocians or Halians.

The envoys returned to Athens in July 346, some five weeks after their departure. Demosthenes denounced his fellow-envoys to the Boule, which was sufficiently impressed by his information to refuse the envoys the customary vote of thanks and public dinner – which, as Demosthenes notes, had not even happened to Timagoras (Dem. 19.18, 31–2). But when the Assembly met, Aeschines outmanoeuvred Demosthenes, suppressing the Boule's *probouleuma* and making much play with a letter from Philip promising to settle the Phocian question to Athens' satisfaction (Dem. 19–24, 35–41). On the motion of Philocrates a *psēphisma* was passed extending the alliance with Philip to his descendants and pledging Athens to use force if the Phocians refused to give up their occupation of Delphi (Dem. 48–50). Phocis surrendered to Philip and Aeschines joined Philip in celebrating the event. Philip's savage treatment of Phocis included a decree of outlawry on the grounds of impiety that could have been drafted by an Athenian expert.[77] The Amphictyonic Council resolved to transfer the Phocian vote to Philip. The Athenians were so disgusted that they refused to send representatives to the Pythian Games; but Aeschines was there (Dem. 128).

Matters came to a head when Philip asked Athens to recognize his election to the Amphictyonic Council. Aeschines supported the request but was shouted down by the Assembly (Dem. 111–13). At this stage members of the second mission to Macedon were called on to undergo their *euthynai*. Aeschines tried to avoid scrutiny, claiming that the clearance given to the first mission covered the second. The auditors may have accepted this,[78] though we are told that when Aeschines was about to render his accounts Demosthenes and Timarchus stood forth to accuse him; Aeschines demanded a preliminary hearing, on the basis that Timarchus had prostituted himself and was debarred from being an accuser (Dem. 19 *Hypothesis* II 10). Timarchus, who may have been Aeschines' principal accuser,[79] was obliged, in 346–5, to submit to a special scrutiny which led into a jury-trial.[80] Demosthenes may have appeared for Timarchus,[81] but Aeschines proved his case and Timarchus was barred.

The disqualification of Timarchus delayed the case against Aeschines, and it was not until late in 343 that the case came to trial. It might not have been reinstated on the roll even then had it not been preceded by two other skirmishes in the forensic war, both in the earlier part of 343. A certain Antiphon, an agent of Philip, was caught by Demosthenes trying to sabotage the Piraeus dockyard. Demosthenes arrested him and took him before the Assembly, but Aeschines made a great fuss about democratic rights and entering premises without authority, and Antiphon was released. However, the Areopagus arrested him and brought him before the people, and he was tortured and executed (Dem. 18.132–3). Next, Philocrates was charged by Hyperides with *parapresbeia* in connection with the Macedon mission; he was condemned to death *in absentia*. Aeschines cites the case in his defence, asking how he can hope to be acquitted when the city has already condemned Philocrates; he answers himself by comparing Philocrates' self-incriminating flight with his own appearance to stand trial (Aesch. 2.6). He adds that the main thrust of the allegations in regard to the mission is against Philocrates and the other envoys, but he is being dragged into it (Aesch. 8). The point is reminiscent of that which was in issue at the Arginusae trial. There, too, every accused was held responsible for the acts of his colleagues, the only difference being that they were tried together, whereas Philocrates and Aeschines were tried separately. Aeschines makes a similar point later in the speech when he complains that by blaming both Philocrates and himself Demosthenes is making a divided accusation (Aesch. 121).

Aeschines' problems were compounded by another incident shortly before his trial. In c. 343 Athens was involved in a dispute with Delos concerning the sanctuary on the island, then administered by Athens but claimed by Delos. The Assembly appointed Aeschines to appear before the Amphictyonic Council to argue the case on Athens' behalf, thus displaying what Demosthenes describes as 'the sort of unintelligence which has so often dogged public affairs'.[82] Aeschines may have written a speech for the occasion (Plut. *Mor* 840E) but he was never able to deliver it, because the Areopagus reversed the appointment, dismissing Aeschines as a traitor and nominating Hyperides; the vote was taken on the altar and Aeschines did not receive a single ballot, which was taken as a proof of his guilt (Dem. 18.134–6). Hyperides won the case (Plut. *Mor.* 849F).

It was in this favourable climate that Demosthenes brought Aeschines to trial – or is generally assumed to have done so, for there is a problem that has largely gone unnoticed. Both Plutarch and Pseudo-Plutarch learnt from Idomeneus that Aeschines was tried, was defended by Eubulus, and was acquitted by the narrow margin of thirty votes (Plut. *Dem.* 15.3, *Mor.* 840C). But both sources note a tradition according to which the two orators composed their speeches but did not deliver them, the reason being that the case could not come on because of Chaeronea. Plutarch is also worried by the fact that in Ctesiphon's case[83] neither Demosthenes nor Aeschines says unequivocally that it did come to trial. However, the story about Chaeronea is plainly false unless there was a battle there in 343 in addition to the well-known engagement of 338. At any rate, Dionysius of Halicarnassus had access to a version which enabled him to date the trial with precision to 343–2 (*Letter to Ammaeus* 1.10).[84]

Despite the speeches of Demosthenes and Aeschines there is

a lot that we do not know about the trial. In general terms the charge was *parapresbeia*, but when it comes to the specific ways in which Aeschines committed that crime we have to rely heavily on Demosthenes' opening summation, when he lists the following as an envoy's responsibilities: (i) his reports; (ii) the advice that he tenders; (iii) compliance with his instructions; (iv) prompt completion of his mission; (v) above all, his integrity (Dem. 19.4). The First Argument to the speech lists three counts against Aeschines: supporting Philocrates' proposal for a disgraceful peace; wasting time and contributing to the loss of Thrace; making false reports and contributing to the Phocian disaster. The Second Argument notes a main head and a supporting head: the main head is the Phocian disaster, which is fortified by a number of presumptions; the supporting head is that the main head was done for money, and again there are presumptions.[85] Aeschines himself says that the allegation of *prodosia* annoyed him most (Aesch. 2.146), but whether that was formally charged is a moot point. Suidas sums up his professions as 'actor, orator and traitor, because he betrayed Cersobleptes and the Phocians', but Suidas is not speaking technically. The best guess is that the indictment closely followed the five heads in Demosthenes' summation.

How did Aeschines manage to get off scot-free when Philocrates, who cannot seriously be held to have been more guilty, was forced into exile? Aeschines himself raises this question when he claims that by remaining in Athens to stand trial he has displayed the *bona fides* that Philocrates lācked (Aesch. 2.4). He knew that if the jury were disposed to acquit him they would need a peg to hang the acquittal on. Another possible reason for Aeschines' good fortune is that Demosthenes was in a most ambiguous position. If all the envoys were to be tarred with the same brush, an exception could not easily be made in Demosthenes' case. In Philocrates' case, on the other hand, Hyperides, who accused, had no personal involvement, and that enhanced his credibility. Another difference between the two orators is that Hyperides was a better lawyer than Demosthenes. His exposition of the *eisangelia* law (Hyp. 4.1–9) achieves a degree of concision and clarity that one finds rarely, if ever, in Demosthenes. And Hyperides himself tells us how carefully and accurately he drew up the indictment against Philocrates (Hyp. 4. 29–30). There is nothing to compare with it in Demosthenes' speech against Aeschines, perhaps not anywhere in the Demosthenic corpus.

There were other factors that also contributed to Aeschines' success. Some of the credit is due to his defenders, who included the former treasurer Eubulus, whose influence Demosthenes found so embarrassing (Dem. 19.289–90), as well as the highly respected Phocion (Aesch. 2.184). Also, public opinion played an important part. The narrow margin of the acquittal, a mere thirty votes on a jury numbering anything from 501 to 1501,[86] testifies to the sharp division between those who favoured co-operation with Macedon and those who opposed it. The swing in the polls over the interval since Philocrates' case was very slight.

4 RESTRAINTS ON ILLEGALITY

There were two judicial restraints on illegality, the *graphē paranomōn* and the *graphē nomōn mē epitēdeiōn theinai*. The *graphē paranomōn*, which will be the main focus of our attention, was largely a fourth-century remedy, for though cases occur in the late fifth century they make up only a small proportion of the total.[87] The remedy has been defined as 'A public action against a rhetor who had . . . carried a *psēphisma* of the Boule or the Demos that was contrary to the laws in force and/or inexpedient'.[88] The *graphē nomōn mē epitēdeiōn theinai*, which was literally an action for making an 'unsuitable' or 'inexpedient' law, is not easily distinguishable from the *graphē paranomōn*. The best guess seems to be that the *paranomōn* was used against *psēphismata*, the *mē epitēdeiōn* against *nomoi*.[89]

The *GP*[90] was based on the idea that it was for the proposer of a law to satisfy himself that it was not contrary to any existing law. It thus saddled rhetors with a responsibility equivalent to that resting on the holders of public office, so that in a certain sense it can be described as the non-office-holder's *euthynai*. But it was more flexible than the process which called officials to account, and it had a more drastic immediate effect. It could be brought either before or after the passage of a proposed law; in the former case it suspended a vote until the issue had been tried, in the latter it suspended the operation of the law. All that the accuser need do was to lodge a sworn declaration (*hypōmosia*) of his intention to bring a *GP*.[91] He risked a fine of 1,000 drachmae and possibly disfranchisement if he either abandoned the action or failed to obtain one-fifth of the votes,[92] but if the tactical advantage was important enough that was no deterrent. If his motive was personal enmity rather than tactical advantage he could look forward to the satisfaction of seeing his enemy punished.[93]

The first known use of the *GP* dates to 415, when Andocides' father, Leogoras, brought the action against Speusippus for having proposed to the Boule that Leogoras be imprisoned as an accessory to the profanation of the Mysteries. Leogoras claimed that the proposal was based on a false allegation to the effect that he had been present at a profanation, and on the strength of this he persuaded a jury of 6,000[94] to overrule Speusippus' decree (Andoc. 1.17, 22). The case thus appears to have turned not on the illegality of the decree but on a question of fact,[95] but the usual explanation, that in 415 legal argument was less well developed than in the fourth century,[96] does not carry conviction; if their jurisprudence was so backward, how did they manage to invent the *GP*? A better answer is that the same allegation of a false statement in a public record underlay the leading case on the *GP*, namely, Aeschines' prosecution of Ctesiphon, to which we shall advert presently. It may also be possible to clarify Leogoras' case by comparing it with the proceedings, in 415, against two Bouleutai who had taken part in the mutilation of the Hermae.[97] It was proposed, and accepted by the Boule, that Scamander's *psēphisma* forbidding the torture of citizens be suspended (Andoc. 1.43). The thought occurs that a similar use of torture may have been implicit in Speusippus' decree against Leogoras, in which case there was a mixed question of law and fact in Leogoras' *GP*. Speusippus' decree will only have contravened Scamander's law if Leogoras had not attended the Mysteries; if he had attended, the equation of the profanation with treason in the form of *katalysis tou dēmou*[98] overrode Scamander's law. Thus the resolution of the question of fact was a condition precedent to the resolution of the question of law.

The case of the two Bouleutai may serve another important purpose. It has been observed that there is something odd about the case, since the conflict with Scamander's *psēphisma* ought to have encouraged the accused to avail themselves of the *GP* instead of merely seeking sanctuary at an altar.[99] But instead of devising an esoteric explanation[100] we should draw the obvious inference that the *GP* had not yet been devised when the attack on the Bouleutai was mounted. It was used for the first time by

Leogoras when the accusers turned their attention to him, still in 415 but *after* the Bouleutai.[101]

Of the other fifth-century cases, the only one calling for mention is the notorious Arginusae affair.[102] As we have seen, Callixenus' proposal for a single trial of the eight generals inspired a charge of illegality, but strong-arm tactics by the prosecution forced the abandonment of the action. Then, when the defence moved for trial under Cannonus' *psēphisma*, the response was a GP by the prosecution. This case interferes with an interesting theory propounded by Sealey. He suggests that where Roman law recognized that whatever the people had last ordered was valid, fourth-century Athenian law required the express repeal of the earlier law, failing which a GP lay.[103] To this perfectly correct statement of the position Sealey adds that a similar position cannot be maintained for the fifth century because of the Arginusae case, because if express repeal was all that was needed, Callixenus could simply have included a repeal of Cannonus' law in his proposal, instead of resorting to intimidation. But if express repeal was not required under the GP as first devised, two things follow. First, there must have been two versions of the GP, with express repeal only included in the later. Second, if express repeal was not included in the earlier version, what objective test was prescribed? A better answer to the Arginusae case is that although express repeal was required, its use against Cannonus' law would have created a dangerous situation. That law had adumbrated a broad category of treason by way of 'doing wrong to the people' (Xen. *Hell*. 1.7.20), and however determined Callixenus may have been, he was not about to declare an open season for treason. Thus the alternative of intimidation may have been forced on him by practical considerations.

The fourth century, to which we now turn, displays a heavy concentration of cases in which the proposal under attack dealt with the conferment of honours. Of thirty-four cases listed by Hansen down to 322, no less than fourteen fall under that head, while six deal with foreign affairs, four with finance, three with citizenship, two with impiety, one with *nomothetae*, and four with unknown matters.[104] The cases in which *psēphismata* conferring honours were attacked are not only the most numerous, they also include the leading case on the GP, Aeschines' indictment of Ctesiphon for proposing the award of a gold crown to Demosthenes in recognition of his services to the city. This case will be the main focus of our discussion of the *GP* in the fourth century. (Other cases in the Demosthenic corpus could be cited. One thinks, for example, of the use of the *GP* in cases involving abolition of fiscal immunities, crowns for a group of councillors, grants of personal inviolability, bail for state debtors, false entries of debts (Dem. 20, 22–5). But Aeschines v. Ctesiphon offers the best overview of the institution.)

Aeschines lodged his indictment of Ctesiphon in 336 at the time of the latter's proposal of the honour for Demosthenes, but the case did not come to trial until 330. As with the charge of *parapresbeia* against Aeschines, we possess the speeches of both Demosthenes and Aeschines, but whether the obfuscations resulting from the embarrassment of riches are any less on that account remains to be seen.

Aeschines raised three heads of accusation, though there is some uncertainty as to the order in which he presented them. The most coherent account is in the copy of the indictment included in the transmitted text of Demosthenes' speech (Dem. 18.54–5), and despite the disfavour in which documents in the orators are held[105] we would do well to take note of this particular document. An abridged version runs as follows:

> Aeschines indicted Ctesiphon for an illegal proposal, namely
> 'That Demosthenes be crowned with a gold crown and that
> it be proclaimed in the Theatre at the Great Dionysia that
> he is being crowned for his merit and goodwill towards all
> Greeks and towards the Athenian Demos, and also for his
> rectitude and constant promotion of the best interests of the
> Demos', all these proposals being false and illegal because
> the laws forbid, *first*, the entry of false statements in the
> public records, *second*, the crowning of an official liable to
> audit, and *third*, the proclamation of a crown in the Theatre
> at the Dionysia. Fine demanded: fifty talents.

The first count is the one on which Aeschines places the most reliance, though he only deals with it after he has completed his address on the other two counts (Aesch. 3.49). He admits that he has kept it out of its proper order; Demosthenes scores a point on this, saying that *he* will follow the order of the *graphē*, starting with the part of the proposal in which his merits are recited (Dem. 18.56–7). But let us follow Aeschines' order. The thrust of the second count is that it is not lawful to crown a man who holds public office and has not yet undergone *euthynai*. This refers to the fact that Demosthenes was one of the ten Commissioners for the Walls (*teichopoioi*) and was a trustee of the Theatrical Fund. Aeschines cites a law forbidding the proposal of a crown for an official whose *euthynai* are still pending, the reason being that if the honour were awarded before the audit a jury would be reluctant to convict for embezzlement (Aesch. 3.10–11). This can be circumvented by making the award subject to completion of the *euthynai*, but Ctesiphon's proposal omits this saving clause (Aesch. 11–12). The third count condemns the proposal to make the award at the Dionysia, for a law requires proclamation to be made before the Boule or the Assembly, and nowhere else (Aesch. 32–3).

On the all-important first count Aeschines is much less specific as to what law has been infringed. He simply says, 'Every law forbids false entries in public *psēphismata*' (Aesch. 50). The general meaning is that the recital of Demosthenes' merits was false, for far from deserving well of the city, his entire career is a denial of such virtues. Aeschines thus purports to provide legal underpinning for a comprehensive attack on Demosthenes' policies, performance, and character. He thus makes his hated rival the real defendant, with Ctesiphon only filling that role in a nominal capacity. One suspects that this technique was frequently employed, hence the preponderance of honorary decrees amongst the known uses of the *GP*. But there is something suspicious about Aeschines' assertion that 'every law' forbids false entries. Why not '*a* law', as in the other two counts? It has been suggested that there was a statute penalizing the falsification of public documents, but that this was not the same thing as a false preamble.[106] But that argument does not impress, for if there had been such a law it would have been an easy interpretation to extend it to preambles. However, it is significant that Demosthenes makes no attack on the indictment on this ground. He assumes the statutory basis. The *graphē* having been read by the clerk, Demosthenes observes, 'These are the clauses of the *psēphisma* at which this prosecution is aimed' (Dem. 18.56–7). He then embarks on a detailed exposition of his public career, pointing out that it is Aeschines who has put that vast subject in issue (Dem. 59). The only objection that he raises is to Aeschines' incorporation of his private life in the debate; he says that is extraneous to the indictment, but he will reply to it so that the jury's decision be not distorted by irrelevancies (Dem. 8–9, 34).

The outcome of the trial was a sweeping victory for Demosthenes. The dicasts voted an acquittal by better than a four-fifths majority, thus exposing Aeschines to a fine of 1,000 drachmae and partial disfranchisement.[107] Aeschines left Athens for Rhodes, never to return,[108] and Demosthenes' crown was duly voted by the Assembly.

Demosthenes' triumph was due to his successful exploitation of the issue raised by the first count, for he devotes the greater part of his speech to a vindication of his public career, so as to show that there is no question of any false entries in the public records in that regard. Aeschines had attacked his career under four heads – the period ending with the Peace of Philocrates of 346, the renewal of the war with Philip in 340, the battle of Chaeronea in 338, and the period after Chaeronea. Demosthenes replies to the first head in 18.18–52, concentrating on Aeschines' responsibility for weaknesses in the peace treaty. He broaches the second head in 60–109, claiming special credit for the trier-archy law of 340–39. His answer to the third head (160–251) defends his advocacy of resistance to Philip and makes much of his role in forging the alliance with Thebes; but he says very little (320–3) in reply to the fourth head.

The opening that enabled Demosthenes to capitalize on his record was handed to him quite gratuitously by Aeschines, for if the debate had been kept on an austere technical level his room for manoeuvre would have been seriously curtailed. That Aeschines had committed a bad tactical error by including the first count was recognized in antiquity,[109] but Demosthenes should still have been hard put to find an effective answer to the second and third counts. In his brief reply to those counts (110–21) he floats a large red herring in the shape of the personal contribution that he made to the expenses of his commissionership, on the strength of which he seeks to rebut the *euthynai* point, claiming that the law does not require an audit of donations. Perhaps so, but what he fails to say is whether any funds other than donations were involved.

It is idle to ask why Aeschines chose such an unfavourable course. Perhaps the need to 'play to the gallery', to give the jurors the entertainment to which they were accustomed, outweighed tactical considerations. But the more important question is why the trial was delayed for six years. It is true that the previous encounter between Demosthenes and Aeschines had also been delayed, but in that case the delay had been engineered by Aeschines for good and sufficient tactical reasons. The same cannot be said of the instant case. Neither side tried to embarrass the other by an interlocutory prosecution. Indeed Demosthenes taunts Aeschines with his failure to indict him for his alleged misdeeds at the time when he had committed them. He also notes with scorn that Aeschines had no part in the *GP* which had been launched in *c.*338 against the proposers of an earlier gold crown for Demosthenes – a case which met with the identical fate to that which overtook Aeschines' attempt.[110]

It has been suggested that the assassination of Philip shortly after the lodging of the *graphē* against Ctesiphon cautioned a delay until Alexander's policy became known,[111] but it did not take six years to clarify that. There have been attempts to identify events that Aeschines would have considered unpropitious for a resumption of the case, such as the destruction of Thebes in 335, which might have swung Athenian opinion behind Demosthenes, or Alexander's departure for Asia in 334, which might have aroused hopes of his defeat.[112] But his victory at Issus in 333 was a favourable portent for Aeschines,[113] yet he still waited another three years.

If speculation is in order one might cite Alexander's demand, in 335, for the extradition of Demosthenes, Lycurgus, and others, in order (as I suggest) to have them tried by the *synedrion* of the League of Corinth on charges of being responsible for Chaeronea, insulting Philip and Alexander by celebrating Philip's death, and being involved in the Theban rebellion.[114] The demand for their extradition might have been suggested to Alexander by Aeschines. And when Demades proposed that a mission be sent to Alexander to plead for the men's lives against an undertaking to try them in an Athenian court if they deserved punishment,[115] Aeschines might well have sided with his friend Phocion in opposing the plan, realizing that the promise to try them at Athens was a sham, since with the possible exception of Chaeronea no Athenian court could claim jurisdiction over the offences in question.[116] In any event Demades was able to persuade Alexander to absolve the men (Diod. 17.15.5), and Aeschines might well have concluded that this was not the time to reinstate his case. But even this does not take us much further, for it is merely another isolated example of an unpropitious time.

There is, I believe, a connection between our case and the trial of Leocrates at about the same time, in 331–0. That case is well worth a glance, even though it does not bear directly on the *GP*. After Chaeronea, Leocrates left Athens with his money and his mistress and fled to Rhodes, where he spread the rumour that Athens had been occupied and Piraeus was under siege. He later moved to Megara, where he continued to prosper, but in 331–0 he returned to Athens, hoping that his cowardly flight had been forgotten. But he reckoned without Lycurgus, a leader of the anti-Macedonian forces who had been named with Demosthenes in Alexander's demand for extradition. Lycurgus was a tireless worker in the criminal courts. He had pledged himself to purge the city of treason, and his criminal laws were said to have been written with a pen dipped in blood.[117] He charged Leocrates with *prodosia* immediately on the latter's return, but the prosecution failed, for Leocrates was absolved on a tied vote.

Why did Lycurgus fail when operating in his own special preserve and against someone in such low standing as Leocrates? For some reason his act of *prodosia* was constituted solely by his hurried departure, though one might have thought that the rumours which he had spread at Rhodes were a clear enough act of betrayal.[118] Be that as it may, the probable answer to the puzzle of his acquittal is not that the law applicable was only enacted after his departure,[119] but that the law in question was uncertain and Lycurgus was unable to drive home his interpretation of it.

That the case depended on legal interpretation is established by the Argument to Lycurgus' speech, from which we learn that far from denying the facts, Leocrates merely tried to put a different interpretation on them.[120] The law that was being discussed is described in the Argument as a *psēphisma* of the Demos after Chaeronea, which forbade citizens to leave the city or to remove their wives and children. This is the emergency decree cited by Lycurgus himself; he says that after Chaeronea the people ran in haste to the Assembly and decreed that the women and children be brought from the countryside within the walls and that the generals allocate both Athenians and metics to defence duties as they thought fit (Lyc. *Leocr.* 16). The Argument over-simplifies the decree by having it impose a straightforward ban on departures and removals. In fact the decree cited by Lycurgus imposed a prohibition of uncertain interpretation, and that was the trouble.

101

Lycurgus' difficulties can be pieced together from his speech quite easily. He makes three points in quick succession. First, he tells the jurors that they do not have the power to acquit Leocrates because the act in question[121] has already been judged and condemned, by the Areopagus when it seized and executed fugitives who had abandoned the city to the enemy (*Leocr.* 52).[122] Lycurgus then cites the case of Autolycus, an Areopagite whom Lycurgus had prosecuted in 338 for removing his wife and children to safety although Autolycus himself had remained at his post (*Leocr.* 53). This, too, was a precedent resting on the Areopagus' emergency powers.[123] But those powers were only temporary,[124] and Lycurgus needed a law which was still operative in 331-0. He found it (or thought he had) in the *psēphisma* passed by the Demos in 338:

> If you punished one whose only crime was to send away non-combatants, what should your verdict be on one who, though a man, did not pay his country the price of his keep? The people, too, were appalled at what was happening and *decreed that those who ran away from facing danger on behalf of their country* [125] *were guilty of prodosia and deserved the extreme penalty.* (*Leocr.* 53)

The criminal provision in the *psēphisma* was in regard to those who avoided military service by leaving, and that was where an ambiguity arose. Did any departure fall under the decree, or only a departure for the purpose of avoiding service? Leocrates claimed that he had left for the purpose of trade. The Argument tells us so: 'Some classify it as an inference from intention, for it is admitted that he left the city, but his purpose is doubtful. Did he contemplate *prodosia* or trade?' By citing the Areopagite precedent Lycurgus hoped to persuade the jurors to read an absolute ban independent of intention into the *psēphisma*, but he failed, though only on a tied vote. The narrowness of the result says much for the increased judicial sophistication that had been ushered in by the reforms of 403-399.

So much for the law in Leocrates' case. But what is the connection between that trial and Ctesiphon's? In his speech against Ctesiphon Aeschines notes bitterly that a private citizen who had sailed to Rhodes after Chaeronea[126] because he could not master his fear was very recently subjected to an *eisangelia* and was only saved from exile or death by a tied vote, whereas an orator deserted his post in the army and ran away from the city but now claims a crown (Aesch. 3.252-3). Aeschines is referring to Demosthenes' absence after Chaeronea, when he may have gone off to raise money for Athens abroad,[127] though he was impeached (unsuccessfully) after his return (Dem. 18.249-50).

Another possible link with Leocrates' case is supplied by Lycurgus, who delivers a long harangue against the *synēgoroi* who are going to speak for Leocrates (Lyc. *Leocr.* 135-40). Lycurgus does not name the defenders, but he does make an interesting statement. He says that if any of them wish to cite their own public services in favour of Leocrates they should not rely on horsebreeding or chorus funding; they should concentrate on services which benefited the city rather than themselves, such as serving as a trierarch, or building walls to protect the city, or spending one's own money for the public safety (ibid., 139-40). This is an extraordinarily accurate preview of issues that would very soon be canvassed at Ctesiphon's trial on the question of Demosthenes' qualifications for a crown. It is even more than that, for the references to what a *synēgoros* should *not* rely on can also be brought into focus. The horsebreeder is Lycurgus' sworn enemy, Lycophron,[128] against whom Lycurgus took the unusual step of bringing a charge of adultery by way of *eisangelia*.[129] But who is the funder of choruses? Two things point to Aeschines. First, his career as an actor[130] makes it very possible that the reference is to him; Lycurgus is sketching the *dramatis personae* of the forthcoming *cause célèbre*, the reinstatement of which will already have been known at the time of Leocrates' trial. Second, after leaving Athens to avoid paying the loser's fine which resulted from Ctesiphon's trial, Aeschines established himself at Rhodes (Plut. *Mor.* 840D). Rhodes had been Leocrates' first choice. Moreover, while at Megara, Leocrates had done business with Alexander's sister, Cleopatra (Lyc. *Leocr.* 26). There is no need to recapitulate the evidence for Aeschines' links with Alexander. It looks very much as if Aeschines was one of Leocrates' defenders. If so, he deserves a belated crown for his legal expertise.

There is also a possible link between Demosthenes and Leocrates' trial, apart from Lycurgus' graceful tribute to his colleague and political associate. When dealing with the aftermath of Chaeronea in his speech for Ctesiphon, Demosthenes says that immediately after the battle, in the midst of anxiety and danger, the people adopted his proposals for the safety of the city; all the precautions – strongpoints, trenches, maintenance of the walls – were decreed in *psēphismata* moved by him (Dem. 18.248). This is not the *prodosia* decree under which Lycurgus indicted Leocrates (and which, as its possible author,[131] he tried so hard to interpret), but it is contemporaneous with that decree, and suggests that Demosthenes was an active supporter of the *prodosia* decree even if he was not its author. It would seem that the aftermath of Chaeronea was the burning issue of the day, and Aeschines, fresh from his successful defence of Leocrates, saw an opening for yet another service to his Macedonian masters. Lycurgus had used the occasion of Leocrates' trial to launch a revival of the memory of Chaeronea (Lyc. *Leocr.* 39–51) as a counterweight to Alexander's renewed attempts to get the Athenians on side, and with one victory already chalked up Aeschines was eager to press home his advantage by defusing the democrats' weapon. Hence, very possibly, his decision to reinstate a case which had been gathering dust for six years.

VI

FOURTH-CENTURY ATHENS: *ASEBEIA*, THE WILLING WORK-HORSE

1 PRELIMINARY

In addition to a general examination of fourth-century impiety trials, two special questions will be considered from time to time. The first is suggested by a feature of the fifth-century trials for *asebeia*, namely the preponderance of cases with political connotations. This is very clear in the cases of Anaxagoras and other Pericleans, and also of Alcibiades and his co-defendants. It is equally clear in the case of the Arginusae eight, which ranks marginally as an impiety trial, and we have argued plausibly for a political component in the cases of Protagoras and Diagoras. For Aeschylus a political reason is less certain, but still arguable. The closest to being apolitical is Euripides' case, but it is also the closest to not being a trial at all; which is a pity, because one of the questions that we ask when we contemplate the fourth century is whether there was such a thing as a 'pure' trial for impiety. Did it ever happen that the outraged religious sentiments of the Athenian people demanded satisfaction as such, irrespective of political currents?

Our second question is prompted by the strong contingents of philosophers who were tried for impiety in both the fifth and the fourth centuries. Did the people dislike them *because* they were philosophers, thus giving their cases a distinct anti-intellectual tinge, or did what they were doing just happen to be particularly offensive to religious sentiment, although no different in principle from the impiety of non-philosophers? In other words, was

105

the statutory form of *asebeia* which had been created by Diopeithes' *psēphisma*, and which continued to regulate the trials of philosophers in the fourth century,[1] similar to, or different from, the laws governing the trials of non-philosophers?

2 SOCRATES AND ANDOCIDES

The most famous impiety trial of all time was held in 399, when Socrates was condemned to death. What is not so well known is the contemporaneous trial of Andocides, the man who escaped a death sentence for impiety in 415 by turning informer, and was exiled for *parapresbeia* in 392.[2] His trial for impiety in 400–399 interacts instructively with that of Socrates, and the two should be considered together.

The attack on Socrates was launched by a *graphē asebeias* lodged by Meletus with the support of two co-accusers, Anytus and Lycon. The indictment ran, according to a copy seen in the archives by Favorinus, as follows:

> This is the charge drawn up and confirmed by Meletus, son of Meletus, of the deme Pitthus, against Socrates, son of Sophroniscus, of the deme Alopece. Socrates is guilty of not believing[3] in the gods in whom the city believes and of introducing new divinities; he is also guilty of corrupting the young. Penalty: Death. (Diog. Laert. 2.40)

Xenophon attests the same charge (*Mem.* 1.1.1), except that he substitutes 'to the following effect' for Favorinus' categorical 'this is the charge', and uses a different verb for 'introducing'. But the heated debate about these *minutiae*[4] is mere hairsplitting. One might point with slightly more justification to the brevity of the Favorinus document compared with the detailed *eisangelia* against Alcibiades (Plut. *Alc.* 22.3), but that is simply due to a difference in procedure. One of the uses of *eisangelia* was for crimes for which no written law existed, therefore the indictment had to supply a 'definition'.[5] But when the *graphē asebeias* replaced *eisangelia* in impiety cases there was probably a concomitant law defining *asebeia* in comprehensive terms,[6] and individual indictments lost their quasi-legislative function.[7]

One divergence in the sources is important. Plato reverses the order of the charges, putting corruption of the young before disbelief in the gods (*Apol.* 24B), and this has a bearing on the canons of construction applicable to the case. On the Favorinus/ Xenophon version it can be argued that the corruption charge is *eiusdem generis* with the disbelief charge – the young were corrupted by being taught disbelief.[8] In other words, the pernicious teachings were capable of being subsumed under the *asebeia* statute by a fairly simple interpretation. But Derenne argues that the pernicious teachings covered not only impiety but also attacks on social and moral values and arguments contrary to justice.[9] That is very possibly right, but Derenne is on less safe ground when he goes on to say that two different jurisdictions were involved, one for impiety, which fell under the king-archon, and the other for pernicious teaching, which fell under the thesmothetes. Derenne is not able to explain how the two jurisdictions integrated their combined operation,[10] and it should be concluded that everything fell under the *asebeia* statute and the *graphē asebeias*, and that Plato has reversed the correct order of the charges. But he is not to be condemned for this, because corrupting the young may have been the main thrust of the accusation. The charges of disbelief and new beliefs may have been the vehicle by which pernicious teaching was made actionable, since by itself it was not a crime.[11]

We now turn to the actual trial, but with some misgivings, for the details have been so overlaid by the war of words which turned the trial into a legend[12] that one cannot hope for more than an approximation to the truth. Modern interpretations depend largely on the observer's point of view. The Socratic Corpus is mainly a creation of the philosophers, and only occasionally is the emphasis on the history and the law. The dividing-line is admittedly unclear. How can we tell when the principal source, Plato's *Apology*, is using the trial as a vehicle for philosophy, and when it is portraying historical reality? Is Xenophon's *Apology* more, or less, accurate than Plato's? There is no simple answer. That Socrates did make some sort of defence despite the late tradition that has him stand mute is probable.[13] And that Plato has seized the general thrust of the defence is also probable.[14] It would be nice if one could take Xenophon's down-to-earth account as a true picture, and he does furnish some important details not provided by Plato.[15] But if only one of the two versions could be preserved for posterity, which would one choose?

Socrates did not deny the facts - not because of the alleged imprecision of the charge of *asebeia*,[16] but because all the facts were common knowledge and it was merely a question of whether they were to be given a guilty or an innocent interpretation. He begins by replying to 'the first accusers', that is, the calumnies that had been circulating against him for many years. He then turns to the present accusers, attacking the charges on the grounds that Meletus is a young man who does not know what his case is.[17] Socrates says very little on the merits. In Plato he passes over his alleged atheism in silence, though in Xenophon he denies it (Xen. *Apol.* 11). His reply to the charge of pernicious teaching is an essay in irony, including the assertion that he never taught his pupils anything. He claims credit for his way of life, presenting himself as a successor to Achilles who defies death in defence of justice. He says that on the advice of his 'demonic voice' (*daimonion*) he takes no part in politics, and adds that had he done so he would have perished. He cites the attempt to indict him for his stand at the Arginusae trial, and also makes capital out of his refusal to do the bidding of the Thirty by arresting Leon of Salamis (Plat. 32C).

The jury of 501 convicted Socrates, though only by a margin of 281 votes to 220.[18] This being an *agōn timētos*, a trial for which no statutory penalty was laid down,[19] Socrates was at large to propose an alternative to the death sentence demanded by the accusers. But instead of exile, which might have been accepted, he proposed free meals for life in the city's sacred hearth, the Prytaneum. As this privilege was reserved for those who deserved well of the city, his friends urged him to propose a fine. He did so, but in the derisory amount of one *mina* of silver. His friends persuaded him to propose thirty *minae* and offered to guarantee the amount. But the jury had had enough of the irony of Socrates, and decreed sentence of death by the large majority of 361 votes to 140. Socrates was led away by the Eleven, rejected a plan of escape, spent some time in discourse with his friends, drank the hemlock and died. It is said that the Athenians soon changed their minds, closed the gymnasia as a sign of mourning, and punished the accusers, sentencing Meletus to death and Anytus and Lycon to exile. But this late tradition lacks credibility.[20]

What was the background to the case? We begin with the accusers. Plato says that from the ranks of the slanderers came Meletus, who nourished a grievance on behalf of the poets,

Anytus on behalf of the artisans and politicians (*dēmiourgoi*, *politikoi*), and Lycon on behalf of the orators (*Apol.* 23E). The principal accuser, Meletus, was a tragic poet of sufficient consequence to be satirized by Aristophanes, despite Plato's portrayal of him as an unknown.[21] He is very possibly the Meletus who obeyed the Thirty's order to arrest Leon of Salamis[22] – hence Socrates' citation of his own courage on that occasion (Plat. 32C). Most important of all, this Meletus was a member of the team that prosecuted Andocides, and was probably the author of the speech against Andocides that is erroneously credited to Lysias.[23] Meletus' involvement in two major *asebeia* trials in the same year[24] makes him something of a specialist. For further clarification of his role at this time we must interrupt our discussion of Socrates' trial in order to glance at Andocides' case.

Despite the immunity that turning informer in 415 had secured for him, Andocides had been stigmatized as a confessed perpetrator of impious acts and had been precluded by the *psēphisma* of Isotimides from access to sacred sites and the Agora. He was now accused of contravening that *psēphisma* by attending a celebration of the Eleusinian Mysteries. This was a straightforward statutory charge, but there was a subsidiary charge of depositing a suppliant's bough on the altar of the Eleusinion, and this gave rise to a furious debate. In terms of an inscribed (written) law the penalty was a fine of 1,000 drachmae. A preliminary hearing was held before the Boule, but in view of the quantum of the fine that council could not be seised of the definitive trial (cf. *AP* 45.1). But Callias, who was guiding the prosecution, cited an ancestral law (*nomos patrios*) to the effect that placing a suppliant's bough in the Eleusinion attracted the death penalty without a formal trial (Andoc. 1.115–16). Callias asked the Boule to pronounce sentence of death without any more ado. He declared that his father, Hipponicus, had once given a similar interpretation 'to the Athenians' (i.e. officially). Thereupon Cephalus, a friend of Andocides, declared that by giving an interpretation Callias had acted impiously, since he was a Keryx, not a Eumolpid to whom alone belonged the right of interpretation. Cephalus also criticized Callias for citing an ancestral law when the case was governed by a written law (ibid.).

The legal issue did not have to be decided, since it was proved that the bough had not been deposited by Andocides, but by Callias himself in order to incriminate Andocides. The legal question is, however, of great interest. Why did Callias think that the ancestral law was still enforceable despite the ban on unwritten laws in the revision of 403–399? And why was he accused of usurping the Eumolpid exegetic function?

The answer is speculative, but it does turn on a known fact, namely the jurisprudence of the Eumolpidae, a hereditary priestly clan which claimed an interpretative monopoly in connection with the Eleusinian Mysteries.[25] It is also clear that Callias stirred up a conflict of laws, and in a case of *asebeia* expressly linked to the Mysteries. And that conflict of laws is identified by Pseudo-Lysias (that is, Meletus) in his speech against Andocides, when he says that Pericles had once advised the Athenians to enforce against impious persons not only the written laws but also the unwritten laws which the Eumolpidae followed in their expositions.[26] For further clarification we turn once more to the *eisangelia* against Alcibiades,[27] where the legal basis of the charge was that Alcibiades had contravened 'the laws and institutions of the Eumolpidae, Kerykes and Priests of Eleusis'. These were unwritten laws, but in 415 they were enforced by a secular court, and in a case in which the impious acts were seen as evidence of treason (*katalysis tou dēmou*).[28] What is more, that enforcement of the priestly laws and institutions was incorporated in a *psēphisma* of the Demos inflicting the punishment of death, confiscation, and curses on Alcibiades.[29] Callias was therefore able to argue that as the priestly laws and institutions had been backed by the Demos, the rule authorizing an immediate death sentence against Andocides without trial was enforceable in spite of the great revision of 403–399, which was very recent indeed at the time of Andocides' trial. It is a pity that Callias' chicanery resulted in the case going off on a question of fact, leaving us in the dark as to how the latest argument based on the democratization of religious law would have been decided.

Cephalus' other criticism of Callias, namely that he was usurping the right to interpret and was guilty of *asebeia*, turned on an ambiguity. Alcibiades' case went, on a literal interpretation, further than the Eumolpidae, for it was based on the laws and institutions 'of the Eumolpidae *and* the Kerykes *and* the Priests' (Plut. *Alc.* 22.3). Callias, a member of the clan of the Kerykes,[30] might have argued that as the Kerykes and Priests had not been excluded they ranked as interpreters alongside the Eumolpidae. But this argument would not have succeeded even if the case had been decided on the law. The Eumolpid monopoly was well established, and its full significance is brought out by a comparison with Rome. As is well known, the original inter- preters of the law at Rome were the members of the pontifical college, who appointed one of their number to respond to con- sultants every year; these priestly respondents were the ancestors of the Roman jurisconsult.[31] When we find the Eumolpidae not only interpreting under what they claim as a monopoly,[32] but appointing three of their number to exercise the exegetic func- tion on behalf of the clan[33] and, most significantly, having their rulings clothed with normative efficacy in the secular sphere, it would be perverse to deny the force of the parallel with Rome.

The exegetic function of the Eumolpidae brings us back to Socrates' accuser, Meletus. In the speech against Andocides, Meletus cites an interpretation of *asebeia* by his grandfather, Diocles, whom he describes as a Hierophant (Lys. 6.54). The Hierophant was always a Eumolpid, and it has been plausibly conjectured that the speaker was himself a member of that clan.[34] The example of Diocles adds a further dimension to the normative efficacy of Eumolpid interpretations, for when Diocles interpreted 'to the Athenians' he did so officially. Meletus, who was in the forefront of the two great impiety trials that ushered in the fourth century, was a proto-jurisconsult and the spiritual ancestor of Theophrastus.[35]

Of Socrates' other accusers, Lycon, the orators' representative, is described as a demagogue (Diog. Laert. 2.38), which points to a continuation of the populist link with *asebeia* going back to Cleon and Androcles; though nothing else about him is of immediate interest.[36] But Anytus, the driving force behind the prosecu- tion,[37] is important. The upwardly mobile son of a wealthy tanner, he is said to have included Socrates in his hatred of the sophists because of the philosopher's denigration of the great men of Athens (Plat. *Meno* 90–4E), and also because of his derogatory references to Anytus' origins (Libanius *Apol. Socr.* 25–6). None of this is surprising in a fervent patriot who was only one genera- tion away from obscurity. He was well versed in courtcraft, as he showed in 410–9 when he was charged with *prodosia* for fail- ing to relieve Pylos; he claimed that a storm had forced him to abort the mission, but his acquittal was thought to owe more to bribery.[38] His close links with Theramenes[39] suggest that he may have been on the prosecution's side at the Arginusae trial,

111

perhaps as an expert witness on the effect of storms on military operations; Socrates refers to his own role in the Arginusae case in the same passage as that which contrasts his conduct in Leon's case with that of Meletus (Plat. *Apol.* 32). But Anytus was a defence witness at Andocides' trial (Andoc. 1.150), and at first sight that is awkward. Andocides couples him with Cephalus, and we end up with Anytus and Meletus in opposite camps in that case. But on reflection this does not damage our equation of the Meletus of Andocides' case with the Meletus who accused Socrates. If Anytus could take up different positions in two *asebeia* cases, then *a fortiori* Meletus could take up a consistent position in which the only variable was the identity of his allies. It may well be that Anytus, impressed with Meletus' work in Andocides' case, prevailed on him to undertake a similar accusationary mission against Socrates.

What were the motives of Socrates' accusers? It is time to say that with all its faults the Athenian popular jurisdiction was something more than a mere outlet for personal ambitions and animosities. An accuser had to be able to tune in to public opinion; he had to propose something that a majority of citizens found acceptable. The real villain of Arginusae was not Theramenes; it was the Demos which was prepared to tolerate the destruction of its heroes. This pinpoints the ultimate riddle of Socrates' trial. The acquittal of Andocides shows that there was not, in the popular perception, a blind acceptance of the wrongness of impiety. Others had taught astronomy besides Anaxagoras, others had mocked the Mysteries before Alcibiades, but only at certain times and under certain conditions were offenders brought to book. Callias found to his cost that the Mysteries were not a matter of special concern in 400–399, but Anytus read the people's mood correctly. What, then, had Socrates done to arouse public opinion so violently?

No solution to the riddle of Socrates can be more than tentative, but that which it is proposed to offer here is at least based on a specific statement in the sources, namely Plato's presentation of the accusers as the representatives of interest groups – Meletus of the poets, Anytus of the artisans and politicans, and Lycon of the orators (*Apol.* 23E–24A). Meletus described himself as a good patriot (ibid., 24B), and no doubt the others did the same. We thus have a coalition representing a substantial cross-section of Athenian society. But what was omitted from the coalition is just as important as what was included, for there is no mention of the Establishment, the landed aristocracy. They were not opposed to Socrates; understandably so, for his enemies were their enemies, and it was actually on their behalf that he had launched his attacks over the years. His prime target was what may, for want of a better word, be called the middle class,[40] the class which more than any other had benefited from the twin institutions of democracy and empire but had been the hardest hit by the defeat and the resultant economic stagnation.[41] Their top priority was economic recovery, and their weapons included strong religious feelings and a strong family structure,[42] traditional peasant values which were still cherished by the upwardly mobile. They were most suspicious of Socrates' educational methods, for by encouraging his pupils to expose everything to the cold light of reason he was being 'clever', and cleverness was the quality that they distrusted most.[43] Their natural ally in the drive for national recovery was the little man, whose modest slice of the imperial cake through such avenues as pay for public service had come under threat whenever an oligarchic regime was in power. Those to whom pay for jury service was as indispensable as the modern dole remembered with acute anxiety how the Five Thousand had attacked government spending in 411 (Thuc. 8.97.1). Now, with the empire gone, the little man lent an attentive ear to anyone who promised him a return to the days of wine and roses.

But even if this is what was threatened by Socrates, did they have to kill him for it? And even if the threat that he had posed for so many years had become more acute in the wake of defeat, why had they still waited another four years before taking action against him? The short answer to the first question is, according to Derenne, that the accusers did not really want the death penalty; they would have been satisfied to consign Socrates to exile, but his intransigence ruled that out.[44] There is, however, more to it. We are once more in the grey area between *asebeia* and treason which we encountered in Alcibiades' case. There is not a specific link between impiety and *katalysis tou dēmou* as there was in 415, but the idea is there.[45] The charge of *asebeia* was beginning to foreshadow the role that it would play in the Hellenistic world. Acts potentially subversive of the state no longer needed to be tied to express categories of treason like *katalysis tou dēmou* and *prodosia*. Those were still the preferred

113

categories against those who were politically active, but not against an apolitical figure like Socrates. Yet the threat that he posed was just as real as the regular forms of treason. They therefore cast around for an alternative remedy and came up with *asebeia*, which could generate the death penalty which they proposed – and wanted, because in the last resort you did not execute anyone whom you did not want to execute.

It is often complained that *asebeia* was undefined and uncertain, and charges were extremely difficult to defend.[46] But this misses the whole point. The categories of wrongful acts were set out in detail (cf. the Alcibiades indictment) and as a rule there was no uncertainty as to whether the accused had committed Acts A, B, and C. The uncertainty lay in a superimposed factor. Thus in Socrates' case it was common cause that he had done certain things, but it was not certain that by doing them he had 'corrupted the young' – that is, that he had instilled ideas which threatened to destabilize the socio-political order which his enemies knew as the Demos. Teaching *per se* might be quite innocuous, but teaching which threatened the existing order was not, and the appropriate penalty was death. Where the objective of the act was innocuous, as with a minor offence against the Eleusinian gods, then it was 'pure' *asebeia* for which a sub-capital penalty was (under the secular statute) appropriate.[47] That is why there was such a heated debate at the meeting of the Boule which preceded Andocides' trial. The secular statute treated bough-depositing as a relatively minor offence, but Callias wanted to make it a crime against the state. It was in the interpretation of the objective of an act that the uncertainty principle came into play, because different interpreters interpreted differently according to their own predilections. This gave *asebeia* great flexibility, but the actual categories of wrongful acts were in no way capricious.

Our second question now claims our attention. Why did Anytus delay so long before taking action against Socrates? Having put up with him for so many years, why did he suddenly change? The answer is that some recent event was the last straw, the ominous harbinger of real danger. That event was the fact that Socrates' pupil, Critias, had headed the Thirty during its worst period.[48] He was the concrete proof of the dangers inherent in Socratic education. But then why had they not charged Socrates in 403-2, immediately after the fall of the Thirty?

Again there is a simple answer: Socrates was protected by the amnesty of 403-2. His teachings made him an accomplice in Critias' crime, and to prosecute him would have violated the amnesty. What was needed was a new cause of action, one which had only come into existence in the post-amnesty period. This meant a new statute, a law passed since the archonship of Eucleides. On the advice, we may well think, of Meletus, Anytus may have secured the passage of a comprehensive *asebeia* statute. Its date will have been 400-399,[49] after the acquittal of Andocides had exposed weaknesses in the existing law.

But how, it will be asked, could the new statute have helped? Were not Socrates' acts still pre-amnesty? Indeed they were, but under the Athenian judicial system laws were received in evidence in exactly the same way as facts.[50] There was a sort of source competition amongst pleaders, with each one citing the law which suited his case best. We have seen it in operation in the debate between Cephalus and Callias. Consequently, if certain conduct was declared culpable by a post-amnesty statute it did not matter that the original factual basis had arisen before 403-2; it was possible by an optical illusion to charge Socrates under the new statute without violating the amnesty. It had taken the middle class some time to work its way around the amnesty, but it got there in the end.

We conclude with a further note on Andocides' case. Isotimides' *psēphisma*[51] testifies to his having been exposed to odium for fifteen years after turning informer in 415, but was the odium due to his political importance or to his unpopularity on religious grounds? Did they legislate against him because they were horrified at his having escaped punishment for profaning the Mysteries, or was it just another case of political enemies using *asebeia* as an instrument? His subsequent career, with its repeated but vain attempts to regain the favour of the Athenians,[52] suggests a general sense of outrage rather than routine political machinations. But a staunch traditionalist like Anytus did not hesitate to support him at his trial. Is there any evidence of a personal motive on the part of his accusers – not the banal dispute with Callias about a girl[53] but an issue which had been smouldering since 415? There is one possibility, centring on the ubiquitous Meletus. He, or another man of the same name, was denounced in 415 for taking part in the mock Mysteries and the mutilation of the Hermae, and only escaped death by flight;

Andocides worked with Meletus in those enterprises, though there were always doubts about Andocides' loyalty.[54] That this is the Meletus who accused Andocides in 400–399 has been suggested[55] but is not essential. What is important is that the Meletus who accused Socrates and Andocides had a father of the same name (Diog. Laert. 2.40). There is thus reason to believe that the Meletus family had been looking for Andocides ever since the great betrayal of 415. In his speech Andocides is at pains to deny that he had informed against his father, Leogoras (Andoc. 1.22). The denial may have been correct, but it is clear that the accusers used the rumour against him. Interestingly enough, it amounted to his having committed asebeia in one of the forms reputedly defined by Aristotle.[56] Be that as it may, the background to Andocides' case suggests that it is no more a case of 'pure' asebeia than that of Socrates is.

3 SOME NON-INTELLECTUALS

Three-quarters of a century elapsed between the trial of Socrates and the next attack on a philospher, Aristotle. But there was no shortage of charges of asebeia against other categories of defendants. Some of the cases have obvious political ramifications. Archias, a Hierophant of Eleusis, sacrificed during the festival of Haloa in order to oblige a courtesan, Sinope; he was condemned to death because animal sacrifices were forbidden during the festival, and also because sacrificing was the work of a priestess, not of a Hierophant (Dem. 59.116). In 379 Archias had disclosed the plot to smuggle Theban exiles into Thebes (Plut. *Pelop.* 10.3). This frustrated Athens' collaboration with Epaminondas, but Archias could not be charged with treason; his city dared not disclose its role. A solution was found in asebeia. Similarly, in 340 Phano, the illegitimate daughter of the courtesan Neaera, was allowed by her husband, the king-archon Theogenes, to perform sacrifices to Dionysus and to administer the oath to priestesses. The Areopagus punished Theogenes, whose explanation that he thought Phano was the daughter of Neaera's husband, Stephanus, was not accepted. The case was part of the attack on Stephanus, a prominent orator and politician.[57]

The pollution of rites and temples by women of ill-repute had been treated as asebeia ever since Aspasia, and the charge surfaced yet again at some time prior to 322 when Phryne, the courtesan who was so beautiful that she did not need cosmetics, was charged with *asebeia*. Hyperides, who defended her, secured an acquittal by suddenly stripping his client and calling on the jurors to spare 'Aphrodite's prophetess'.[58] As for the background, neither her attempt to seduce Xenocrates nor her high tariff for her favours[59] looks political. But her offer to rebuild Thebes, which Alexander had destroyed, and the placing of Praxiteles' statue of her between those of Archidamus III and Philip II at Delphi (Athen. 591B–D) locate her squarely in the anti-Macedonian lobby alongside her defender, Hyperides; that orientation is confirmed by the appearance of Anaximenes, a strong supporter of Macedon, as her accuser.[60]

Religious pollution was not the only basis for charges of *asebeia* against women. An Athenian priestess named Ninos was put to death for conducting initiations in a cult of foreign gods, leading bands of revellers through the streets in celebration of a foreign god, and preparing potions for the young.[61] The case is almost a pastiche of Socrates' trial, charging both the introduction of new gods and corruption of the young. A political component is conjectural. Another Ninos was the founder of the Assyrian empire,[62] but that is not enough to link the case with Alexander's campaigns. However, Demosthenes does compare Ninos' cult activity with that of the mother of that dedicated friend of Macedon, Aeschines (Dem. 19.281). The theme fascinated Demosthenes, for he appeared as the accuser when the Lemnian woman, Theoris, was charged with dabbling in magic drugs and incantations (Dem. 25.79–80) and also with teaching slaves (by means of magic?) to deceive their masters (Plut. *Dem.* 14.4). It has been suggested that Theoris practised magic arts under cover of a mystery cult and that her case is on all fours with that of Ninos.[63] She was sentenced to death and her whole family shared her fate[64] – as accomplices in the cult, unless it was put on a broader basis, seeing that her teaching destabilized an economy based on slave labour, as Socrates' teaching had destabilized traditional values.

Our last case traverses quite a different line of country. In 376–5 some Delians expelled the Athenian administrators from the temple of Apollo on Delos; they were charged with *asebeia* and sentenced to exile and fines of 10,000 drachmae each (*IG* ii[2] 1635.134–40). It has been surmised that they were tried at Athens under Athenian law,[65] but this needs to be tested. The case was tried shortly after the formation of the Second Athenian Alliance, the charter of which included judicial provisions. The *koinon synedrion* of the Alliance was empowered to try those who attempted to abrogate or alter the confederacy, and to sentence to death or banishment from Alliance territory (*GHI* 123.51). Although we do not have all the provisions, it is most unlikely that there was mention of an exclusively Athenian court. The forcible expulsion of the Athenians on Delos could well have been seen as an attempt to alter the terms of the Alliance. The case was heard a mere six years after the trial of Ismenias by a *koinon synedrion* at Thebes.[66] If a charge of 'not being good for Greece' stood up against Ismenias, why not against the Delians? Besides, could a decree of exile from *Athenian* territory have made any sense against the Delians?

The cases in this section do not reveal any clear examples of 'pure' *asebeia*. But it is fair to say that political motives could not have given *asebeia* its special position in the criminal calendar if the charge had not touched the deepest wellsprings of the people's religiosity. The secret of the accusers was their ability to detect the vast and elastic possibilities that the people's receptivity to this charge opened up. The label of the charge was as important as the content, though this is not always realized. Some investigators have expressed surprise, for example, at the fact that Theoris' accusers attacked her by a *graphē asebeias* rather than by a *graphē pharmakeias*,[67] but this is to miss the whole point. The accusers wanted the jury to be predisposed to convict as soon as they heard the name of the charge.

Finally, on the second question posed at the beginning of this chapter, as to whether there was any technical difference between the charge of *asebeia* as preferred against philosophers and the charge as preferred against non-philosophers, the probable answer is that there was a comprehensive statute at the turn of the fifth century which encompassed *asebeia* in all its aspects (cf. n. 49). But even if there was not a comprehensive ordinance, no difference in principle can be detected between the statutory form as defined in Diopeithes' *psēphisma*, for example, and a form such as the secularized version of the principles evolved by the Eumolpidae.

4 ARISTOTLE, DEMADES, AND THEOPHRASTUS

The first post-Socratic use of *asebeia* against a philosopher was when charges were brought against Aristotle. But in order to put that case in proper perspective it is proposed to begin with the trial of the orator Demades, which preceded Aristotle's case by a few months.

In 324–3 Demades proposed a decree granting Alexander the Athenian component of the divine honours that he sought from all members of the League of Corinth. At first Demosthenes opposed the proposal, but after the Olympic Festival of July 324 he agreed to the divine honours although he opposed Alexander's proposal for the return of all exiles.[68] After Alexander's death Demades was charged with having made Alexander the thirteenth god although he was a mere mortal; Aelian, to whom we owe that important (and almost certainly correct) piece of information, adds that the Demos could not tolerate this excess of impiety and fined him a hundred talents (Ael. *Var. Hist.* 5.12).[69] Athenaeus makes the fine ten talents and merely says that it was for introducing Alexander as a god (Athen. 251B). Derenne thinks that the charge was specifically *asebeia*,[70] but this needs to be considered. Plutarch says that Demades was convicted under the *graphē paranomōn* seven times and was unable to pay the fines.[71] It may well be (and is so assumed by Hansen)[72] that Alexander's deification was charged under the *graphē paranomōn*; it was illegal to propose any alteration of the primacy of the twelve gods. If we could be sure that the *graphē paranomōn* was used in this case it would place Alexander's installation as a thirteenth beyond any doubt; the prior law whose violation gave rise to the *graphē* will have been a law dealing exclusively with the twelve, not with gods in general. When Aelian says that the Demos could not tolerate this excess of impiety he is noting the special considerations, namely the twelve-gods law, that influenced the jury in this case. But this raises an awkward question: Can we ever be sure that the charge was technically *asebeia* just because a source uses the word? However, the difficulty may be a limited one. The *graphē paranomōn* only lay against those actively engaged in the political process, and of the *asebeia* defendants whom we have noticed so far, only Alcibiades and Andocides can be so described; and neither of them was charged in connection with legislative proposals.

119

Demades is also said to have been condemned in connection with the Harpalus affair (Deinarch. 1.89, 2.15), but the link, if any, between that corruption scandal and the deification case is far from clear.[73] The only connection that springs to mind is suggested by Aelian's belief that Demades was fined one hundred talents for the deification, that is, exactly ten times the fine attested by Athenaeus. Now, Deinarchus tells us that one of the penalties for bribery was a fine of ten times the amount of the bribe (Deinarch. 1.60). This suggests that Aelian may have thought that the amount of ten talents known to Athenaeus as the fine was in fact the amount of the bribe; he therefore did his own arithmetic. Other than this there is no discernible link between the two cases.

Why was the *graphē paranomōn* used against Demades? Why was the *graphē asebeias*, which was well established by this time, not used? The easy answer is that there was nothing in the *asebeia* statute to cover the case of divine honours to a mortal. But Aristotle's case casts doubt on this explanation.

Aristotle got into trouble – or narrowly escaped doing so – soon after Demades. His close links with Macedon were remembered after Alexander's death, and in 323–2 the anti-Macedonian lobby decided to bring him down. The accusers[74] uncovered a number of impious acts allegedly committed by Aristotle. The most important arose out of Aristotle's friendship with Hermias, the philosopher-ruler of Atarneus and Assos to whose kingdom Aristotle had moved in 348–7. When Hermias was lured to the Persian Court and killed in *c*.345–4, Aristotle composed both a hymn in his honour and an inscription for his statue at Delphi.[75] The accusers claimed that the hymn was a paean, a choral song addressed exclusively to gods, and Aristotle was alleged to have intoned it every day at mealtimes (Athen. 696A–B). He was also alleged to have sacrificed to Hermias (ibid., 697A). Another charge was that after the death of Pythias, the adopted daughter of Hermias whom Aristotle had married, he sacrificed to her in the same way as the Athenians sacrificed to Demeter of Eleusis.[76] It was not for nothing that the Eleusinian Hierophant, Eurymedon, was included amongst the accusers.[77]

Aristotle decided not to remain in Athens for the trial. Saying that he did not want the Athenians to make the same mistake about philosophy twice (Ael.*V.H.* 3.36), he fled to Chalcis, where he died. This, at any rate, is the accepted tradition,[78] but there are some loose ends. Favorinus (*ap.* Diog. Laert. 5.9) said that

Aristotle was the first to compose a court speech in his own defence; Athenaeus quotes from a document described as *Apology to the charge of asebeia* in which Aristotle replied to the allegation about Hermias, though Athenaeus is not sure whether it is genuine (Athen. 697A). It is possible[79] that Aristotle saw the *graphē asebeias* and drafted his reply to it, only to find that the case was hopeless and that only flight remained.

How do we reconcile the charges against Demades with those against Aristotle? On the face of it Aristotle was charged with the same type of offence as Demades, that of introducing a new god, the only difference being that Demades added a thirteenth to the official list, whereas Aristotle established a private cult. And Socrates and Ninos, it seems, were also charged with introducing new gods. But in fact there is an important distinction between Socrates and Ninos on the one hand and Demades on the other. Socrates and Ninos introduced entities which were already divine, and they did not try to make any of their imports a thirteenth god in the pantheon. But Demades had to do two things – to convert a mortal into a god and to include that god in the pantheon. Aelian makes it clear that the mortality of the new god was the decisive factor against Demades: 'they fined him because he had enrolled Alexander, a mortal, amongst the Olympians' (Ael. *V.H.* 5.12). Nothing like that stood in the *asebeia* statute as it had been restated at the turn of the century. Nor had the statute contemplated the special way of introducing a new god by Olympian enrolment. On both grounds, therefore, the use of the *graphē paranomōn* against Demades still makes sense.

They could not use the *graphē paranomōn* against Aristotle for a very simple reason: he had not made any official proposal. But does this mean that they charged impiety *faute de mieux*, or were they logically able to bring him within the scope of the *graphē asebeias*? If we divide the case into two parts, the cult of Hermias and the cult of Pythias, the latter immediately gives a viable statutory basis for a charge of *asebeia*. Let us recall Diogenes Laertius' words: 'He married her and sacrificed to her in his transports of delight, as the Athenians did to Demeter of Eleusis' (Diog. Laert. 5.4). This exposed him to a rule against mocking the Mysteries that went back to Alcibiades' case. Derenne condemns Diogenes for embellishing sacrifices which, according to Eusebius' source, were only offered to her after her death.[80] But is it an embellishment? Or has Diogenes revealed one of the

121

Eleusinian secrets? His source was the younger Aristippus of Cyrene (Diog. Laert. 5.3), who was at least as reliable as Lycon, who reached Eusebius via Aristocles. Aristippus would not have made the comparison with the Mysteries if he had not had some knowledge thereof. It is safe to assume that the part of the indictment relating to Pythias was fully covered by the *asebeia* statute, and this helped the other part relating to Hermias; once the Pythias charge had given the accusers a secure footing, they simply added the Hermias charge for good measure. We conclude, therefore, that up to this time the *graphē paranomōn* was uniquely needed for Demades.

Our next trial, of Theophrastus who succeeded Aristotle as head of the Peripatetics, was held at some part of the period 317–315.[81] The principal accuser was Hagnonides, a sycophant who had prosecuted Phocion for *prodosia* in 318 but had resisted a proposal to torture him before putting him to death (Plut. *Phoc.* 29, 33, 35). Demosthenes' nephew, Demochares, also had a part in Theophrastus' prosecution. The charge was *asebeia* (Diog. Laert. 5.37), but the factual basis is not available. We may be able, however, to deduce something from Aelian's account of how Theophrastus lost the thread of his argument when addressing the Areopagus and explained that he had been overawed by the council's prestige, on which Demochares commented: 'Theophrastus, it was the Athenians, not the twelve gods, who were judging you' (Ael. *V.H.* 8.12). It would seem that he had offended against the pantheon in some way, though it is not possible to be more specific. The outcome of the case was that Theophrastus was acquitted, and Hagnonides only just managed to secure one-fifth of the votes (Diog. Laert. 5.37).

The fact that the trial was held before the Areopagus, and during the ten-year regime of Demetrius of Phalerum,[82] helps to identify the political background, for the links between Theophrastus and Demetrius were particularly strong. Theophrastus was Demetrius' teacher, and when Demetrius carried out his revision of the laws in *c*.317–6 he relied heavily on Theophrastus' *Nomoi*;[83] he also consulted his old teacher in person, especially on the law of property.[84] Demetrius got more out of it than Theophrastus, for he was celebrated as the third lawgiver of Athens, and after his explusion in 307 went on to compile a code for Ptolemy Soter.[85] But Theophrastus did receive some recompense, for by restoring the Areopagus' jurisdiction to compensate for Demades' virtual abolition of the *dikastēria*[86] Demetrius provided a court which gave Theophrastus a sympathetic hearing despite his (typical) ineptitude in a court situation.[87]

Theophrastus' links with Demetrius supply a general political ambience for the attack on him, but can we identify a more specific *casus belli*? The best guess is his part in Demetrius' revision of the laws, especially the law of property, including Theophrastus' advocacy of a system of registration in order to ensure that successive mortgages as recorded on boundary stones (*horoi*) were made enforceable in the correct order of priority.[88] *Horoi* had been a focus of contention ever since Solon 'liberated the black earth'; they had epitomized the gulf between the Haves and the Have-nots, and now they epitomized the middle-class ideology of Theophrastus and Demetrius.[89] The same middle class that had destroyed Socrates was once more in the box-seat, and the new science of comparative law, of systematically recording the laws and evaluating them,[90] was one of their most important tools. As the democrats saw it, an attempt should be made to check this pernicious development, hence the employment of that willing work-horse, the charge of *asebeia*.

We pause at this point in order to glance at Ferguson's explanation for the attack on Theophrastus. The theory is that the Peripatetic school was seen as a centre of aristocratic influence and disloyalty at which thousands came under 'the dangerous teaching of Theophrastus' – in effect a variant of the Socratic corruption of the young. The democrats will have singled out the Peripatetics as their special target, hence the law proposed by Sophocles of Sunium in 307, after the expulsion of Demetrius of Phalerum. Sophocles' law prohibited philosophers, on pain of death, from presiding over schools without the express permission of the Boule and the Ecclesia (Diog. Laert. 5.38). When this law was passed Theophrastus left Athens (ibid.). But in 306 Philon, a Peripatetic, brought a *graphē paranomōn* against Sophocles; the democrat was convicted and fined five talents, his law was repealed and Theophrastus returned (ibid.). The illegality of Sophocles' law resided in the fact that a law of Solon had given certain associations official recognition; there was also an element of impiety in Sophocles' proposal, inasmuch as Theophrastus' school was seen as a religious club dedicated to the service of the Muses.[91]

123

Except for his description of Theophrastus' ideology as aristocratic, Ferguson makes an arguable case. But one or two points need elucidation. Is it correct to claim that the attack was aimed primarily at the Peripatetics? Diogenes has 'all the other philosophers' leave with Theophrastus (5.38). This is an exaggeration, since Diogenes himself says that the law was aimed only at heads of schools, but the point is that according to Athenaeus members of both the Academy and the Peripatetics were attacked by Demochares on behalf of Sophocles (Athen. 509). In fact the democrats had no option but to make the law applicable to both schools, for Athenian law undoubtedly banned *privilegia*, or laws of individual rather than general application; Rome's Twelve Tables had (traditionally) taken such a ban over from the laws of Solon (XII Tables 9.1).

Ferguson thinks that Demochares, who spoke for Sophocles at the latter's *graphē paranomōn* trial, heaped abuse on philosophers because he was unable to mount a defence on the law,[92] but is this right? One would like to think that there was a legal issue of substance on which the absent Theophrastus had briefed Philon.[93] A legal issue can perhaps be conjectured from Ferguson's rendering of a garbled passage in Athenaeus (509): Demochares said that if Sophocles' law meant embarrassing Plato's school in addition to destroying the nest of Peripatetic traitors it could not be helped, because the interests of the state were paramount.[94] Demochares may have been trying to plead a higher legality – *salus rei publicae suprema lex*, bypassing the normal statutes in order to save the state. But Theophrastus, whose strict interpretation of *eisangelia*[95] is only one example of his preference for firm statutory norms in which the law could be anchored, was able to arm Philon with the arguments needed to maintain the supremacy of statute law.

Theophrastus was, through his legal expertise, the most political of the philosophers. It is surprising that he was not charged more often, for he made enemies more easily than most. A misogynist and lifelong bachelor,[96] his contribution to Demetrius' laws regulating the affairs of women[97] was that of an architect rather than a mere consultant. If any advice was needed by the friends of Macedon who accused the courtesan Phryne,[98] they would have been well advised to ask Theophrastus.[99] Despite his prodigious capacity for research, which prompted Aristotle to say that he needed a bridle for his excessive astuteness

(Diog. Laert. 5.39), he was not on very good terms with the 2,000 pupils who flocked to his lectures (ibid., 37), for when he died in *c*.288–7 at the age of 85 he neither bequeathed his library to the school nor left any directions as to the appointment of a successor.[100] Aristippus' criticism of him for having a relationship with Aristotle's son, Nicomachus, while the latter was his pupil (*ap.* Diog. Laert. 5.39) may reflect the tensions which eventually caused him to reject everything that he had built up.

Our last two trials, of Stilpo and Theodorus, give us our last opportunity to uncover an unequivocal case of 'pure' *asebeia*. Stilpo, a Megarian philosopher working in Athens, had said of Pheidias' statue of Athena that it was not a god, because Athena was by Zeus whereas the statue was by Pheidias. When summoned before the Areopagus he claimed that his statement was correct because Athena was not a god but a goddess. Thereupon Theodorus posed a distinctly Rabelaisian question as to how Stilpo knew this: 'Did you pull up (*anasyras*) her dress and have a look?' (Diog. Laert. 2.116). The witticism was probably responsible for the strait-laced Theophrastus using the word *anasesyrmenos* ('pulling up one's clothes') as a synonym for 'obscene'.[101] At all events, Stilpo was ordered to leave Athens. Some time after 320 is favoured as the date of his trial,[102] but it may be possible to be more precise. Given that Demetrius Poliorcetes, who drove Demetrius of Phalerum out of Athens, preserved Stilpo's house at Megara for him (Diog. Laert. 2.115), we would expect Demetrius of Phalerum to have been in power at the time of Stilpo's expulsion. This is supported by the choice of the Areopagus as the forum for the trial, and also by the fact that Stilpo was so good at enticing students away from other schools that he deprived Theophrastus of two outstanding students (ibid., 2.113). Theophrastus may well have had a hand in Stilpo's expulsion, capitalizing on the Megarian's notorious atheism[103] and using the Areopagus, which could be relied on to reach the right decision.

Our last accused, Theodorus of Cyrene, presents as the most determined atheist since Diagoras of Melos (Cic. *Nat. Deor.* 1.2). He claimed the right to commit theft, adultery, and sacrilege as he chose, and had a pungent, if bawdy, wit, but was a scholar of some consequence (Diog. Laert. 2.99, 97). He was well qualified for the role of defendant in an *asebeia* suit, but the tradition as to what actually happened to him is very confused. Diogenes offers us three alternatives: he escaped trial by the Areopagus thanks to Demetrius of Phalerum; he was sentenced to drink hemlock; he took up residence at the court of Ptolemy I and admitted to Lysimachus of Thrace that he had been banished from Athens (Diog. Laert. 2.101–2). Athenaeus (611A) has him put to death, Plutarch (606B) has him banished from Cyrene, and Philo (884) has him banished pursuant to a conviction for atheism and corruption of the young. The probabilities are that Demetrius of Phalerum, who surrounded himself with philosophers and accorded them his protection,[104] connived at his escape before a death sentence that had been imposed by the Areopagus could be carried out. Perhaps Theophrastus supported that solution; there is no record of Theodorus having stolen his pupils.

5 *ASEBEIA:* 'A CRIME AGAINST PARENTS AND COUNTRY'

Our conclusion regarding 'pure' *asebeia* is that in a narrow sense two or three cases – Ninos, Stilpo, Theodorus – appear to meet the required standards of purity. In all those cases there was a general perception of the need to insulate Athenian society against the encroachment of religious innovations, irrespective of any momentary political motivation. One can probably add Socrates to this list. But in a broader sense none of these cases qualifies, because the charge of *asebeia* is always the instrument of a particular socio-economic group for the protection of Athenian society according to that group's definition of society, though not according to the definition of an opposing group.

The charge of *asebeia* was well equipped to take its place alongside treason proper in the battery of defences against the forces threatening the dissolution of society. The fact that there were two schools of thought as to when impiety became actionable does not matter; there were also two schools of thought as to whether a given act amounted to *katalysis tou dēmou* or *prodosia*. The *mariage de convenance* between *asebeia* and *katalysis tou dēmou* in 415 produced a rapidly proliferating progeny, and by the time Theophrastus came to put Aristotle's notes on virtues and vices into descriptive form[105] the ground-plan for the future Hellenistic concept of *asebeia* was securely in place: '*Asebeia* is an offence against gods and spirits, or against the departed, or against parents and country' ([Arist.] *On Virtues and Vices* 7.2). The juxtaposition of parents and country was deliberate: it defined the duty of loyalty in terms that everyone could understand.

VII

ALEXANDER IN ASIA

1 THE FOOTHILLS OF HELLENISTIC ASEBEIA

In the Hellenistic kingdoms, especially Ptolemaic Egypt, the concept of *asebeia* served as a broad umbrella under which were subsumed all offences against the state, which meant offences against the god-king who was identified with the state. Taubenschlag instances stirring up violence in the Boule or Ecclesia in such a way as to violate the duty of reverence owing to the ruler and his house; revolting or raising sedition against the ruler; and swearing a false oath by the ruler.[1] *Hierosylia* (sacrilege or temple-theft) and violation of asylum are classified by Taubenschlag as sacral delicts not falling under *asebeia*, and *prodosia* in the sense of external treason is not listed by him at all; but that can only be due to the absence of papyrological evidence on which he depends for his findings. These few strands, together with even more exiguous material for the Seleucid kingdom, are all that need be noted here for developments subsequent to the fourth century.[2] We therefore take up our theme, the trials under Alexander and his immediate successors. The theme can appropriately be described as a prelude to the judicial history of the Hellenistic period proper.

As foreshadowed in our Introduction, our purpose is to discuss the trials both for their intrinsic interest and for the light that they are able to shed on the early history of Hellenistic *asebeia*. That concept did not arise spontaneously. There must have been a period of germination, and Alexander is a likely starting-point for that. Also, it may be supposed that the sophisticated *asebeia* jurisdiction evolved by Athens played a part in the process. Given the progress made by Athens towards amalgamating offences against the gods with offences against the state, we might expect there to have been a flow-on to neighbouring jurisdictions. Athens may have been the only Greek city to attack philosophers for impiety,[3] but charges under that head were by no means confined to philosophers.

The first question to be considered is whether the word *asebeia* is used in the sources in such a way as to suggest that Alexander incorporated charges of impiety in the Macedonian judicial system. After that it will be a matter of proceeding with our exposition of the trials and being on the alert for pointers to *asebeia* as we go along.

2 THE TERMINOLOGY OF THE TRIALS

In principle one would expect *asebeia* to be prominent in Alexander's trials. His brief sojourn amongst the gods of the Athenian pantheon put him in touch with *asebeia* headquarters, so to speak, for as the thirteenth Athenian god he was not just another cult figure, he was one of a select company for whose protection the full resources of the Athenian judicial system had been available for more than a hundred years.[4] There was also a feature of the Macedonian kingship that might have favoured an adoption of the charge of *asebeia*. The Macedonians cherished an inborn reverence for their kings, a sentiment which invested the ruler with a religious aura and ensured the stability of the state.[5] Quintus Curtius notes that apart from their innate veneration for their kings – *ingenitam illi genti erga reges suos venerationem* – they had a special regard for Alexander (3.6.16). This is, of course, a non-Athenian element in the early history of Hellenistic *asebeia*. But it is an important element.

Despite the promising background, however, the requisite terminology is not found in the Greek sources for the actual trials. The great conspirators of the reign – Philotas, Parmenio, Alexander the Lyncestian, the Royal Pages, Callisthenes – are usually said to have 'plotted against him' (*epibouleuein*), and the word *asebeia* is not used.[6] Plutarch could have described Philotas' verbal attacks on Alexander as 'impious' easily enough, but he merely reports 'improper words [*logous anepitēdeious*] against the king' (*Alex.* 49.1). And when he has Alexander judging harshly in cases in which he has been maligned (ibid., 42.2) the phrase is simply *kakōs akouōn*. We find much the same thing in Arrian's account of Cleitus' death, when the veteran general's belittlement of Alexander evokes no stronger epithet than *hybris*, 'insults' (Arrian 4.8–9). It is only in Curtius that the word *impius* is found, and even then it refers to conspiracies rather than to lack of reverence.[7] Conspiracies would certainly be part of Hellenistic *asebeia*, but in the early stages one might expect the concept to be applied primarily to violations of reverence, either by verbal insults or acts of denigration.[8] You could not assail the traditional gods physically, and the subsumption of physical assaults on the god-king under *asebeia* was likely to occur somewhat later than the subsumption of the non-physical.

Although the appropriate terminology is lacking, some of the underlying ideas were developed under Alexander, as will become clear in due course.[9] There is, however, one other matter that should be mentioned here. It arises out of Alexander's visit to Siwah, when he may have been formally recognized as the son of Ammon. If that is in fact what happened,[10] it is worth noting that under native Egyptian law a usurper or an instigator of sedition was 'an Enemy of the God X', 'a Godless Enemy of the Gods', 'a Rebel against the Gods'.[11] If the son of Ammon also happened to be the Pharaoh, treason against him was also a crime against the gods. This incorporates a native Egyptian element in Ptolemaic *asebeia*. That link may have been forged as early as Alexander. But this possibility is speculative, and in the last resort either it will be possible to piece together a case for charges of *asebeia* under Alexander from individual trials, or it will remain unproven.

3 PHILOTAS AND PARMENIO

The execution of Philotas and his father Parmenio in 330 is the first *cause célèbre* of the reign. A conspiracy by Philotas, commander of the Companion Cavalry and long-standing friend of Alexander, was reported to the king in 330, following an earlier report some two years before, while he was in Egypt. He had discounted the earlier report, but now he was more cautious. Philotas was brought before the Macedonians, with Alexander appearing as his accuser. This conformed to the traditional pattern whereby the Macedonian Assembly, that is, the Army, rendered the verdicts, leaving the king with the role of prosecutor.[12] Philotas was found guilty and was executed by being shot down with javelins.[13]

So much for the bare bones of the story; but there is a lot more to it. Arrian follows the account of Ptolemy, a member of the Royal Bodyguard who later became Ptolemy I of Egypt and wrote a history of Alexander. Arrian considered him one of his best sources, because he not only campaigned with Alexander but was, as a king, less inclined to falsehood (Arrian 1. Pr.2). If anyone was interested in an *asebeia* component in the case it ought to have been Ptolemy, in whose reign the link between Greek and Egyptian concepts of impiety began to be forged in earnest, but his account as cited verbatim by Arrian is silent on that score:

> Ptolemy states as follows: Philotas was summoned before the Macedonians, and after a vigorous accusation by Alexander was heard in his defence. The informers proved his guilt and that of his accomplices by many clear proofs, especially the fact that he had received information of a plot against Alexander and had failed to pass the information on to him though he saw him twice a day. Philotas admitted that he had received the information. He was shot down with javelins by the Macedonians, as were other conspirators. (Arrian 3.26.2–3)

The charge as noted by Ptolemy not only lacked an *asebeia* component, it also lacked direct proof, since the only one of 'the many clear proofs' that Ptolemy bothered to spell out was the inference of guilt that was drawn from Philotas' failure to pass on information. But whether this justifies the acquittal that a number of modern scholars bestow on Philotas remains to be seen.

Other sources go into greater detail. Diodorus (17.79–80.2) forges a chain of conspiracy and disclosure stretching from Dimnus, the disgruntled Friend who launches the plot, via his lover Nicomachus, to the latter's brother Cebalinus who first reports the matter to Philotas, but when he fails to act Cebalinus briefs Metro, a Royal Page, to bring the information to Alexander's attention. The king arrests Dimnus and learns everything from him. He then sends for Cebalinus and Philotas and elicits the whole story. Dimnus kills himself. Philotas admits that it was careless of him to disregard the report but denies that he had any part in the plot. Alexander refers the trial to the Macedonians. After hearing many arguments they condemn Philotas and others to death. Amongst them is Philotas' father, Parmenio. Philotas is tortured and confesses and is then killed 'in the Macedonian manner'. Diodorus locates the torture and confession *after* the Army's verdict; prior to that, at Alexander's pre-trial interrogation, he has Philotas deny his guilt.

Curtius weaves a broad and colourful tapestry (6.7.18–11.40). The important facts not mentioned by Diodorus include the following: Alexander summons a council of Friends to hear Nicomachus' evidence (6.8.1). Craterus, a close confidante of Alexander, leads the attack. The council decides to torture Philotas to force him to name his accomplices (6.8.15). Elaborate precautions are taken by the king's Friends and Bodyguards, including a road-block to prevent anyone going to Parmenio in Media. Alexander arrests Philotas and assembles 6,000 Macedonians. After an address by Alexander that gives Curtius ample scope for his creative talents, Philotas speaks. He argues that the only case against him rests on his failure to pass on the information (6.10.11–37). The trial is adjourned. The council of Friends recommends that Philotas be stoned according to ancient custom,[14] but Hephaestion, Craterus, and Coenus want the truth to be forced out of him by torture (6.11.10). After a lurid account of the torments suffered by the unfortunate Philotas, Curtius has him incriminate his father, Parmenio, while also admitting his own part (6.11.22–34). Philotas and others are executed. Curtius adds a curious note: the primary purpose of torturing Philotas is to uncover the names of accomplices, but it also saves Alexander from odium by extracting a confession, for without that Philotas could not have been condemned without arousing the indignation of the Army, since the case was doubtful until he confessed (6.11.39–40). The first objective of the torture, to identify accomplices, makes perfect sense, but the second objective defies all logic. There is no Roman parallel that Curtius could be retrojecting, nor does it look like a genuine Macedonian institution. Could the Army have returned a conditional verdict, or could Alexander have incurred odium by following the regular trial procedure?

Plutarch's version (*Alex.* 48–9) introduces a radical new element. For some time Alexander had been suspicious of Philotas' arrogance, and had persuaded the latter's mistress, Antigone, to act as an *agent provocateur*. Philotas confided many improper words against the king to her, claiming that the king's achievements were the work of Philotas and his father, and Alexander was a mere stripling who owed his throne to them.[15] These manoeuvres are described by Plutarch as a plot *against* Philotas (*Alex.* 49.1). But Alexander takes no action until the plot gets under way. Philotas fails to report to the king, but the informers eventually get the message to him. Dimnus is killed before he can be questioned (*contra* Diodorus). The informers assert that Dimnus was only a tool, and lodge many charges against Philotas. He is tortured (before the trial). The account ends abruptly with an oblique reference to Philotas' execution ('after he had been put to death Parmenio was despatched'), but there is no mention of a trial.

It is a pity that Curtius draws on his imagination so profusely, because when he does happen to attest a genuine fact not found elsewhere we tend to reach for the salt-cellar anyway. A case in point is his assertion that in his prosecuting speech Alexander said that when his cousin Amyntas made an impious plot against him, Philotas was his accomplice (6.9.17). The reference is to the trial and execution of Amyntas, son of Perdiccas II, in 335, shortly after Alexander's accession.[16] Then, when Philotas speaks he says that he does not deny his friendship with Amyntas, and is even prepared to admit that he venerated him, but that was unavoidable in view of Amyntas' lofty position as the king's relative – *in illo fortunae gradu positum etiam venerari necesse erat* (6.10.25).[17] Philotas was not charged with Amyntas in 335, but can we be so sure that accusations of having plotted with him and rendered him cult (*asebeia* in the basic sense) were not dredged from the past to be used in 330? But the trouble is, as always, that the Greek sources do not confirm this possible charge of *asebeia*.[18] We must also bear in mind Curtius' possible recollection of the charges against Cassius Longinus, who offended Nero by rendering cult to a statue of his ancestor who had killed Caesar (Tac. *Ann.* 16.7.3).

Was Philotas guilty? The question is glibly answered in the negative by many moderns,[19] but as Hammond points out, we have no evidence on which to retry his case.[20] Admittedly we have only one concrete fact, his failure to report to Alexander, but it was a fact of crucial importance, one well able to provide a foundation for an inference, especially when supported by the amount of corroboration that we have here – Parmenio's letter from Philotas, Philotas' friendship (with or without cult) with Amyntas, his marriage alliance with Attalus, and his denigration of the Ammon connection (Curt. 6.9.13–19). A modern court would consider this enough in the absence of a satisfactory explanation for Philotas' failure to report. To take it all as an elaborate charade on the strength of Plutarch's claim that Philotas was plotted against strains credulity. It requires the fictitious *mise en scène* of a plot by Dimnus and at least a dozen others whose names have been preserved,[21] followed by a gross breach of faith with the Army/Assembly, which believed that there was a genuine plot.[22] Unless and until Philotas' friends offer a better explanation for his failure to report than carelessness or underestimation of the gravity of the news, the inference of guilt must stand.

Indirect confirmation of the basic fairness of Philotas' trial is furnished by the case of Amyntas, son of Andromenes, and his brothers. They were charged with complicity in Philotas' plot, and much was made of their close links with him, and of the fact that one of the brothers, Polemon, had defected to the Persians when Philotas was arrested. The Macedonians acquitted Amyntas by acclamation, whereupon he asked leave to go to Polemon and bring him back. He duly brought him back, and Polemon was acquitted.[23] The adverse inference failed in this case because of insufficient corroboration. The Army/Assembly was far from being a mere rubber-stamp.

The use of torture against Philotas does not make his trial anything out of the ordinary. That the evidence of slaves was admissible only if elicited under torture was axiomatic in both Greek and Roman law,[24] and free men were not always in a better position. At Athens foreigners could be tortured when the security of the state was involved, and the fact that Scamander introduced a *psēphisma* forbidding the torture of citizens proves that it had been used against that category as well.[25] Cicero certainly believed that free men had been tortured by the Athenians and the Rhodians (*Part. Orat.* 113). There was admittedly some resistance, because when Phocion was convicted of treason by the Ecclesia in 318 the attempt to add to the verdict a rider that he be tortured before being executed was opposed by Hagnonides; but even he agreed that torture could be used when they caught the villainous Callimedon (Plut. *Phoc.* 35). The sequence in Phocion's case is the same as that in Diodorus' version of Philotas' trial, whereas Plutarch and Curtius have Philotas tortured before the trial. The latter makes better sense to modern eyes, but in any case the purpose was to uncover the names of accomplices; if it also induced the accused to confess, so much the better.

Ultimately, of course, the validity of Plutarch's claim that Philotas was the victim of a plot depends on the case of his father, Parmenio, to which we now turn. Parmenio's downfall began, according to Diodorus, when the Macedonians condemned him *in absentia* at the time of Philotas' trial; this will have happened because he was the master-mind behind the plot, and his execution will have been carried out by messengers sent to Media by Alexander (Diod. 17.80.1). Strabo also has Parmenio killed as an accomplice (15.2.10). Justin makes a valiant attempt to supply an *asebeia* component when he says that Parmenio was tried and executed for criticizing Alexander for subverting Macedonian traditions (Just. 12.5.1-3). Curtius has Philotas refer to his father as a co-accused (6.10.30). But Arrian says nothing about a trial; he says that Alexander sent Polydamas, one of the Companions, with a letter to three commanders serving in Parmenio's army in Media, namely Cleander, Sitalces, and Menidas. The three put Parmenio to death. Arrian surmises that this was done either because Alexander refused to believe that Parmenio was not implicated, or because it was dangerous to leave such a powerful man alive after putting his son to death (Arrian 3.26.3-4). As for Plutarch, he simply says that Alexander sent someone to Media to kill Parmenio, but he does not say whether this was pursuant to a trial (*Alex*. 49.7). Curtius, who has already attested a trial, has Alexander entrust Polydamas with letters to the three commanders, plus a letter from Alexander to Parmenio and a letter purporting to have been written to Parmenio by Philotas. Polydamas disguises himself as an Arab and sets out with two Arabs as his companions. Before reaching his destination Polydamas reverts to Macedonian dress. While Parmenio is walking in a grove reading his two letters he is set upon by the three officers and killed. When his troops hear the news they threaten mutiny, but Cleander calms them down by reading Alexander's letter concerning Parmenio's part in the plot (Curt. 7.2.11-34).

Everyone except Arrian and Plutarch attests a trial *in absentia*, and those two agree in any case with the others in so far as the execution is carried out in Media on instructions from Alexander. Two questions therefore arise. First, are we to believe those who say that there was a trial, or those who say nothing on that score but attest the same sequel? Despite anguished cries of 'Murder most foul!'[26] there is nothing obviously wrong with the statement that there was a trial. If Alexander knew that Philotas' death was going to evoke a violent reaction by Parmenio, it was surely better to give his counter-measures a colour of right by securing a verdict *in absentia*. That he hastily arranged the father's assassination as an afterthought does not accord well with the patient preparation that went into the son's case. More important, on what basis except a verdict of the Macedonians could he have ordered Parmenio's death? If the king did not have the power to try cases of treason against himself, can he reasonably be credited with the far more arbitrary power of ordering summary execution?

In the last resort, however, we do not need a trial in order to absolve Alexander of the charge of murder. There is a valid alternative principle under which he could have kept within the bounds of Macedonian law. Curtius says that during the investigation of Philotas, near relatives of Parmenio, fearing the Macedonian law whereunder the relatives of those who plotted against the king were executed with the plotters, either killed themselves or fled. To stop the panic Alexander suspended the law (Curt. 6.11.20). The account rings true; Themistocles' family had, we recall, been punished with him.[27] But how long did the suspension last? In his account of another trial which was held several years later Curtius again refers to the Macedonian law and the anxiety of relatives (8.6.28). It is easy enough to say that Curtius had simply forgotten what he had written earlier, but it is at least possible that the law, which had only been suspended, was reinstated.[28] It may thus have been back on the statute-book by the time Alexander got around to dealing with Parmenio.

One feature of Parmenio's death remains. Was he still in command in Media, or had he been replaced by the three officers who eventually killed him? The first alternative must be ruled out at once, because it is inconceivable that the officers would have killed their commanding officer; it would also have been an extremely unwise precedent for Alexander to set. We must therefore agree with Robinson that Alexander deposed Parmenio from his command,[29] but probably after learning of his involvement in the plot rather than earlier. Alexander notified the three officers of this, and also told them that the rule regarding relatives had been reinstated. They were thus able to kill this particular relative with a clear conscience.

4 ALEXANDER THE LYNCESTIAN

The Philotas/Parmenio case was followed within a short time by the execution of Alexander the Lyncestian. This scion of the Lyncestid royal house had been accused of treason in connection with Philip's death in 336, but where his two brothers were put to death on the same charge he was saved by Alexander, whose accession he had been the first nobleman to acknowledge. In 334–3 it was reported that he was negotiating with the Persian king, Darius, to assassinate Alexander and take his place on the Macedonian throne. The Persian intermediary fell into Parmenio's hands and was sent to Alexander. The king consulted the Friends, who felt that the Lyncestian should be dispatched as soon as possible before he rose up with the Thracian cavalry, to whose command Alexander had appointed him. Parmenio arrested the Lyncestian and sent him to the king, but Alexander would not refer him to the Macedonians for trial and kept him in prison.[30] Three years later, after the deaths of Philotas and Parmenio, the Lyncestian's luck finally ran out. One of the generals, Atarrhias, asked that he be brought before the Macedonians. When ordered to speak[31] he could manage only a few incoherent words and was put to death.[32]

The case has some points of interest. It indirectly confirms the gravity of the Philotas/Parmenio affair, for nothing short of that extreme danger could have caused Alexander to reverse the leniency that he had hitherto shown the Lyncestian. Curtius is surprised that he was unable to speak although he had three years to work on his defence (7.1.8); his confusion is also noted by Diodorus (17.80.2). We might therefore think that an entirely new *casus belli* had arisen. But the silence of the sources rules this out. Who was the accuser at the trial? Hammond notes that Alexander is not mentioned as such,[33] but could it have been anyone else? Curtius reminds us that in an earlier (lost) book of his history he described how information was laid against the Lyncestian by two informers; in accordance with the practice in Curtius' own day *a duobus indicibus delatus* (7.1.6) means giving information, not appearing as the formal accuser. Could the *duo indices* have been

Alexander's mother, the formidable Olympias, and the Persian arrested by Parmenio?[34]

5 THE POSTHUMOUS TRIAL OF CLEITUS

'Black' Cleitus, a somewhat disillusioned commander of an older generation, attended a dinner given by Alexander at Samarkand in 328. As the wine began to flow singers denigrated generals who had recently been defeated by the Persians, and flatterers compared Alexander with Castor and Pollux, to whom he had begun sacrificing in preference to Dionysus. Cleitus could not stomach these insults to divine beings, or the belittlement of the heroes of old (Arrian 4.8.4). He reminded Alexander that his achievements were not his but Macedon's. When the company began denigrating Philip, Cleitus could contain himself no longer. He reminded Alexander that he had saved his life at the River Granicus, 'when you, god-born as you are, were turning your back on the Persian's spear' (Plut. *Alex.* 50.6). Cleitus added, 'It is by the blood of Macedonians that you have become so great as to disown Philip your father and make yourself the son of Ammon' (ibid.). The king tried to attack Cleitus, but was restrained by other members of the company. Alexander called out to the elite guards, the Hypaspists, in the Macedonian language, the use of which indicated a crisis; he also ordered a trumpeter to sound a general alarm, and hit him when he failed to obey (ibid., 51.4). Cleitus was forced out of the hall but tried to force his way in again. Thereupon Alexander seized a spear from one of the guards and ran him through. When he sobered up he was stricken with remorse and was inconsolable for three days.

If this were all, the incident might not qualify for consideration here, but there is more to it. Curtius says that in order to assuage the king's guilt the Macedonians decreed that Cleitus had been lawfully killed: *iure interfectum Clitum Macedones decernunt.* The Macedonians added that they would have denied him burial if the king had not ordered otherwise (Curt. 8.2.12). The temptation to charge Curtius with a reminiscence of Scipio Aemilianus' famous pronouncement on the death of Tiberius Gracchus (Vell. 2.4.4) should be resisted; the differences between the two episodes are much greater than the similarities. Nor is Curtius' credibility affected by the fact that the Gracchans were, as enemies of the state, denied burial in 133; a similar rule was well known at Athens (Thuc. 1.138.6) and can safely be posited for Macedon as well.

Curtius has told us that the Macedonians formally ratified Alexander's killing of Cleitus. But this decision of the army in its judicial mode was not prompted only by a wish to help the king in his predicament. There were also legal grounds. In other words, Cleitus' conduct was treated as treason. This raises a nice point. Was it treason because he had assailed the king by words, making light of his divinity, suggesting that the son of Ammon was a coward, accusing him of defiling Castor and Pollux by being compared with them, and even implying that he was only fit to rule barbarians and slaves?[35] Or was it because his attempt to force his way back into the hall had assailed the king by acts, being seen as a prelude to an attempt on his life? The latter was the last link in the chain of events, but it was not the only link. Plutarch has Alexander make his first attempt to kill Cleitus when he has uttered only verbal insults, although it is only at the second stage when Cleitus tries to force his way back in that he actually kills him (*Alex.* 51.3,5). Arrian found a similar version in Aristobulus (4.8.9). Even more important is Arrian's description of how Alexander, no longer able to tolerate Cleitus' insults, cries out that he is in the same plight as Darius when he was imprisoned by Bessus; he now has nothing left of a king but the name (4.8.7–8).[36] This makes Cleitus' case one of the crucial phases in the early history of Hellenistic *asebeia*. By 'cutting the king down to size' with his insults Cleitus threatened the entire edifice of kingship. We may classify the Macedonians' posthumous trial of Cleitus[37] as a landmark in the evolution of the new kind of impiety.

6 CALLISTHENES AND QUESTIONS OF JURISDICTION

The case of Callisthenes is, or appears to be, the great watershed in Alexander's judicial history. Callisthenes of Olynthus, great-nephew and pupil of Aristotle and fellow-pupil of Theophrastus, was Alexander's official historian.[38] But his relationship with Alexander was equivocal. On the one hand he portrayed the king as a possessor of divine attributes, but on the other hand he claimed that the king's divinity and place in history depended not on his mother's fantasies but on what his history would present to the world; and he praised Athens' stand against tyranny (Arrian 4.10.1–4). After his death at Alexander's behest (below) Theophrastus wrote his obituary,[39] and one wonders whether the friendship between the jurist and the historian imbued the latter with an unshakeable faith in the authority of *nomoi*. This is suggested by passages in Arrian and Plutarch in which Anaxarchus the Sophist tries to console Alexander for the death of Cleitus by reminding him that everything done by a ruler is just and lawful, since he is both law and the measure of justice.[40] This precursor of the Hellenistic notion that the king is law incarnate (*nomos empsychos*)[41] was not altogether favoured by Plutarch, who says that it encouraged Alexander to ride roughshod over the law (*Alex.* 52.3–4). It may also not have been favoured by Callisthenes, for when he in turn consoles Alexander he sedulously avoids Anaxarchus' advocacy of unbridled power (ibid.). Callisthenes may have disliked the idea of a freewheeling autocratic legislator.

The year 327 ushered in the events that were to lead to Callisthenes' downfall. Anaxarchus, vigorously pursuing his ideal of the unfettered autocrat, initiated a discussion at Bactria on the subject of Alexander's divinity; he proposed that as a first step towards deifying the king in his lifetime the Persian ceremony of prostration (*proskynēsis*) should be introduced. Callisthenes strongly opposed this, arguing against divine honours in general and *proskynēsis* in particular; to confer it on mere mortals would diminish the majesty of the gods and provoke them to even greater anger than that to which a private individual's usurpation of the royal prerogatives would provoke Alexander.[42] The analogy was carefully chosen: this particular act of *asebeia* against the gods would be even more serious than the sort of act that had made Alexander feel that he retained nothing of his kingship except the name.[43] The juxtaposition is not accidental; Arrian or his source knew of the native Egyptian law which stigmatized a usurper as 'an Enemy of the Gods'.[44]

Callisthenes forced the abandonment of the proposal for *proskynēsis* as far as the Macedonians were concerned (Arrian 4.12.1), but Alexander did not forget. When Callisthenes became embroiled in the case of the Royal Pages the king reacted harshly.[45] One of the Royal Pages, Hermolaus, had a grievance against Alexander and organized a plot amongst the Pages serving at Bactria. The attempt on his life was to be made when the turn of the Pages came to stand guard over him. But Alexander was forewarned by a wise woman, and spent the night with friends. Details of the plot came to the ears of Ptolemy, who reported to the king. The conspirators were arrested and tortured. After they had revealed the names of accomplices they were stoned by the Macedonians. The sources were not sure whether Callisthenes' name was amongst those disclosed by the conspirators. Arrian's two main sources, Aristobulus and Ptolemy, had the conspirators declare that Callisthenes had put them up to it (4.14.1), but he found no confirmation of this elsewhere; 'most authorities' simply said that Alexander's dislike of Callisthenes led him to draw an adverse inference. In Plutarch, Hermolaus asks Callisthenes how to become illustrious, to which the historian replies, 'By killing the most illustrious'. But Plutarch adds that neither Hermolaus nor his associates denounced Callisthenes. He cites letters written by Alexander to Craterus, Attalus, and Alcetas, three Macedonian officers serving in Pareitaene, informing them that the youths had admitted that they had made the attempt themselves and that no one else was implicated (Plut. *Alex.* 55.2–3). Arrian, on the other hand, says that when the youths were put to the question they revealed their own plot and implicated others, though he does not name them (Arrian 4.13.7). Arrian thus does not seem to know of the letters cited by Plutarch. The latter also cites a letter from Alexander to Antipater, regent of Macedon, in which the king accused Callisthenes of the crime and said that where the youths had been stoned by the Macedonians, he would personally punish Callisthenes (*egō kolasō*); he would also punish 'those who sent him to me and those cities which harbour men who are plotting against me'. Plutarch takes the concluding words as a threat against Aristotle, in whose house Callisthenes had been brought up (Plut. *Alex.* 55.3–4). 'Those who sent him to me' is of course an allusion to the fact that Aristotle had presented Callisthenes to Alexander (Diog. Laert. 5.5); and 'the harbouring city' is Athens.[46]

Can the sharp conflict between the letters to the three officers and the letter to Antipater, who was deputizing for Alexander in Europe, be resolved? The sovereign remedy of pronouncing the letters forgeries should be avoided,[47] if possible. Indeed the discrepancy may be more apparent than real, for the letters to the officers may have had quite a different purpose from the letter to Antipater. The officers were interested in the Pages' plot only in so far as it might lead to trial by the Macedonians. Only Macedonian citizens were subject to that jurisdiction, as Curtius makes clear when he has Hermolaus ask Alexander to give Callisthenes a hearing, to which the king replies that if the historian had been a Macedonian he would have presented him to the Army along with Hermolaus; but as an Olynthian he is not subject to the same jurisdiction – *Olynthio non idem iuris est* (Curt. 8.8.19). It follows, then, that the three officers only needed to know whether the Pages had incriminated any Macedonians; they had no interest in Callisthenes.

Antipater had a much broader interest in the case. The crux of the communication to him is that Alexander will personally punish Callisthenes. What did Alexander mean by this? As usual, comprehension is blunted by source conflict, in this instance regarding Callisthenes' ultimate fate. Plutarch cites Chares for the statement that Callisthenes was kept in prison for seven months in order to be tried by the *synedrion* with Aristotle present, but before that he died of squalor and natural causes; his death occurred at about the time that Alexander was wounded in India (Plut. *Alex*. 55), that is, in 326–5. Chares was partly corroborated by Aristobulus, from whom Arrian learnt that Callisthenes had been imprisoned and led about with the army, only to die of squalor and disease (Arrian 4.14.3). But Arrian got a different version from Ptolemy, according to which Callisthenes was tortured and then hanged (ibid.). Plutarch also knows of that version, and in fact notes it before Chares' version, though he does not credit it to Ptolemy – 'some say' (*Alex*. 55.5). Curtius has Callisthenes die under torture (8.8.21), which looks like a garbled version of Ptolemy's account. Diogenes Laertius, never at a loss for an embellishment, has Callisthenes carried around in an iron cage until, infested with vermin, he is thrown to a lion (5.5). But this Roman punishment was not known in Greece or Macedon.

The key to the riddle of Callisthenes' fate lies in the question as to what Alexander meant when he said that 'I will punish him'. There are three possibilities. First, that he would refer the trial to the *synedrion* of the League of Corinth of which he was *hēgemōn*.[48] Second, that he would try Callisthenes under his personal jurisdiction, seeing that the Macedonians could not try a Greek. Third, that he would simply put Callisthenes to death arbitrarily and without any semblance of judicial process.

Trial by the League *synedrion* is what Chares said was intended, although Callisthenes died before that plan could be put into effect. There is nothing inherently improbable in this. Irrespective of whether Callisthenes was to be charged with plotting against Alexander or merely insulting him, the *synedrion* had jurisdiction, for when the Greek cities participated in the Common Peace with Philip of Macedon in 338–7 they swore an oath not to conspire against or subvert the kingdom of Philip and his descendants;[49] insults had been tantamount to subversion of the kingdom since the death of Cleitus at the latest.[50] Nor is there any difficulty in taking Alexander's 'I will punish him' in his letter to Antipater as an intention to refer the case to the League. Although the delegates from the member-states made up the panel of judges in the League *synedrion*, Alexander's duties as hegemon included the preparation of the agenda for meetings;[51] in effect, therefore, he framed the charges and decided what offenders, and what offences, were to be listed. When Alexander wrote to Antipater to alert him to the possibility that Callisthenes would be sent to Europe for trial,[52] he also told him that Aristotle was to be tried with Callisthenes; for when Chares said that the historian was to be tried 'with Aristotle present' (Plut. *Alex*. 55.5) he meant present as a co-accused, not as an interested spectator.[53] A show-trial was contemplated, for in the same letter to Antipater, cities which harboured Alexander's enemies, that is, Athens, were also to be punished; there was no difficulty there, for the *synedrion* was competent to deal with inter-city disputes.[54] But what would have been the most sensational trial in Greek history did not come to pass, because of Callisthenes' premature death.

There remain, then, the second and third possibilities that we have adumbrated – trial by Alexander personally or arbitrary execution without trial. Either of those possibilities is consistent with Ptolemy's statement that Callisthenes was tortured and hanged (Arrian 4.14.3). Arrian quotes Ptolemy with extreme brevity – 'Ptolemy son of Lagus says he was tortured and put to death by hanging'[55] – and goes on to observe that the conflicting accounts of Ptolemy and Aristobulus (who had him kept in prison until he died of disease) show that even trustworthy witnesses who were with Alexander at the time are unable to agree about events of which they had full knowledge. Plutarch, who also notes both versions (though without naming the sources) adds a detail which was either omitted by Ptolemy or suppressed by Arrian, namely, that the hanging was carried out on Alexander's orders (*Alex.* 55.5). There is no reason to query Ptolemy's evidence.[56] If he thought that death in squalor reflected badly on Alexander, why fabricate an equally unpalatable death by hanging instead of simply recording that 'he died in custody'? It is therefore proposed to accept that Callisthenes was hanged, and on Alexander's orders. But the sources do not say whether those orders were given pursuant to a trial or at discretion, and that is what we must now try to decide.

In principle we should expect Alexander to have preferred the judicial option. Given his acute anxiety not to be branded as a murderer, as shown most clearly by his procural of Macedonian ratification in Cleitus' case, why would he have wanted to jeopardize his gains by an act of naked force against Callisthenes? A ruler who wished to be seen as law incarnate[57] should not act capriciously, as Isocrates reminded the Macedonian kings: 'The king must not live lawlessly, [and] his own judgments should be as fixed and just as the best of laws.' (*Philip.* 31, 18).[58] It is true that the extreme hostility of the Peripatetic school to Alexander as a result of Callisthenes' death[59] is consistent with an arbitrary act, and it has even been argued by Schachermeyr that the proposed synodal trial was merely designed as a smokescreen pending the completion of arrangements for Callisthenes' summary dispatch.[60] But this suggestion founders on two obstacles. First, if Alexander intended to eliminate Callisthenes as an example to all Greeks who opposed his plans for an autocratic empire, as Schachermeyr says, then the obvious way to transmit the message would have been by a genuine plan to hold a show trial, as we have suggested, not by a hole-in-corner assassination. Second, what was the point of the elaborate charade if the truth was going to come out in the end? Admittedly we do not have an explanation for the failure to hold the trial other than Chares' statement that he died before it could be put into effect, but why should that not be true? If an alternative possibility is wanted, we might suggest that Alexander had doubts about Antipater's impartiality towards a relative of his friend Aristotle, doubts that might have been planted in the king's mind by Antipater's enemy, the indefatigable Olympias.[61] All in all, there are much better grounds for thinking that Alexander sought a legal basis for Callisthenes' elimination. But the crucial question is, was such a basis available?

The answer that it is proposed to offer is that the necessary basis was available, in the shape of the king's personal jurisdiction. This, however, requires careful consideration. The basic Macedonian jurisdiction in cases of treason saw the Army/Assembly seized of the power of decision, with the king appearing as a prosecutor without any legal authority to influence decisions, though he might do so indirectly through his prestige. Curtius, to whom we owe this information, states the position crisply as follows: *de capitalibus rebus vetusto Macedonum modo inquirebat <rex, iudicabat> exercitus* (6.8.25).[62] The cases that we have discussed confirm the position attested by Curtius: Philotas, Parmenio (possibly), Alexander the Lyncestian, and the Royal Pages were all convicted by the Macedonians; even Cleitus' death required a posthumous trial by the same tribunal. Curtius introduces a slight complication when he has Amyntas' brother, Polemon, acquitted by the soldiers by acclamation, but then has them unanimously (*una vox*) call on the king to spare him; the Friends support this, whereupon Alexander declares, 'I myself also [*et ipse*] acquit Amyntas and his brothers by my vote [*mea sententia*]' (Curt. 7.2.7–8). It is said that Alexander added his *sententia* only to show that he was in agreement,[63] but I am not sure that we need go as far as that. Curtius was influenced by trials by acclamation in the Early Principate, when the soldiers expressed a view to which the emperor gave effect.[64] Arrian's account of Amyntas' case has no trace of the Curtius scenario: he stands trial before the Macedonians, is acquitted by them, and seeks leave from them to fetch his brother (3.27.2).

The crisp question now is whether we can find room for an exercise of personal jurisdiction by the king within the Macedonian system. For this we must go to Plutarch. He notes that at first, when trying capital cases, Alexander used to put a hand over one ear while the accuser was speaking in order to keep it free for the accused; but later on the profusion of charges so exasperated him that he believed the false because so many were true; he was especially thrown off balance when he was maligned (*kakōs akouōn*) and became cruel and inexorable, because he valued his good name more than his kingdom or his life (*Alex.* 42.2). That this is not a mere pastiche of the tradition for Tiberius or Domitian is guaranteed by the part about Alexander putting a hand over

one year; there is no parallel in the tradition for the Early Principate. We therefore have here a portrait of a man sitting in
judgment, not merely acting as an accuser. It is also a man sitting
as a judge in his own cause: he is not reacting harshly against
insults in cases in which the complainants are persons other than
himself. We note that within the 'bad' period Alexander reacted
more strongly against statements derogatory of his character or
divinity than he did against conspiracies. Plutarch is thus placing
special emphasis on the nascent new strand in the *asebeia* genre.
But Curtius, discussing the same 'capital cases' as Plutarch, gives
exclusive jurisdiction to the Macedonians. Has Plutarch invented
a personal jurisdiction in treason cases, or has Curtius mistakenly
deduced a general rule against such a jurisdiction from individual
cases?

Against Curtius is the fact that although the Greek sources
supply ample examples of individual cases being judged by the
Macedonians, no source puts it in the form of a general rule as
Curtius does. But Curtius is usually quite good on specific laws
and institutions. If Plutarch did invent personal jurisdiction he
did it by crediting the ruler with verdicts which in fact emanated
from another tribunal; the sources for the Roman Principate made
that into an art. But this almost accidental perversion of the truth
should not have produced the anecdote about keeping one ear
for the accused. It is time to see whether other passages in
Plutarch cast any light on the problem. The word *aparaitētos*
(inexorable), which Plutarch uses to describe Alexander's reaction to malignment, appears again on the eve of the drive into
the Hindu Kush, when Plutarch says that Alexander was greatly
feared and was inexorable against wrongdoers. He cites two
examples: Menander, one of the Companions who had been
posted to a garrison but had refused to remain there, for which
Alexander put him to death; and Orsodates, a Persian who
defected and was shot down by Alexander with his own hand
(*Alex*. 57.2). Orsodates is a case of personal jurisdiction (if he
was given a trial at all), but he was not a Macedonian: Menander
was. Is Plutarch telling us that Alexander judged him personally?
That is quite understandable if he was not so much judging a case
of treason as punishing a military infraction in his capacity as
commander-in-chief. But why should he be condemned as
'inexorable' for punishing insubordination? The fact that the
criticism was ventilated suggests that there was an irregularity,

that he did judge personally in a case which some thought should have been referred to the Macedonians.

There is one more allusion to jurisdiction in the *Alexander*, when Plutarch lists judging (*dikazōn*) as one of the pursuits that filled Alexander's day (*Alex.* 23.2). Here Plutarch is probably referring to cases involving other people rather than the king himself. A selection of such cases is given in the *Sayings of Philip* section of Plutarch's *Moralia*. Of the six items listed, five deal with civil suits or criminal acts not amounting to treason,[65] but the sixth[66] has a bearing on our problem. Plutarch says that when some of Philip's entourage stigmatized Lasthenes and his followers, who had betrayed Olynthus as 'traitors', Philip refused to entertain the charge that the Olynthians sought to bring, saying 'The Macedonians are rustics who call a spade a spade'. The basis of the proposed charge was, I suggest, that the remark about Olynthian traitors was a slur on Philip, who had to rely on such dubious collaborators; if it had merely been a case of the Olynthians vindicating their own reputations Philip would have had no reason to refuse them an action. This case authorizes an important conclusion, namely that Philip refused to treat verbal attacks as treason. At first Alexander followed a similar policy,[67] but later on he was less tolerant, and that is the stage to which Plutarch refers in *Alex.* 42.2.

At this point we may profitably glance at some modern theories in regard to Alexander's personal jurisdiction. Berve has him presiding over a *consilium* of officers, which tries Macedonians for minor crimes but has an unfettered jurisdiction over non-Macedonians.[68] Berve cites the case of Bessus who killed Darius and usurped the Persian throne. Alexander summoned members of his entourage, brought Bessus before them, accused him of *prodosia* towards Darius, commanded that his nose and the tips of his ears be cut off, and decreed that he be taken to Ecbatana to be executed before the assembled Medes and Persians (Arrian 4.7.3, Curt. 7.5.36–43). Hammond does not agree that Bessus was tried by Alexander and his Macedonian Friends; he thinks that Alexander was merely the accuser, and those of his entourage who judged the case were Persians.[69] It is indeed surprising to find a Macedonian court pronouncing on *prodosia* committed against Darius, but Arrian quite clearly gives Alexander the presiding role; moreover, he takes him to task for over-punishing Bessus (4.7.4). Finally there is the theory of Briant, who holds

147

that the Council of Friends, which he calls the *synedrion*, was regularly summoned by the king for the preliminary consideration of cases; where the misdemeanour was of an administrative nature and the miscreant was a satrap or high dignitary the Army/Assembly was not summoned at all, and the matter was disposed of by the king – but by him alone, for Briant does not allow the Friends more than a deliberative role.[70]

The question is whether Berve's imperial court gives us what we need for Callisthenes. If the only evidence for that court is the trial of Bessus and a generalization by Athenaeus,[71] can we be sure that it was the personal jurisdiction that ultimately decided the historian's fate? There is one fact that indirectly lends support to that possibility. It is the fact that hanging was the mode of execution in Callisthenes' case. The traditional Macedonian modes of execution were shooting down with javelins and stoning, and when we find another mode being used we may well argue that if the punishment inflicted on Bessus was of an experimental nature, hanging could have been another experiment by a new jurisdiction which was free of the constraints of Macedonian tradition. The Roman Principate furnishes confirmation of the proposition that a change in jurisdiction inspired a change in penalties.[72] The reason why there had to be a change was given by Alexander when he refused to present Callisthenes to the Army: *Olynthio non idem iuris est* (Curt. 8.8.19).

Our search for the court that tried Callisthenes ends, then, in his being too ill to go to Europe and being hastily tried by the Council of Friends presided over by Alexander. Whether the Friends had only a deliberative role as postulated by Briant, or participated in the verdict as implied by Berve, is not certain. Similar uncertainty clouds current thinking about the Roman emperor's judicial *consilium*.[73] At all events the new jurisdiction disposes of the apparent conflict between Curtius and Plutarch in regard to 'capital charges'. They are not talking about the same thing. Plutarch is no longer looking at the traditional jurisdiction. He is looking at the new jurisdiction, which was, at least in embryo, an imperial court that might have supplanted the traditional jurisdiction completely if Alexander's empire had retained its cohesion after his death. Even amidst the disintegration it had some survival, since the principle of one jurisdiction for Macedonians and another for the rest was perpetuated in Ptolemaic Egypt, where separate courts for Greeks and Egyptians were the rule. But the two compartments could not be entirely watertight. Once the Greek concept of *prodosia* was charged against Bessus in respect of his actions against Darius, an interface between the two jurisdictions inevitably began to form. Was Bessus judged by the standards of loyalty expected of Macedonians and Greeks, or by the standards expected of subjects of the Great King? Arrian makes this very point in his criticism of Bessus' trial:

> I do not approve of this excessive punishment of Bessus. I consider the amputation of the extremities barbaric, and I agree that Alexander was carried away when he aped Medic and Persian wealth and the discriminatory treatment of their subjects by barbarian kings. (4.7.4)

If Appian here reflects fourth-century criticism, as seems likely, we may suppose that the trial of Callisthenes by the same embryonic imperial court also evoked criticism and contributed to the unfavourable Peripatetic assessment of Alexander. One of the factors in that assessment may have been the inclusion in the charge-sheet of allegations of *asebeia* based on Callisthenes' frustration of Alexander's divine aspirations. But the indictment also alleged conspiracy, thus combining the two strands of the *asebeia* concept. To make matters worse, the attacks were not seen as an assault on the hegemon of the League of Corinth, which might have been tolerated, but as an attack on the embryonic god-king.[74]

We conclude with a note on the equivocal reaction of the Macedonians themselves to the king's exercise of personal jurisdiction. During the mutiny at Opis in 324, hence within a year of the delegation from the Greeks which had brought him golden crowns and divine honours at Babylon (Arrian 7.23.2), Alexander was stung to action against the mutineers by their taunt that he had better discharge them and campaign with his father, by which Arrian takes them to mean Ammon (7.8.3). Alexander pointed out thirteen of the most vociferous agitators and ordered the Hypaspists to arrest and execute them (ibid.). This is a classic example of the harsh reaction to verbal abuse to which Plutarch alludes, and if Curtius (10.4.1) is to be believed, one of the ringleaders reproached him bitterly with putting his soldiers, his citizens, to death without trial (*incognita causa*). Elsewhere (10.3.3) Curtius wonders whether the Army's passive acceptance of their comrades' execution was due to veneration for the name of king, since those who are ruled by kings cultivate them as gods, or to a special veneration for Alexander, or to his confident assertion of his authority. The reproach about *incognita causa* is of special interest because of the *asebeia* connotation. The mutineers did not mean that Alexander should have tried them. Their complaint was that he should not have dealt with them at all. Their crime was a new kind of treason rather than a breach of military discipline, and should have been referred to the Macedonians.

VIII

FROM PERDICCAS TO POLIORCETES

1 THE CHAOTIC SUCCESSION

The long period of infighting that followed Alexander's death saw the elevation of the political trial to new heights as a political weapon. In Alexander's time the overriding consideration had been security; only in Callisthenes' case was there possibly a broader objective in the shape of a message to the Greek world. But now the horizons were expanded. The security of the titular heads of state was to a large extent a minor consideration; Philip III Arrhidaeus and Alexander IV owed their survival, such as it was, to chance equilibria amongst the warring forces rather than to the law. In the forensic area, as in so many others, the centre of gravity had shifted to the Diadochi, the great satraps and dynasts caught up in the maelstrom of the struggle for power. In their hands the law was not a mechanism for their protection as heads of state, for they were not heads of state. But they made much greater use of the law than ever before, nominally in defence of the sovereigns but in reality in furtherance of their personal ambitions. And though the death of a rival was always a consummation devoutly to be wished, it was no longer the only goal. Very often charges were lodged against a rival without any expectation of being able to bring him to trial. What was aimed at was a propaganda exercise, the advancement of one's own claims and the undermining of his. The result was the emergence of a curious hybrid. Although the Diadochi were, throughout our period, still members of a single empire, they began displaying

151

the marks of independent rulers. In this quasi-capacity the law assumed some of the characteristics of international law, inasmuch as the ultimate sanction was provided by war rather than by any domestic enforcement agency. But it was all done in the name of the sovereign, except that here too anomaly found fertile ground, since there was very little agreement as to who the sovereign was. The one stable factor should have been the Army/Assembly of the Macedonians, for that was virtually the only jurisdiction at this time; there was no effective exercise of personal jurisdiction by the king, for Arrhidaeus was too retarded and Alexander IV was too young. Yet such was the state of fragmentation that even the Army/Assembly was an uncertain quantity, for fractions of the Army under different commanders claimed to be the repositories of a jurisdiction which strictly speaking belonged only to the whole. The whole scene bears an eerie resemblance to the 'closely united' Roman Empire at the turn of the fourth century AD.

2 PERDICCAS AND NEW TECHNIQUES

The first major contender for power was Perdiccas, chiliarch of Asia[1] from 323 until his death in 321 and initiator of the new direction taken by political trials, being involved in forensic confrontations with Meleager, Antigonus, Cynnane, and Ptolemy and finally succumbing to such a confrontation himself.

Meleager, taxiarch of the phalanx and as such an infantry officer, became at some point Perdiccas' subordinate, although the latter held a cavalry command.[2] The two men were sharply divided on the succession question. Meleager and the infantry favoured Alexander's retarded half-brother, Philip Arrhidaeus, while Perdiccas and the cavalry supported the unborn son of Alexander and Roxane. Meleager got the phalanx to acclaim Arrhidaeus, thus dividing the forces into two armed camps and threatening civil war. The antagonists immediately began resorting to judicial process. Arrhidaeus having been saluted as king, Meleager sent men to summon Perdiccas in the king's name to appear for trial, and failing compliance to kill him; but Perdiccas overawed them and they abandoned the attempt (Curt. 10.8.1–3). The Macedonians resented the exposure of Perdiccas to mortal danger and decided to punish Meleager (Curt. 10.8.5). This probably means that he was arraigned on a charge of usurping the functions of the Army/Assembly.[3] But Meleager got Arrhidaeus to confirm that he had authorized Perdiccas' arrest and the charge was dropped (Curt. 10.8.6–7). If the gravamen of the phalanx's complaint was indeed the by-passing of its jurisdiction rather than concern for Perdiccas' welfare,[4] we have evidence of resistance by the soldiers (not for the first time) to the king's personal jurisdiction.[5]

The crisis was resolved by a compromise in terms of which Arrhidaeus' kingship was recognized by Perdiccas and the cavalry, the right of Roxane's unborn child (if a son) to share the throne with Arrhidaeus was conceded by the infantry, Perdiccas was made regent, and the great Asian satrapies were allocated.[6] But the reconciliation was to be sealed by a solemn ceremony purifying the Army of pollution, and this gave Perdiccas an opening. In the presence of Arrhidaeus he called on the phalanx to surrender those who had led the insurrection, and when this was done he put a number of them to death. Then came Meleager's turn. Diodorus says that Perdiccas punished Meleager, who had been a traitor during the insurrection[7] and was now brought up on the pretext of a private quarrel and charged with plotting against Perdiccas (Diod.18.4.7). Diodorus' *katēgorias* points to a trial, and Curtius confirms that there was some sort of official action when he has Meleager, in despair at the fact that his enemies are acting in the name of the man whom he had made king, take refuge in a temple, only to be killed in violation of sanctuary (Curt. 10.9.20–1). But neither source attests an actual trial, and it is to be supposed that Perdiccas sent men to arrest Meleager in the king's name,[8] thus returning the compliment, whereupon Meleager tried to seek sanctuary. If the trial had taken place it would have underwritten an important new principle: plotting against the king's minister was being treated as plotting against the king himself.

Perdiccas next crossed swords with the formidable Antigonus Monophthalmus ('One-Eye'), satrap of Western Asia Minor.[9] Relations between Perdiccas and Antigonus were soured when Antigonus disobeyed an order to help Eumenes against Ariarathes, who refused to give up the area marked out for Eumenes' satrapy.[10] Perdiccas tried to prosecute Antigonus, but without success. According to Arrian (*Succ.* 20) Perdiccas summoned Antigonus to court (*eis dikastērion*) but Antigonus refused to obey the summons. Diodorus (18.23.3–4) has a more detailed account. After Antigonus had got wind of Perdiccas' plan to jilt Antipater's daughter and marry Alexander's sister, Cleopatra, Perdiccas decided that this most active of the commanders must be put out of the way. He brought false slanders and unjust charges in order to destroy him.[11] Antigonus let it be known that he wanted to defend himself against the charges, but he secretly fled in Athenian ships and joined Antipater in Europe.

The procedural details of the case are discussed at some length by Briant.[12] He correctly takes Arrian's *dikastērion* as the king's court and makes the interesting point that the armies of the satraps were only relics of the full Army/Assembly and did not represent that body. But he falls badly into error when he says that Antigonus' disobedience in the matter of Eumenes did not come under the Army/Assembly's jurisdiction because it was not a capital charge. Athenian generals who had paid for their disobedience with their lives would not have been impressed, nor would Menander whom Alexander put to death. Antigonus did not flee to Athens in order to avoid a fine. Moreover, it need not be assumed that disobedience was the only charge. In his biography of Eumenes, Plutarch has Antigonus brush Perdiccas' orders aside because he already cherishes lofty ambitions and looks down on his colleagues (*Eum.* 3.3). This means that by setting the king's servants at naught he denigrated the king himself. We are again in the foothills of Hellenistic *asebeia*.

Antigonus' strategy gained him time to arrange for his escape to Athens, but from Perdiccas' point of view the exercise had been well worth it, for it left him with a free hand in Asia. And he soon made it clear that he was not going to let anything stand in his way, for later in 322 he staged his most dramatic forensic foray of all when he had Cynnane put to death. Cynnane, daughter of Philip II and half-sister of Alexander, took her daughter Eurydice to Asia in order to marry her to Arrhidaeus. On her way to Perdiccas' camp she was intercepted by Perdiccas' brother, Alcetas, who had brought the Macedonians with him. Polyaenus, to whom we owe most of our knowledge of the case, goes on to say that the soldiers were overawed at the sight of Philip's daughter and Alexander's sister, and changed their minds. Cynnane reproached Alcetas for the wrong done to her but refused to be intimidated, and suffered her throat to be cut rather than see Philip's race stripped of power (Polyaen. 8.60). To this Arrian adds that Perdiccas shared the responsibility for her fate (*Succ.* 23–4); Diodorus (19.52.5) merely notes that Alcetas killed her.

In interpreting this episode we must again join issue with Briant, who writes a scenario in which the Macedonians are not assembled by Alcetas; they are either convened by Cynnane or assemble spontaneously. Cynnane appears as an accuser,[13] charging Alcetas with treason by reason of his opposition to the marriage, which is seen as an attack on Philip's race. To save himself Alcetas kills her, hoping that by taking only Eurydice to Perdiccas he will satisfy the soldiers without embarrassing his brother. But the plan misfires, because discontent spreads to the whole Army and Perdiccas is cornered.[14]

Briant's elevation of the attack on Philip's race to treason dovetails with our findings on *asebeia* well enough, but there is an incurable weakness in Briant's case, due partly to his facile assumption that a woman could be an accuser[15] and partly to his failure to address the question of what the soldiers were doing there in the first place. Berve, reflecting the confusion that admittedly bedevils Polyaenus' account, says that the troops refused to fight her.[16] But in spite of her astonishing military prowess[17] it is perhaps better not to assume that this is what Polyaenus means when he says that the Macedonians changed their minds. It is at least possible that they had been convened by Alcetas to try her but changed their minds about finding her guilty. The charge against her may have been based on her having raised a force and confronted Antipater on the Strymon as part of her drive into Asia (Polyaen. 8.60).[18] The fact that that occurred outside Perdiccas' territory makes no difference, for we are entitled to suppose[19] that the Macedonians were still able to operate as a court anywhere in the king's domains. We therefore conclude that Perdiccas and Alcetas hoped to secure Cynnane's legal condemnation, and only when that proved impossible did Alcetas kill her.

Perdiccas' meteoric career came to an end in 321, but not before he had become embroiled in yet another judicial encounter, this time involving Ptolemy, the son of Lagus, who held the satrapy of Egypt and would become the first Hellenistic king of that country in 305. Perdiccas invaded Egypt in the hope of eliminating what he considered the weakest link in the coalition that had been put together against him,[20] and at some point he tried to bring Ptolemy to trial. According to Appian (*Succ.* 28) Perdiccas entered

Egypt with the kings (Arrhidaeus and Alexander IV) to make war on Ptolemy. He accused Ptolemy, but the latter cleared himself before the army. However, in spite of being held to have brought an unjust accusation Perdiccas began the war, although the army was against it. Diodorus only adverts to the case in his notice of the day after Perdiccas' death, when Ptolemy appears before the Macedonians and speaks in his defence regarding the accusations against him (Diod. 18.36.6). The trial, after being accepted almost unanimously for many years,[21] came under attack in 1930 when Schwahn argued that Arrian's account went back to an invention by Duris; it was said to be incredible because Ptolemy would not have risked appearing before Perdiccas' troops, nor would he have got away alive had he done so, for Perdiccas would easily have secured a conviction on the basis of Ptolemy's seizure of Cyrene, his appropriation of official funds to pay his mercenaries, his murder of his hyparch Cleomenes, and his theft of Alexander's body.[22] Schwahn's first point had been anticipated by Bouché-Leclerq, who had Ptolemy appear by proxy rather than in person.[23] In principle it might be thought that if an accused could be condemned *in absentia* he could be acquitted in the same way, but we recall that Amyntas had to fetch his brother before the Macedonians would absolve him of complicity in Philotas' plot. In any event an acquittal by proxy is just as unlikely, given the strength of the case against Ptolemy. Volkmann tried to meet Schwahn's arguments by claiming that Ptolemy's great popularity with the Army would have guaranteed him against any underhand move by Perdiccas,[24] but Seibert points out that Antigonus had not had enough confidence in Perdiccas' justice to stay in Asia to stand trial.[25] An eccentric solution was proposed by Fontana, who thought that the trial had been held earlier than is usually supposed, in 322–1 when the coalition between Ptolemy and Antipater was still being negotiated; Perdiccas will have tried to block the negotiations by staging a show trial with a pre-ordained acquittal, which would prove his good faith.[26]

The solutions meriting serious consideration are those of Seibert and Briant.[27] Seibert argues that although Arrian (as epitomized by Photius) and Diodorus both have a Ptolemaic bias, Arrian is the more favourable because he has Perdiccas go to war in spite of Ptolemy having cleared himself at the trial. In Diodorus, Ptolemy still has a twinge of conscience after Perdiccas' death, thus the decision to go to war was not against the Army's wishes. As Seibert locates the trial (in Arrian) prior to Perdiccas' arrival in Egypt[28] it ought to follow that the purpose of the trial was to furnish Perdiccas with a viable *casus belli*. But Seibert is not quite sure what he thinks Arrian means, for he goes on to say that the war had already broken out and therefore the trial had no point.[29] He adds (against Bouché-Leclercq) that it could not have been designed to give Perdiccas' campaign an official character, because the Army/Assembly was not competent to do that.[30] Seibert rejects Arrian and opts for Diodorus' version of a defence speech by Ptolemy the day after Perdiccas' death; the argument is that although Perdiccas was dead his successor might continue the war, therefore Pompey had to defuse the accusations.

Briant argues that Arrian and Diodorus go back to a common source, Hieronymus of Cardia, whose account is accurately preserved by Diodorus but is distorted in Arrian because of clumsy epitomizing by Photius, who has mistakenly made Perdiccas' formulation of charges and Ptolemy's exculpatory speech contemporary. In reality Perdiccas summoned Ptolemy when he arrived in Egypt, but Ptolemy did not respond; it was only after Perdiccas' death that he went to the soldiers to answer the allegations. As to Perdiccas' motives, there was disaffection in his army before the first confrontation with Ptolemy. Perdiccas calculated that by having Ptolemy convicted he could convert the campaign from a personal undertaking into a Macedonian objective. The charges portrayed Ptolemy as an enemy of the policy of Alexander, hence of the two kings accompanying Perdiccas. In short, the whole thing was a propaganda exercise.

The propaganda motif goes to the heart of the matter, and Briant is closer to the mark than Seibert.[31] There are weaknesses in Briant's case, especially the improbability of Perdiccas' expectation that the Army would endorse in its judicial mode what it was resisting in its military mode. But two things are common cause between Briant and Seibert: Perdiccas did frame charges against Ptolemy, but the latter did not appear and only replied to the charges after Perdiccas' death. We need only add that Perdiccas did not expect Ptolemy to appear. He knew that he had to eliminate Ptolemy by force, but force had to be clothed in legality. Putting one's case by way of an accusation had special advantages; it crystallized the debate, presenting the issues in a way which forced the adversary's replies into a mould of the accuser's choosing, while at the same time preserving a semblance of fair play by offering the adversary a right of reply. Moreover, if the charges were not going to be subjected to judicial scrutiny because of the non-appearance of the accused, one had a great deal of latitude in framing them, and Perdiccas was able to give a quasi-judicial coloration to the magnification of Alexander that had occupied his mind ever since Alexander's death.[32] The indictment included a charge of stealing Alexander's body,[33] and the thrust of that accusation was much more than a mere violation of a decision of the dynasts. Alexander dead was a god of the Macedonians, a status that had eluded him during his lifetime,[34] and if Ptolemy's theft of his body could be charged as a crime against the state it would give the burgeoning concept of Hellenistic *asebeia* a considerable boost. Furthermore, by vindicating Alexander, Perdiccas was defending the integrity of the empire, hence divisive acts like the murder of Cleomenes whom Alexander had made satrap of Egypt, and Ptolemy's alliance with the four kings of Cyprus,[35] could be included amongst the charges. The whole episode thus becomes a striking example of the special uses to which political trials could be put. But Perdiccas' advantage was ephemeral. He was killed, and Ptolemy's ultimate refutation of the charges *validated* his possession of Alexander and encouraged him to emulate the latter's charismatic hold on power.[36] It is no accident that the Egyptian variety of *asebeia* looms largest amongst the successor kingdoms.

Perdiccas' death is the subject of a confused tradition.[37] His disastrous attempt to cross the Nile near Memphis precipitated a conspiracy, probably by a fairly small group of officers, and he was assassinated. The question that concerns us is whether it was outright murder or execution pursuant to a trial verdict. The latter possibility is canvassed by Briant,[38] who argues that Pithon, Antigene, Seleucus and the others legalized the execution by accusing Perdiccas before the Macedonians. Briant's evidence is Diodorus' statement that many officers joined together and accused Perdiccas (*katēgoroun*), to which the phalanx responded with threatening shouts (Diod. 18.36.4). To Briant this is an example of what he considers the regular process in trials by the Army/Assembly: deliberation by the *synedrion* (in this case the council of conspirators) followed by condemnation by the soldiers. But Diodorus' sequence does not support this: he locates Pithon's defection *after* the phalanx's expression of hostility. Even more puzzling, after that defection some cavalry officers make a compact, go to Perdiccas' tent and stab him to death (Diod. 18.36.5). This is not the regular mode of execution by shooting down with javelins, nor is it clear how the cavalry came to carry out a verdict of the phalanx.

The sequel may help. Two days after Perdiccas' death the victory of his ally, Eumenes, over Craterus and Neoptolemus became known; the news, says Diodorus, would have saved Perdiccas if it had been known sooner (18.37.1). The Macedonians now passed the equivalent of a sentence of death on Eumenes and some fifty of his officers.[39] They also sentenced Perdiccas' brother Alcetas, his sister Atalanta, and a number of his most loyal supporters to death (Diod. 18.37.1). As for Perdiccas himself, one way out of the dilemma posed by Diodorus is to suppose that news of Eumenes' victory reached some of Perdiccas' entourage early and they formed a conspiracy to kill Perdiccas before Eumenes could intervene. Later on when they prosecuted the Perdiccans they might have included a posthumous charge against Perdiccas.

3 THE SKILLS OF POLYPERCHON AND CASSANDER

When Antipater died in 319 his place as regent was taken by Polyperchon, an old officer of Philip II. Antipater's son, Cassander, became chiliarch. The two men became involved in a bitter struggle for control of mainland Greece in which political trials played an important part.

The first shot was fired by Cassander shortly before his father's death. After Demades had undertaken a mission to Macedonia on behalf of Athens, Deinarchus of Corinth denounced him to Cassander; the denunciation was prompted by the discovery, after Perdiccas' death, of correspondence in which Demades had asked Perdiccas to rid Greece of Antipater. Cassander had Demades and his son extradited to Athens, where they were presumably tried before being put to death.[40] Plutarch notes with satisfaction that Macedonia was the instrument of revenge for Demades' part in the destruction of Demosthenes (*Dem.* 31.3). He might have added that Demades was poorly rewarded by Macedonia for his services in sponsoring Alexander's membership of the Athenian pantheon. But perhaps that sponsorship contributed to Demades' downfall, for the god Alexander was the showpiece of Perdiccas' ideology, and not exactly welcome to Cassander. Demades' act of *asebeia*, for which the Athenians had punished him some years earlier, seems to have haunted him till the end of his days.

Polyperchon soon made it clear that he was not in the same camp as Cassander. The decree which he issued in the name of the king, Arrhidaeus, liberating all Greek cities from the oligarchies imposed by Antipater,[41] included a provision restoring all exiles except those who had been lawfully banished for murder, *asebeia* or (in the case of five cities) *prodosia* (Diod. 18.56.4,7). The inclusion of *asebeia* is interesting: it was being classified as a crime against the Macedonian king. Polyperchon also ordered 'Argos and the other cities' to exile those who had headed governments in Antipater's time, and to condemn some of them to death and confiscation (Diod. 18.57.1). The cities in question included Athens, and the Athenian specially singled out for punishment was Phocion (Plut. *Phoc.* 32.1–2). Many Athenians blamed Phocion for their virtual subjugation by Cassander's general, Nicanor, and with the re-enfranchisement of the returned exiles they hoped to bring him to trial.[42] An unexpected colloquium between Nicanor and Polyperchon's son, Alexander, having given the democrats an opening, Phocion was deposed and denounced as a traitor by Hagnonides (Plut. *Phoc.* 33.1–3). Phocion fled to Polyperchon for protection, but his enemies had anticipated this and had sent a mission to the regent to lay charges against Phocion. The proceedings were conducted under the nominal presidency of the king, Arrhidaeus (presumably sitting with Friends in continuation of Alexander's court for non-Macedonians),[43] but everything was orchestrated by Polyperchon. He repeatedly interrupted Phocion when he tried to speak, and eventually arrested him and his associates and delegated someone to take them to Athens; he said that in his opinion the men were traitors, but it was for the Demos to convict or acquit them as it saw fit.[44]

Polyperchon deserves full marks for ingenuity. By extraditing Phocion to Athens he acknowledged the Demos' autonomy, but in fact he dictated the verdict. This is what Diodorus means when he says that Polyperchon told Argos and other cities to exile or execute those who had headed governments under Antipater. Polyperchon had laid the foundation for this exercise in double standards by including in the 'liberation' decree a clause requiring

all cities to enact laws prohibiting war against, or public opposition to, Arrhidaeus (Diod. 18.56.7). In strict law Phocion had to
be a traitor to Athens, not to Arrhidaeus, if he was to be tried
by an Athenian court, but the whole drama was played out
against the background of the 'liberation' decree. The dividing-
line between the Macedonian king and the Athenian Commons
was becoming blurred.

In Athens Phocion and his friends were charged with enslav-
ing the country after the Lamian War, specifically under the head
of *katalysis tou dēmou* (Diod. 18.66.5); Phocion was also charged
in connection with the betrayal of Piraeus to Nicanor (Nepos *Phoc.*
3.3). The trial was a travesty in the best traditions of Arginusae,
though it is only fair to say that his treachery must have been
very great to have aroused such bitterness.[45] A motley assembly
to which slaves, metics, disfranchised, and women were admitted, was set up, and when someone objected he was nearly
stoned. No one dared speak for Phocion, and when he himself
spoke he could scarcely make himself heard above the din. He
admitted his guilt and proposed the death penalty for himself,
but asked that the others be spared. Exile was permissible in terms
of Polyperchon's directive, but Hagnonides produced a *psēphisma*
according to which only sentence of death was competent. As
we saw earlier, an attempt to add a rider providing for Phocion
to be tortured before being executed was resisted by Hagnonides.
Phocion and four others were condemned and executed, while
Demetrius of Phalerum and others who had fled to Nicanor rather
than to Polyperchon were sentenced to death *in absentia*. The case
had what had almost become a standard sequel at Athens: after
a short time Phocion was given public burial despite his conviction, as well as a bronze statue; and the Demos condemned
Hagnonides to death.[46]

It was at about this time that Alexander's mother, the formidable Olympias, made a spectacular farewell appearance.[47]
Polyperchon invited her to return to Macedonia from Epirus in
order to take charge of her grandson, Alexander IV, until he
became of age. This was a response to the plans of the equally
formidable Eurydice, wife of Arrhidaeus, who supported
Cassander and bade fair to become the *de facto* ruler herself.
Eurydice, who had inherited the martial ardour of her mother,
Cynnane, tried to deny Olympias entry into Macedonia by an
armed confrontation, but her troops refused to fight Alexander's

mother. Eurydice and Arrhidaeus fell into Olympias' hands and were put to death, together with Cassander's brother Nicanor and about a hundred Macedonian nobles. Diodorus has a graphic account of Eurydice's death. Walled up in a narrow space with a single narrow opening, she continued to claim that the kingdom belonged to her even after her husband was stabbed to death; Olympias sent her a sword, a noose, and some hemlock and invited her to choose; Eurydice elected to hang herself (Diod. 19.11.4–9). Shortly afterwards, still in 317–6, Cassander overcame Polyperchon's forces and captured Olympias.

Cassander proceeded to put Olympias on trial, though the picture is predictably controversial. According to Diodorus, Cassander prevailed on relatives of Olympias' victims to accuse her in the general assembly of the Macedonians. Olympias neither attended nor had anyone to speak for her, but the Macedonians condemned her to death (Diod. 19.51.1–2). But Cassander secretly advised her to escape and offered to provide a ship to take her to Athens. He did this so that by condemning herself to exile and being killed on the voyage she would be seen to have suffered a just punishment, thus allaying Cassander's fears about her rank and the fickleness of the Macedonians (Diod. 19.51. 2–3). But Olympias refused to flee, and expressed her readiness to be judged before all the Macedonians (§4). Cassander was afraid that if she defended herself the crowd might change its mind. He therefore sent 200 soldiers to kill her, but when they saw Olympias they were overawed and withdrew (§4–5). Thereupon the relatives of her victims killed her (§5). She was denied burial (*FGrH* IIB, 1204).

The crucial question is whether the assembly that condemned Olympias was the Army/Assembly with which we have managed quite adequately so far, or whether it was the Assembly of the People which Curtius says operated in peacetime, and which Justin implies operated specifically in Olympias' case (Just. 14.6.6). The tribunal which condemned her was not the same as that by which she subsequently demanded to be tried,[48] but what was the difference between the two? Briant thinks that the first tribunal consisted of Cassander's soldiers, whereas that demanded by Olympias included all elements of the *ethnos* and was thus an Assembly of the People.[49] This is the distinction drawn by Curtius: 'the army judged but in peacetime it was the business of the people – *in pace erat vulgi*' (6.8.25). Curtius is, of course, using *in pace* in the sense of *domi* – at home rather than abroad (*militiae*). Tarn thought that the first tribunal consisted of the Army on the spot, but that Olympias wanted an assembly of all the soldiers of both Europe and Asia.[50]

Before choosing between Briant and Tarn there is a difficulty that does not seem to have been noticed before. The charge against Olympias was treason – that is guaranteed by the fact that Arrhidaeus was one of her victims and by the denial of burial – but in that case what were the relatives of victims doing as accusers? We have been led to believe that in cases of treason tried by the Army/Assembly the king was the prosecutor; and when the treasonable act achieved its purpose the successor took over the role of accuser, as Alexander did when Philip was murdered. There is no reason to believe that the position was any different in trials by the Assembly of the People, and even if there had been it would not apply here, because the crucial trial at which the relatives accused was held before the soldiers. What if we suppose that the first tribunal was not called on to hear charges of treason at all, it was simply asked to decide charges of murder (not including the death of Arrhidaeus, for that would necessarily have made it treason)? This would have given the relatives *locus standi* as accusers, but Olympias might have argued that a murder court was not competent to try royalty. Unfortunately, however, this will not work either, for the denial of burial could not have been attached to a conviction for murder. We might meet that by supposing that the burial order was voted later, as the Macedonians had tried to do in Cleitus' case, but once we have to start piling supposition upon conjecture the prospects for a convincing solution are not bright. The most that can be said in conclusion is that if it were not for the difficulty with the accusers our vote would go to Briant's solution.

4 THE 'ENEMY OF THE MACEDONIANS' DECLARATION

From 316 until his death in 301 Antigonus Monophthalmus dominated the scene, opposing some sort of policy of preserving the unity of the empire to the fragmentationary coalition of Cassander, Lysimachus, Ptolemy, and Seleucus. Antigonus gave an important new direction to the forensic side of the struggle very early in the piece. In 315 he convened an assembly of soldiers and civilian residents at Tyre[51] and ventilated accusations against Cassander, accusing him in respect of the murder of Olympias, his treatment of Roxane and Alexander IV, his forcible marriage with Thessalonice, his attempts to claim the Macedonian throne, his settlement of the Olynthians in a city called after him (Cassandreia), and his rebuilding of Thebes; the last two were slaps in the face for Philip and Alexander respectively. After the crowd had expressed its indignation, Antigonus introduced a decree (*dogma*) declaring Cassander an enemy unless he destroyed Cassandreia and Thebes, released Alexander and Roxane from prison, and obeyed Antigonus, the duly appointed general[52] and guardian of the king (Alexander IV). The decree also proclaimed the autonomy and freedom from garrisons of all Greeks (Diod. 19.61.1–3).

The decree was *not* a criminal verdict, despite the belief in some quarters that it was.[53] It did not find the absent Cassander guilty of a specific charge or sentence him to death. It declared him an enemy unless he did certain things: τὸν Κάσανδρον πολέμιον εἶναι, ἐὰν μὴ. Those things did not include any action in respect of the murder of Olympias, because that could not be undone; hence its omission from the definitive part of the decree. If Cassander failed to comply with the stipulations he would become an enemy of the Macedonians, and hostilities against him would be a just war. The decree thus anticipated such Roman measures as the *hostis* declaration against Caesar in January 49, which was to come into operation if he failed to disband his army.[54] The mechanism was well known in the Hellenistic world, going back to Antigonus' manifesto of 315, and even earlier than that to the decree against Eumenes and his officers after the death of Perdiccas in 321.[55] But Antigonus' decree represented an advance on that of 321, because the latter did not include a built-in ultimatum; it did not call on Eumenes to do certain things, failing which he would be an enemy. Again there is a Roman parallel, in the earlier version of the *hostis* declaration.[56]

Antigonus' manifesto was a pure propaganda exercise. He had even less expectation of Cassander's compliance than Perdiccas had had of Ptolemy's obedience to a summons, but like the latter it was solidly grounded in the criminal law. And also like the latter, it enabled new definitions of treason to be written into the statute-book without having to prove charges. Insults to Philip and Alexander, through the resettlement of the Olynthians and the restoration of Thebes, were now ready to be charged as *asebeia* if the need ever arose. Meanwhile, as Diodorus knew, Antigonus had provided himself with an excellent pretext for war (Diod. 19.61.4). The Macedonian assembly[57] had come a long way since the days when it had adjudged men traitors by shouts of indignation[58] and had shot them down on the spot. Its new sophistication was a direct by-product of the avalanche of instability that followed Alexander's death.

In 311 events began moving rapidly towards a situation in which entirely new judicial parameters would be required. In that year Antigonus signed a treaty with the hostile coalition, confirming Cassander as *stratēgos* of Europe until Alexander IV came of age, settling the holdings of Lysimachus, Ptolemy and Antigonus, and bringing hostilities to a halt.[59] But the ink on the treaty was not yet dry when Cassander ordered Glaucias, commander of the young Alexander's bodyguard, to murder the king and Roxane, but to conceal the bodies and keep the whole thing secret. This, adds Diodorus, relieved all the Diadochi of anxiety, for now there was no heir to the throne, and each could look forward to royal power over his particular territory (19.105.2–4). Antigonus made no attempt to indict Cassander for this operation, which is hardly surprising. Killing royalty had almost become an annual event, for in 309 Antigonus had Alexander's full sister, Cleopatra, killed while attempting to escape from internment at Sardis (*FGrH* 239B 19); Antigonus brought about her death through the agency of certain women, but covered up his traces by punishing the women (Diod. 20.37.5–6). In the same year Polyperchon murdered Alexander's illegitimate son Heracles.[60]

We would expect the new situation to have had a profound effect on political trials. With the disappearance of the empire-wide king who had hitherto been the theoretical frame of reference for all trials, and his replacement by new monarchs whose juristic co-ordinates had still to be plotted, an entirely new set of ground-rules was required. The Argeads, whose dynasty had come to an end with the murder of Alexander IV, had presided over the first experiments with the new category of treason by assaults on the king's good name and godhead, and it was time to start exploiting the full potential of that category. Hard evidence is not very thick on the ground, but the most promising avenue, the reign of Demetrius

Poliorcetes, is of more than passing interest.

5 DEMETRIUS POLIORCETES: THE RETURN TO ASEBEIA HEADQUARTERS

In 306 Antigonus had himself saluted as king by the Macedonians and conferred the same status on his son, Demetrius Poliorcetes. Antigonus saw himself as the first legitimate successor to Alexander and as heir to the whole kingdom. In 305–4 his example was followed by Ptolemy, though he only claimed to be king and pharaoh of part of the empire, Egypt. Cassander, Lysimachus, and Seleucus soon added their diadems to the regal cluster, but with the possible exception of Cassander they limited themselves to their particular territories as Ptolemy had done.[61]

Demetrius Poliorcetes ('Besieger of Cities') had a special relationship with Athens. In 308–7 he drove Cassander's subordinate, Demetrius of Phalerum, from the city and 'restored the freedom of the Athenians',[62] who promptly proceeded to shower the most extravagant honours on Demetrius and his father. According to Plutarch the Athenians were the first to give the two Antigonids the title of king, and they were the only people to give them the appellation of saviour-gods (*Sōtēres Theoi*). They created two new tribes known as Demetrias and Antigonis, increased the membership of the Boule to 600 to accommodate them, dated the year by a priest of the *Sōtēres* instead of by the eponymous archon, styled envoys to the *Sōtēres* 'sacred deputies', renamed the Dionysia 'Demetria', decreed that when Demetrius visited the city he should receive the same honours as Demeter and Dionysus, renamed the month Mounychion 'Demetrion', sought an oracle from the saviour-god concerning a dedication of shields at Delphi, and conferred numerous other cult honours (Plut. *Demetrius* 10.2.–12.2, 13).[63]

This 'overkill' of honours was intended to reinforce Antigonus' claim to be the true successor to Alexander, but the first trials of the reign did not advance that claim significantly, for the series of *eisangelia* processes against Demetrius of Phalerum and members of his government were fairly routine vindications of the democracy,[64] albeit with less ferocity than usual, perhaps because the accusers deliberately planned it that way.[65]

The breakthrough into new judicial areas came in 303–2, following Poliorcetes' formation of a League of Corinth modelled on the League of Philip and Alexander.[66] The Athenians, believing that their internal liberty was no longer secure,[67] prosecuted Cleomedon, one of Demetrius' partisans; the charge is not known, but he was fined fifty talents (Plut. *Demet*. 24.3). The verdict had an extraordinary sequel. Cleomedon's son, Cleaenetus, submitted to Demetrius' advances in order to obtain from him a letter directing the Demos to remit the fine. The Demos complied, but passed a *psēphisma* laying down that in future no citizen was to bring a letter from Demetrius before it. Demetrius was so angry that the *psēphisma* was rescinded and its authors were either put to death or driven into exile (ibid., 24.4). It was then decreed that whatever King Demetrius ordained would be righteous towards the gods and just towards men (ibid.). Plutarch's language – 'they also voted that it pleased the Athenian people' – guarantees that he is citing from the actual decree. The formula covered all law, and the king would be *nomos empsychos* in respect of both religious and secular affairs. This law was proposed by Stratocles, Demetrius' chief representative at Athens and author of many of the decrees conferring divine honours.[68] Someone said of the *nomos empsychos* decree that Stratocles was mad to propose it, whereupon Demochares of Leuconoe declared that 'He would be mad not to be mad'. The remark earned Demochares a trial and exile (Plut. *Demet*. 24.5).

Can any charges of *asebeia* be uncovered here? It will not have formed the basis of the charge against Cleomedon, for even if he was the author of some of the divinity decrees[69] we know from Demades' case[70] that proposing an impious *psēphisma* conferring divine honours on a mortal only became culpable when the offending *psēphisma* was rescinded. The honours to Demetrius were not rescinded until much later.[71]

The main author of the divine honours, Stratocles, could also not be prosecuted for the same reason, and that is why the conflict between those who favoured democracy and the divine honours which were part of democracy's stock-in-trade, and those who opposed such ideas, was largely fought out in the theatrical arena. In 301 the comic poet Philippides attacked Stratocles by attributing an unseasonable frost that had blighted the crops, and other natural disasters, to Stratocles' impiety in giving men honours that belonged to the gods (Plut. *Demet*. 12.3–4). And when Philippides said, 'This sort of thing, and not comedy, threatens democracy's dissolution', he was referring to exactly the same link between *asebeia* and treason as that which had surfaced in Alcibiades' case more than a hundred years before. A running fight between Demetrius' friends and exponents of New Comedy had been going on for some years. When supporters of the new regime hurled accusations of *katalysis tou dēmou* at Demetrius of Phalerum and his friends, they nearly entangled the poet Menander in that particular forensic net; he was only saved from prosecution by the intervention of Poliorcetes' cousin (Diog. Laert. 5.79, 80). Stratocles had threatened to muzzle New Comedy[72] on the grounds that it was contributing to *katalysis tou dēmou*. Philippides' riposte claimed that *asebeia*, not comedy, was responsible for that danger.

The struggle was not entirely confined to the theatre, however, for the type of *asebeia* which consisted in insulting the god-king is present in some of the cases. Stratocles' *psēphisma* had recognized Poliorcetes as *nomos empsychos*, and for Demochares to exercise his wit on it was an innuendo against Poliorcetes not unlike that which had been aimed at Philip through Lasthenes.[73] But where Philip had refused to treat insults as treason, Stratocles had no difficulty in persuading an Athenian court. *Asebeia* headquarters was living up to its reputation by providing underpinning for the new charge of impiety. Poliorcetes' divinity was also in issue when charges were brought against the sponsors of the *psēphisma* prohibiting any citizen from bringing any letter from Demetrius before the Demos. Here the technical basis will have been the *graphē paranomōn*. The divinity decrees were in the statute-book, including the *nomos empsychos* decree, and the proposal to ban Poliorcetes' letters ran counter to those decrees. But as in Demades' case,[74] the technical charge was one thing and the people's perception was another, and the offence was seen as *asebeia*.

After his sojourns at Athens in 307 and 304–3 Poliorcetes did not see the city again for some ten years. The defeat and death in action of Antigonus at Ipsus in 301 made Europe inaccessible to Poliorcetes; and the Athenians, volatile as ever, passed a decree denying him admission to their city (Plut. *Demet*. 30.2–3). But the death of Cassander in 298–7 reopened Europe to the Antigonid, and by 294 he was king of the Macedonians and once more master of Athens. During the blockade which starved the Athenians into surrender the Demos decreed the death penalty for anyone who so much as mentioned negotiations with Poliorcetes (*Demet*.

34.1). This virtual declaration that Poliorcetes was an enemy of the Athenians does not appear to have generated any trials. Nor is there any trace of charges against the authors of the decree. One might have expected a *graphē paranomōn* if the original divinity decrees were still in force,[75] but on gaining control of the city Poliorcetes proclaimed a reconcilation which set people's fears at rest (*Demet.* 34.3–4). He may have felt that he was not giving much away, for if some of the honours listed by Plutarch were voted at this time rather than earlier, as has been suggested,[76] it is quite on the cards that some of the earlier honours that may have fallen into abeyance since Ipsus were restated alongside the new awards.

Poliorcetes may have condoned acts of impiety against himself, but there were many who still shared Philippides' dislike of impiety against the regular gods, and in 290 they tried to bring some of the culprits to book. When Poliorcetes arrived at Athens he was greeted with an Ithyphallos, a hymn of the type usually sung to Dionysus, in which aspersions on Ptolemy and the Aetolians were mingled with an outright acknowledgement of his divinity:

> The other gods are a long way off, or have no ears, or no existence, or are indifferent to us. But you, a true god rather than one of wood or stone, we see face to face. To you we pray; give us peace. (Athen. 6.253B–C; Duris, *FGrH* 76. F13)

Some might have seen the song as frivolous and merry,[77] but there was also a strong counter-reaction. It is reflected in Athenaeus' citation of the song as a signal example of flattery, and even more clearly in Duris' comment: 'Thus sang the Men of Marathon, though they killed the man who offered *proskynēsis* to the Persian king' (*FGrH* 76.F13). The reference is to Timagoras' mission to Artaxerxes.[78] Duris may well reflect what being said at the time, namely that the flatterers responsible for the hymn should be charged with *asebeia*. Duris was a Peripatetic and a pupil of Theophrastus; he will have remembered Callisthenes, especially on the *proskynēsis* issue, which to him was on all fours with the honours conferred on Poliorcetes.[79] But we have no evidence of an actual prosecution in this matter.

The major entry in Poliorcetes' court dossier is supplied by the trials and legislation of 303–2 – Cleomedon, the *nomos empsychos* decree, and Demochares. They are one of the most important landmarks in the early history of Hellenistic *asebeia*, for they gave the very first Hellenistic dynasty the imprimatur of what was still the most prestigious Greek city. The idea that the king was animate law had been discussed in philosophical circles long enough, but it had not received formal legislative recognition. That was given for the first time by the Athenian Ecclesia when it approved of Stratocles' *psēphisma*. At the same time the action against the sponsors of the decree which had banned letters from Poliorcetes gave notice that the criminal courts would also be enlisted in defence of the *nomos empsychos*. The god-king's most important function would be to make law, for that was ultimately what deification was all about.[80] Whatever the precise relationship between Demetrius Poliorcetes and Athens,[81] his divinity had been written into the constitution of the Athenians.

ABBREVIATIONS

AJP	*American Journal of Philology*
ANRW	*Aufstieg und Niedergang der römischen Welt*
AP	Aristotle (or Pseudo-Aristotle) *Athenaion Politeia*
CAH	*Cambridge Ancient History*
CP	*Classical Philology*
CQ	*Classical Quarterly*
DemAes	*Demosthenes and Aeschines*, introd. T.T.B. Ryder, tr. A.N.W. Saunders, Penguin, Harmondsworth 1975
EOS	*Commentarii Societatis Philologae Polonorum*
FGrH	F. Jacoby (ed.), *Die Fragmente der griechischen Historiker*, 3 parts in 14 vols. Berlin/Leiden 1923–58
Gomme	A.W. Gomme, A. Andrewes, and K.J. Dover, *A Historical Commentary on Thucydides*, 5 vols, Oxford 1948–81
GRBS	*Greek, Roman and Byzantine Studies*
Hist.	*Historia*
JHS	*Journal of Hellenic Studies*
Kl. P.	*Der Kleine Pauly, Lexikon der Antike*
Mus. Helv.	*Museum Helveticum*
OCD	*Oxford Classical Dictionary*, 2nd edn
PSZ	G. Wirth (ed.), *Perikles und seine Zeit*, Darmstadt 1979
RhM	*Rheinisches Museum*
RE	*Real-Encyclopädie der classischen Altertumswissenschaft*

Symposion	H.J. Wolff (ed.), *Symposion 1971: Vorträge zur griechischen und hellenistischen Rechtsgeschichte*, Cologne/Vienna 1975
Tod *GHI*	M.N. Tod, *Greek Historical Inscriptions*, 2 vols, Oxford 1946, 1948
ZAG	H. Will (ed.), *Zu Alexander d. Gr.*, Fschr. G. Wirth, 2 vols, Amsterdam 1987

NOTES

I INTRODUCTION

1 Macedonian law will be discussed when dealing with
   Macedonian trials.
2 Hansen 1975, 9.
3 See *AP* 3.6, 4.4. On the authorship of that work see Rhodes
   1981, 58–63. I assume Aristotle's authorship but am not
   dogmatic about it. On the Areopagus generally see Lipsius
   1905, 121–9; Bonner and Smith 1938, vol. 1 *passim*;
   MacDowell 1971, *passim*; Rhodes 1981, *passim*. See also Chapter
   III 1, p. 32.
4 On these jurisdictions see Lipsius 1905, 11, 68, 374, 627; Bonner
   and Smith 1938, vol. 1 *passim*; Harrison 1971, 8–9, 12–17;
   MacDowell 1971, 24–6; Hansen 1987, 60–1, 63–4, 225.
5 Lipsius 1905, *passim*; Calhoun 1927, *passim*; Bonner and Smith
   1938, vol. 1 *passim*; MacDowell 1978, *passim*; von Wedel 1971,
   passim; Hansen 1987, 215; Sealey 1987, 60–70, 118–9; Sinclair
   1988, 19–20. See also *AP* 9.1 with Rhodes 1981 ad loc.
6 The distribution of sovereignty between the Ecclesia and the
   dicasteries has been assiduously investigated by M.H. Hansen.
   See for example Hansen 1987, 94–124; also his 'The political
   powers of the people's court in fourth century Athens' (advance
   copy kindly supplied by the author). His proposal is that in the
   fourth century ultimate sovereignty rested with the *dikastēria*
   rather than with the Ecclesia. I need not express a final opinion
   on this proposition here, and therefore reserve judgment.
7 *AP* 68.1. See also Antiphon *Chor*. 21, Andoc. 1.27. M.H.
   Hansen, *Class. et Med*. 33 (1981-2), 9–47 would deny Heliaea
   any meaning other than 'the unambiguous old designation for
   the people's court'. Thus to him 'the heliastic courts' means
   only the *dikastēria* manned by jurors, membership of whose
   panel was restricted to citizens over thirty who took a solemn
   oath. The alternative understanding of Heliaea as the Ecclesia as a
   whole in its judicial mode is ruled out by Hansen. But there is
   considerable support for the view that the Heliaea was, at least

originally, the Ecclesia sitting as a court. See MacDowell, 1978, 30 and the citations by Hansen himself, *Class. et Med.* 33, n. 83. See also Chapter V n. 8.

8 Bauman 1967, *passim.*
9 Thonissen 1875, 196–201; Lipsius 1905, 374–7; Bonner and Smith 1938, 1.298; Harrison 1971, 53–5; MacDowell 1978, 175–6. Also *AP* 8.4, 16.10; Plut. *Solon* 19.4.
10 Xenophon speaks of ἐάν τις τὸν τῶν ᾿Αθηναίων δῆμον ἀδικῇ and adds that the wrongdoer is to make his defence before the people in chains, and if convicted of doing wrong (*adikein*) is to suffer execution and confiscation. Thonissen 1875, 169–70 and MacDowell 1978, 180–1, do no more than cite the passage. Lipsius 1905, 43, discusses it but does not ask what 'doing wrong' means.
11 See Lipsius 1905, 105–10, 176–211, 286–98; Bonner and Smith 1938, 1.294–309, 170–2; MacDowell 1978, 56–65, 170–2 and *passim*; Sealey 1987, 82–90; Hansen 1975, *passim*, 1987, 212, 215.
12 In the fourth century a distinction was drawn between a *nomos* ('a law') and a *psēphisma* ('a decree'), the former a general and permanent enactment, the latter one of limited scope and duration. Sealey 1987, 32–52; Hansen 1987, 219–20; Sinclair 1988, 84. Whether the distinction was always observed is a moot point, and whether it is fully understood today is even more debatable. The Romans carefully preserved separate terminology for the *lex* and the *plebi scitum*, but the only distinction observable in the developed law is a technical difference in the composition of the assembly enacting the two types.
13 Lipsius 1905, 931 and n.3 distinguishes between being at risk *peri tou sōmatos* ('in life and limb') and *peri tēs ousias* ('in property'). A third category was *peri tēs epitimias* ('in civic rights'). Aeschin. 3.210. Cf. MacDowell 1978, 176–7.
14 Quintilian *Inst. Orat.* 2.15.30 says of Socrates' trial that the law forbade representation – *(ius) quo non licebat pro altero agere* – but the use of *ius* rather than *lex* suggests custom rather than a statute. Bonner 1927, 135, cites Aristotle's advice about a man using his tongue as well as his hands to defend himself, but does not claim that Aristotle is attesting a law.
15 A circumvention, of course. But so was speech-writing in Quintilian's view.
16 Lipsius 1905, 907–10.
17 ibid., 206–7.
18 MacDowell 1978, 251.
19 On which see for example R.A. Bauman, *Lawyers in Roman Republican Politics*, Munich 1983, *passim*.
20 Calhoun 1944, *passim*; Jones 1956, 292–308; E.A. Havelock, *The Greek Concept of Justice*, Cambridge, Mass. 1975; Allen 1980, 22–32; Bauman 1986a, 100–1 and *passim*. Some optimism is displayed by U.E. Paoli, in Berneker 1968, 39–57; H.J. Wolff, in

Symposion, 1–22; ibid., *Seminar* 3 (1945), 93–109. See also n. 22 below.

21 See e.g. A. Watson's volumes on the law of the Roman Republic.

22 Bonner 1927, 1–25, is generally pessimistic, endorsing Pollock's assertion that 'A civilized system of law cannot be maintained without a learned profession of law'; but Bonner then proceeds to find that profession in the orators with special reference to Ps.–Plutarch's Ten. A better assessment, because based on a better appreciation of what constitutes a legal professional, is that of Jones 1956, 292–308.

23 R.A. Bauman, *ANRW* II 13 (1980), 112–16.

24 Bonner and Smith 1938, 1.85–8; Rhodes 1981, 102.

25 On the thesmothetes, Rhodes 1981, 102. On the nomothetes, Clinton 1982, *passim*; Hansen 1987, 55, 98, 220; Sealey 1987, 35–41.

26 K.J. Dover, *Lysias and the Corpus Lysiacum*, Berkeley 1968, 148–74, sees the speech-writer as a consultant who sometimes wrote a speech for the client and sometimes merely gave advice. He cites Ar. *Clouds* 462–75, the possible significance of which is greater than Dover realizes. Strepsiades is told that if he studies rhetoric under Socrates, 'There will always be a crowd at your door, wanting to discuss lawsuits, hoping to consult you on problems to which it will pay you to give intelligent consideration'. One is reminded of the jurisconsult Q. Mucius Scaevola (Augur) whose house was besieged by clients (Cic. *Orat.* 1.200). But that is as far as the similarities go; Strepsiades is not going to study law under Socrates. There is also no suggestion of legal expertise in the portrait of Antiphon (Thuc. 8.68.1). Lysias, with reference to whom Dover propounds his consultative theory, was criticized by Theophrastus (on whom see below) for the artificiality of his style. The Roman lawyers also distanced themselves from the excessive verbiage of the orators (Cic. *Orat.* 1.38–40). For an evaluation of Dover's theories see also S. Usher, *GRBS* 17 (1976), 31–40.

27 Cf. Jones 1956, 292–3, on the limited influence of Greek philosophy on Greek law, though he puts it too strongly. Theophrastus was a philosopher, and Jones (correctly) accepts him as a lawyer. Perhaps a special aptitude for the practical side of law was developed in the Peripatetic School: Aristotle will have been of more use to practitioners than Plato. Book 9 of the latter's *Laws* is perhaps more down-to-earth than some of the other books, with its discussion of such matters as temple-theft, treason, and the difference between intentional and unintentional wrongdoing.

28 Jones 1956, 292–308. See also R. Dareste, *Rev. Legisl. Fr. et Etranger* 1870/71, 262.

29 Previous works on the fragments of Theophrastus' *Nomoi* are superseded by Szegedy-Maszak's work.

30 *Lex. Rhet. Cantab.* s.v. *eisangelia.* Text in Bonner and Smith 1938, 1.295.
31 Szegedy-Maszak 1981, 20–2, thinks he was, and finds the slight differences between the versions of Theophrastus and Hyperides 3.7–9 unimportant. See also Chapter VI n. 95 below.
32 On the great law revision of 403–2 see MacDowell 1978, 46–9; Sealey 1987, 35–41; Sinclair 1988, 83–4; Rhodes *CQ* 35N.S. (1985), 55–60.
33 Ferguson 1911, 40; ibid., *Klio* 11 (1911), 265–77; Jones 1956, 294–5.
34 W. Spoerri, *Kl.P.* 3.326–7.
35 That interest is, of course, not confined to those with Macedonian sympathies. A case will be made for the anti-Macedonian Hyperides, for example, but not for Demosthenes. He was the Cicero of Athens, and Cicero was not a lawyer. Luban 1987, 311–13 has some interesting comments on Aeschylus as a legal theorist.
36 O. Hiltbrunner, *Kl.P.* 1.1469.

II FIFTH-CENTURY ATHENS: EARLY EMPIRE-BUILDERS AND THE COURTS

1 On this case see F. Marx, 'Der Tragiker Phrynichus', *RhM* 77 (1928), 337–60; Bonner and Smith 1938, 1.198–9; von Blumenthal, 'Phrynichos Nr. 4', *RE* 20.911–8; von Wedel 1971, 124–6.
2 Bonner and Smith 1938, 1.199 and nn.; Hignett 1952, 181; Heuss *ap.* von Wedel 1971, 124.
3 E. Meyer, *Gesch. d. Altertums*, vol. 4, 4th edn, Stuttgart 1944, 291–4; von Wedel 1971, 125.
4 Marx, *RhM* 77, 344.
5 Lipsius 1905, 211–9; MacDowell 1978, 194–7.
6 See Bauman 1967, 28–9.
7 Lipsius 1905, 93–5; Busolt-Swoboda 1926, 1118–9; MacDowell 1978, 157–8.
8 C. Roebuck, *The World of Ancient Times*, New York 1966, 330.
9 Busolt-Swoboda 1926, 1118 nn. 3, 4 postulate a law defining the competence of the *agoranomoi.*
10 von Wedel 1971, 126.
11 von Blumenthal, *RE* 20.911 makes the suggestion about *Phoenician Women*, Stoessl *Mus. Helv.* 2 (1945), 148–65 that about *Persians.*
12 See however Chapter III 5, pp. 45–7.
13 Cf. Busolt-Swoboda 1926, 884 n. 1; Bonner and Smith 1938, 1.198. Herodotus' *dikastērion* is not used technically.
14 *OCD*² 688; K. Kinzl, *Kl.P.* 3.1305. *Contra* perhaps Obst, *RE* 15.1683.
15 It would have been different under the fourth-century *eisangelia* law known to Theophrastus. Cf. Chapter I 3, p. 9.
16 References in n. 14.

17 J.A.R. E.g. Munro, *CAH*[1] 4.231-2. On *dokimasia* see Chapter V 1, p. 82.
18 E.M. Walker, *CAH*[1] 4.170-2; Bonner and Smith 1938, 1.198; von Wedel 1971, 126.
19 Walker, op. cit. (n. 18) 171-2. Hignett 1952, 181, envisages an ideological riposte by pro-Persian elements, but the careers of Xanthippus and his son do not indicate a medising phase.
20 Walker, ibid. *Contra* Frost 1980, 77-8.
21 Hdt. 6.134-6; Ephorus *FGrH* 1.263.107; Nepos *Milt*. 7-8. Other sources in K. Kinzl, *Kl.P*. 3.1305.
22 Claudia's brother who had lost a fleet at Drepana (at n. 6 above) was fined 1,000 *asses* for each ship lost. Bauman 1967, 27-8.
23 On the trial as a whole see Thonissen 1875, 169-72; R.W. Macan, *Herodotus*, London 1895, 2.249-58; W.W. How, 'Cornelius Nepos on Marathon and Paros', *JHS* 39 (1919), 48-61; W.W. How and J. Wells, *A Commentary on Herodotus*, Oxford 1928, 120-2; Bonner and Smith 1938, *passim*; Walker, *CAH*[1] 4.252-3; Obst, *RE* 15.1702-4; H. Berve, 'Miltiades', *Hermes Einzelschr*. 2 (1937), 92-101; Burn 1962, 258-9, 265-7; Ehrenberg 1973, 142-4; von Wedel 1971, 127-8; R. Develin, 'Miltiades and the Parian Expedition', *AC* 46 (1977), 571-7.
24 *Proditio*, the Latin equivalent of *prodosia*, in Nepos.
25 Lipsius 1905, 180; Busolt–Swoboda 1926, 884 n. 1.
26 Bauman 1967, 29-30.
27 On the penalties for embezzlement of state funds see Lipsius 1905, 399-401. See also Chapter II 5 below on Cimon's trial.
28 Bonner and Smith 1938, 1.207-9, citing Xen. *Hell*. 1.7.20, which we have already noticed. See Chapter I 2 at n. 10.
29 Bonner and Smith 1938, ibid. *Contra* Lipsius, 43 n. 132, but he mistakenly has Miltiades charged under the law cited in Dem. 20.100, 135.
30 On the death in prison see Ephorus–Nepos; also Plut. *Cim*. 4.3,7, where Cimon gives his sister in marriage to Callias in return for the latter paying the fine. Cimon's vast wealth (*AP* 27.3, Plut. *Cim*. 10.1) came later.
31 Thus a substitute for legal science as a braking mechanism was devised. But that was fairly late, and it was not a very satisfactory substitute.
32 The death sentence being mandatory under the Cannonus *psēphisma*, the *prytanis'* substitution of a fine is hard to explain. A very tentative solution is that if a *psēphisma* was valid only in so far as it did not contradict a *nomos* (Quass, 40-4), and if the *prytanis* had taken an oath to observe the *nomoi*, he may have felt obliged to reject a penalty which conflicted with the *nomos* penalty for *adikia*. On the Cannonus decree in general see Lavelle, *Cl. et Med*. 39 (1988), 19-42.
33 Balogh 1943, 13; Burn 1962, 201.
34 The use of ostracism against Hipparchus was either a remedy

only introduced at that time or the first use of a measure
introduced by Cleisthenes and kept in cold storage for twenty
years. The literature includes Ehrenberg 1973, 99–100; Burn
1962, 286–7. For Raubitschek's contributions see the list in *Cl. et
Med.* 19 (1958), 74–5.

35 Lyc. *Leocr.* 117. Hansen 1975, 70 argues that Hipparchus did
return under the amnesty, but it is not clear whether he means
that he went away again before the trial or stayed to face it. On
Lycurgus' error in having the trial take place before the Demos
see von Wedel 1971, 130 n. 1.

36 This or close to it is the accepted date. Frost 1980, 191; Rhodes
1981, 320; M. Steinbrecher, *Palingenesia* 21 (1985), 18–26.

37 On what follows see G. Busolt, *Griechische Geschichte*, vol. 3.1,
Gotha 1897, 124–8; Bonner and Smith, *passim*; Kahrstedt,
passim; Cawkwell, *passim*; von Wedel, 131–2; Hansen 1975, Cat.
No. 4; Podlecki, 39–40, 189–93; Frost 1980, 187–99. I do not
propose to debate whether the sentence was death or exile,
since both were capital. See however Frost 1980, 197–9. On the
extradition aspect see Balogh 1943, 21–2.

38 Plutarch discusses ostracism in *Arist.* 7, *Nic.* 11 (citing
Theophrastus), *Alc.* 13, *Them.* 22.3, *Cim.* 17, *Per.* 10.
Raubitschek, *Cl. et Med.* 19, 73–109 thinks Plutarch's sources
were Theophrastus' *Nomoi* and *Politika pros tous kairous*.

39 Frost 1980, 31–4.

40 Kahrstedt 1934, 1694.

41 Diod. 11.55.4–56.1. Other sources in Frost 1980, 198. Add
Nepos *Them.* 8.

42 Kahrstedt 1934, 1694.

43 Frost 1980, 183, 196–7.

44 'As it was accustomed to do at that time'.

45 von Wedel 1971, 131–2.

46 There is a curious statement by Thuc. 1.135.3, that when the
Athenians despatched a posse to arrest Themistocles 'they were
accompanied by the Lacedaemonians who were quite ready to join
in the pursuit'. Why were the Spartans so interested if nothing more
than a domestic Athenian trial was contemplated at any stage?

47 Cic. *Fam.* 5.12.5, written shortly after Cicero's own return. The
first alternative, a very late date for the trial, would take it into
the 450s, because room also has to be left for the ostracism.

48 Rhodes 1981, 319–20.

49 Ibid. *Contra* Hansen 1975, Cat. No. 4, arguing that Craterus'
citation proves that there was a decree of the Demos. But can
we be sure that the Areopagus' verdicts were not confirmed by
psēphismata? Do we even know that Craterus recorded only
psēphismata?

50 Kahrstedt 1934, 1694. Cf. Busolt, *Griech. Gesch.* 3.1.126 n. 1.
Kahrstedt consistently refers to the Peloponnesian League when
in fact Diodorus and Plutarch are referring to the Hellenic
League. Cf. Larsen 1966, 48.

51 Cawkwell 1970, *passim*.
52 They may or may not have included Aristides. On the equivocal portrayal of relations between Themistocles and Aristides see Frost 1980, 26–31, 167–8.
53 Despite the rejection of Themistocles' democratic tendencies by Frost 1980, 26–31, *Ath. Pol.* believed them. G. Thomson, *Aeschylus and Athens*, 3rd edn, London 1966, 213–4, thinks that Themistocles sought Persian collaboration because Sparta was the greatest threat to the democracy.
54 *AP* 27.1; Plut. *Cim.* 14.2–15.1, *Per.* 10.5. Nepos *Cim.* 3 notes the ostracism but not the trial. Diodorus has neither. Sealey, *PSZ* 149, thinks Cimon's friends wanted Pericles as one of the accusers.
55 So G. Busolt, *Griech. Gesch.* 3.1.155; Ed. Meyer, *Forschungen zur alten Geschichte*, vol. 2, Halle 1899, 25 n. 1. *Contra* Raubitschek, *Cl. et Med.* 19, 91 n. 7.
56 On this see W.R. Connor, *GRBS* 4 (1963), 107)14, accepting the fragment as genuine.
57 See below on the penalty for aggravated corruption. But although that was equated with treason, it does not intersect with the charge of *katalysis tou dēmou* referred to by Demosthenes. The penalty for that was quite different – outlawry and confiscation. Andoc. 1.96–7.
58 Rhodes 1981, 335–6.
59 The Areopagus: Rhodes 1981, 335–6, 309–22. The Demos: G. Busolt, *Griech. Gesch.* 3.1.245 n. 3; Lipsius 1905, 33; Hansen 1975, Cat. No. 5.
60 Thonissen 1875, 213–21.
61 The device was well known at Rome. See e.g. R.A. Bauman, *Hist.* 22 (1973), 38–9, 41–3.
62 Plut. *Cim.* 14.2 merely says that 'it was thought that he could easily have done so'.
63 There were other warning shots: Ephialtes began his attack on the Areopagus by bringing charges of maladministration. *AP* 25.2. See also Chapter III 1 n. 1.
64 Hansen 1974, *passim*, and in numerous papers since.

III FIFTH-CENTURY ATHENS: THE JUDICIAL SOVEREIGNTY OF THE DEMOS

1 *AP* 25.2. No names can be attached with the possible exception of Cimon. Rhodes 1981, 313–4, thinks trials were used to discredit ex-archons who became Areopagites; charges would be raised at their *euthynai*.
2 The exact nature of Ephialtes' reform is probably irrecoverable. For example, neither Rhodes 1981, 315–9, nor Sealey 1987, 130–1, achieves a secure picture. I have not seen R.W. Wallace, *The Areopagus Council*, Johns Hopkins U.P. 1989. It is proposed to proceed on the working hypothesis in the text. But see Chapter III 5, pp. 45–9.

3 On Cimon's ostracism, Plut. *Cim.* 15.3, 17.3, *Per.* 9.5. The Areopagus' fortunes had been boosted by its contribution at Salamis, and so the period after the Persian wars is made its special *floruit* by Aristotle. *AP* 23, 25.1. That it was basically conservative needs no documentation.

4 In *AP* 25.4 the murderer is Aristodicus of Tanagra, but that was disputed in antiquity. See Rhodes 1981, 322.

5 On Aeschylus' political stance in general see the various views of Ehrenberg 1973, 188–91; G. Thompson, *Aeschylus and Athens*, 3rd edn, London 1966, 229–78; A.J. Podlecki, *The Political Background of Aeschylean Tragedy*, Michigan 1966, 42–62; Rhodes 1981, 311–12; Luban 1987, 294–313. My thanks are due to Associate Professor G.G. Winterton of the School of Law, University of New South Wales, for bringing Luban's study to my notice.

6 A debate flares up intermittently as to whether *Eum.* 741, 752–3 means that Athena's vote breaks a tie or creates a tie. The point is of little practical importance.

7 It may be as well to record the full references to this in *AP*. They are 3.6, 4.4, 8.4, 25.2.

8 *Eum.* 690–706 and *passim.* The renderings are loosely based on H.W. Smyth, Loeb edn 1926, P. Vellacott, Penguin edn 1956, and Robert Lowell, New York 1978. Lowell's professed aim 'to trim, cut and be direct' makes Aeschylus come alive as never before.

9 See Chapter III 5, pp. 45–9.

10 'A Delphia lawyer' according to Luban. Perhaps the best word is 'shyster', which does have the imprimatur of the Oxford English Dictionary.

11 R.A. Bauman, 'Lawyers and Politics in the Early Roman Empire', *Münchener Beitr. z. Papyrusforsch. u. antiken Rechtsgesch.*, 82. Heft (1989), 40–2.

12 On Pericles' possible role see Bonner and Smith 1938, 1.253, 270.

13 On Thucydides see Rhodes 1981, 349–51, 358, arguing that he married Cimon's sister and had a daughter who married the son of another sister of Cimon; the two first cousins were the historian's parents. Rhodes is not sure that Thucydides headed a cohesive political group, but does not quite reject Plutarch. Ehrenberg 1973, 234–5, accepts Plutarch.

14 Burn 1960, 119–21, says that Thucydides attacked both by trials and by ostracism. But the only trial that he cites is Anaxagoras, and that does not date to the period of Thucydides' politicizing. See Chapter III 3.

15 See Chapter V 2.

16 Anon *Thuc. Vit.* 6. H. Gärtner, *RE* 24, 50–1, has reservations but does not quite reject the evidence.

17 This question is not addressed by Connor 1971, 25–9.

18 See Chapter III 4, pp. 42–5.

19 On pay for jury service see, e.g., Bonner and Smith 1938,
    1.226–9; Burn 1960, 76–8.
20 P. Krentz, *Hist.* 33 (1984), 499–504, dates it to 437–6, but that
    adds a new chronological crisis to an already overburdened list.
21 See Rhodes 1981, 271, 342, 350; 284, 34–2.
22 This detail is added by Diod. 12.39.1.
23 The case was set in motion by *mēnysis* (perhaps here used for
    the first time). Menon's indemnity protected him against
    prosecution as an accomplice, but he was not the formal
    accuser. He merely reported to the Ecclesia, whereupon others
    took up the case. Plut. *Per.* 31.2–3.
24 Lipsius 1905, 365, denies that Pheidias was charged with *asebeia*.
    Cf. Mansfeld 1979, 30, and n. 124. MacDowell 1978, 149, thinks
    impiety was possibly charged. Plut. *Per.* 31.4–5 does not say in
    so many words that he was charged on this count, but he does
    say that because of it he was imprisoned. It was undoubtedly
    an element in the case. See also Chapter III 5, pp. 45–9.
25 F. Adcock, *CAH* 5.175, 478; Ehrenberg 1973, 453, n. 113;
    Mansfeld 1979, 32 and n. 130; Stone 1988, 233–4.
26 Burn 1960, 129.
27 Thonissen 1875, 184; Derenne 1930, 9.
28 Dover 1976, *passim* comes perilously close to doing this.
29 E.g. Thonissen 1875, 184; Lipsius 1905, 365; Burn 1960, 176;
    Kienast 1953, 210 and *passim*; F. Kiechle, *Kl.P.* 1.649–50; Frost
    1964, 282–3; von Wedel 1971, 139 n. 145; Ostwald 1986, 194–5
    (probably). *Contra* F. Adcock, *CAH* 5.175, 478; Ehrenberg 1973,
    453 n. 113; Dover 1976, 28.
30 Rudhardt 1960, *passim*, prefers 'cultivating the gods' to
    'believing in them'. Ostwald 1986, 196, has 'pay the customary
    respect to'. See further below.
31 The other two, Hermippus and Hieronymus, add very little. For
    details see Mansfeld 1979, 19–22.
32 Diog. Laert. 2.12 (the sun), 2.8 (the sun and the moon). The
    indictment will have charged both. Cf. Plato *Apol.* 26D. On the
    possible link with Zeus' bolts see Lipsius 1905, 363 n. 22.
33 Frost 1964, 283, 289 n. 40; Dover 1976, 28–34.
34 Dover 1976, 40. See also Stone 1988, 236.
35 See the *scholia* on *Birds* 988, *Knights* 1085, *Wasps* 380. The
    scholiast also does not notice Diopeithes' other legislative act,
    the decree which he promoted in favour of Methone. Cf.
    Derenne 1930, 20.
36 So Derenne 1930, 22; Hansen 1975, Cat. No. 6, n. 5.
37 E.g. Derenne 1930, 19–24; Mansfeld 1979, 32; Ostwald 1986,
    196–8. Dover's attack is almost unique, except for Stone 1988,
    236 and Lefkowitz, whom he cites.
38 On Anaxagoras' instruction of Pericles see Ostwald 1986, 268–9.
    Rudhardt 1960, *passim*, takes *ta theia* in Plut. *Per.* 32.1 to mean
    'the supernatural' rather than 'the gods', but I am not sure that
    a legal statute would have risked such a subtlety.

39 Mansfeld 1979, 84.
40 For an analysis of the *scholia* see Lendle 1955, *passim*.
41 Derenne 1930, 30, 38; Kienast 1953, *passim*.
42 Frost 1964, *passim*; Mansfeld 1979, *passim*; Ostwald 1986, 192, 194-5.
43 Lendle 1955, *passim*.
44 That is, the fifty Boule-members from a given tribe serving as a standing committee for one-tenth of the year.
45 On the date see, e.g., Swoboda 1893, 537. It is not in contention. On the link between the *hierosylia* charge and the eventual trial, see below.
46 Diod. 12.45.4; Thuc. 2.65.3.
47 Ehrenberg 1973, 251.
48 On riders see P.J. Rhodes, *The Athenian Boule*, Oxford 1972, 56, 63, 65, 66-7, 71-2, 278-9, though he does not deal with our problem of the difference between a rider and an amendment.
49 δέ without a preceding μέν.
50 This may seem to indicate that Hagnon's amendment was contemporaneous with Dracontides' proposal, but changed conditions were needed for the amendment. See p. 44.
51 Plut. *Per.* 35.4; Diod. 12.45.4.
52 So Macdowell 1978, 149.
53 The work of Derenne has been an invaluable aid; Ostwald also calls for special mention. But neither scholar approaches the topic quite on the lines being attempted here.
54 Bonner and Smith 1938, 1.258.
55 Sources: Arist. *Nic. Eth.* 3.1, IIII^3 6-10; Heraclid. Pont. fr. 170 Wehrli; Clem. Alex. *Strom.* 2.14, 60.3; Aelian *Var. Hist.* 5.19.
56 Ostwald 1986, 529-30.
57 Barkan 1935, 41-51.
58 For other examples see Barkan 1935, ibid.
59 Ostwald 1986, 530.
60 See below on cases besides Aeschylus.
61 Cf. Chapter III 1, p. 32.
62 Cf. II 2.
63 Cf. II 4.
64 Dover 1976, 42-6; Ostwald 1986, 279-90.
65 So Dover 1976, 29, pointing out that no other play in which Heracles was portrayed as mad is known.
66 I do not understand the Areopagus to have been bound by *res iudicata*.
67 Cf. Chapter III 6, pp. 49-60.
68 According to Derenne 1930, 217-36, and Rudhardt 1960 *passim*, there was a pre-Diopeithes law to which Diopeithes merely added a new category, *ta metarsia*. See further p. 49.
69 Whatever the position prior to Ephialtes, it is agreed today that after his reform *eisangelia* was the exclusive business of the Boule, the Ecclesia and the *dikastēria*. Cf. *AP* 8.4 (Solonic), 25.2 (post-Ephialtean). A coherent picture is not readily obtainable

from Hansen 1975 or Rhodes 1979. For a useful summation see Carawan 1987.

70 It is not included in what was given to the Areopagus by Solon (*AP* 8.4).

71 E.g., the power reputedly given by Solon to try *katalysis tou dēmou*. *AP* 8.4. Cf. on *ta epitheta*, *AP* 25.2 with Rhodes 1981 ad loc.

72 Modern opinions are unclear. For at least a clear exposition of the anomalies (including the intractable problem of whether the Thirty restored the general guardianship but suspended the homicide role) see Bonner and Smith 1938, 1.277–8, 328–32. The crisp question is whether the oversight of the laws given to the Areopagus by the restored democracy – the decree of Teisamenus (Andoc. 1.83–4) – amounted to the retention of that council's full powers as restored by the Thirty, or to something else. On this see Chapter V 1, p. 105.

73 On 'Pericles Monarchos' see the papers of J.S. Morrison and A.W. Gomme in *PSZ* 138, 143.

74 Derenne 1930, 19–21.

75 It does not, however, add anything to the belief (n. 68) that Diopeithes merely added to an existing law. Even if he did, the addition was just as momentous as an entirely new law would have been.

76 Connor 1971, 117–19 at 119.

77 The team is conjectural, but see the speculations of Connor 1971, 128–31.

78 Especially Thuc. 3.36.2.

79 One of the few to note the possibility of a trial, though only in passing, is U. Kahrstedt, *RE* 11 (1921), 714–17. The usual approach is that of A. Andrewes, *Phoenix* 16 (1962), 64–85. Also Gomme, 2.323 ad 3.48.1.

80 See, e.g. R.A. Bauman, *Hist.* 22 (1973), 34 at 37–43.

81 Lipsius 1905, 969, postulates a judicial function. Cf. R. Meiggs, *The Athenian Empire*, repr. Oxford 1982, 220–33. *Contra* Robertson, 26–7, arguing that the Delian League was not so much a true confederacy as a military alliance for a specific purpose. But so was the Hellenic League. However, no Delian League trials are known.

82 On the close links see Hansen 1974, *passim*. On the subordination, Robertson 1924, 29.

83 Robertson 1924, 25–47, especially on Erythrae, Miletus and Chalcis.

84 Ibid., 36–47, on Chalcis.

85 Thuc. 3.37.3, 39.1–2, 39.5–6, 39.40.4.

86 The controversy as to whether Cleon prosecuted Aristophanes or Callistratus will probably never be settled, but the better view is that in the text. See e.g. Croiset 1909, 46–8; Starkie 1909, 247–8. A.H. Sommerstein, *Acharnians*, 1980, 2, leaves it open. On this question see also D.M. MacDowell, *CQ* 32 (1982), 21–6.

87 On this charge see Lipsius 1905, 87, 412, 957. On whether it could have been mounted against Aristophanes with any hope of success see Croiset 1909, 8–9; Starkie 1909, xi–xii; Kaibel, *RE* 2.971–2. Could the poet's dubious birth status have prompted his early use of Callistratus as a front man?

88 So MacDowell 1971, 300. B.B. Rogers had taken Aristophanes as the vine and the Demos as the stake. See A. Chiappe (ed.), *Five Comedies of Aristophanes*, New York 1955, 280.

89 References in MacDowell 1971, 299. He thinks it possible but unproven.

90 See Starkie 1909, 243–5, 247–8; H. Frisch, *The Constitution of the Athenians*, Copenhagen 1942, 277–81.

91 Starkie 1909, 247.

92 To this extent I attempt a more precise definition of *psēphisma* than that noted in Chapter I n. 12.

93 On *adikia* see Bonner and Smith 1938, 1.205–9.

94 Starkie 1909, 244.

95 Cf. Bauman 1974, 25–51.

96 H. Bengtson, *Griechische Geschichte*, Munich 1950, 215; T. Gelzer, *RE* Supp. 12 (1970), 1399.

97 Croiset 1909, 22 and n. 1, 62; Starkie 1909, xxiii; Gelzer, ibid.

98 Ps.-Xen. *Ath. Pol.* 2.18; Cic. *Rep.* 4.10.

99 Croiset 1909, 50; Starkie 1909, 247, 'perhaps with a small fine'; Sommerstein, op. cit. (n. 86) 2.

100 Croiset 1909, 35–51. G. Norwood, *CP* 25 (1930), 1–10, does not succeed in undermining Croiset.

101 This favours his acquittal, or the dismissal of the charge at a preliminary stage.

102 *Wasps* 240–4, *schol.* ad 240, 836–43, 891–1008.

103 Lipsius 1905, 297–8; H. Swoboda, *RE* 12.336–8.

104 MacDowell 1971, 164, 249–54. Cf. Gomme, 2. 430–1.

105 See the interesting demonstration of this by L.A. Post, *AJP* 53 (1932), 265–6.

106 As Gomme is, 2.430–1.

107 See Thuc. 4.103–7. The summary given here is based on that in Bauman 1968.

108 Bauman 1968, *passim*. For other reconstructions see Gomme, 3.584–8; H.D. Westlake, *Hermes* 90 (1962), 276–87; O. Luschnat, *RE* Supp. 12 (1970), 1099–1100, 1103–6.

109 On that charge in general see Lipsius, 380–1. It ought to be as clearly defined as the Roman *male gesta res publica*, but is not.

110 Cf. Luschnat, *RE* Supp. 12, 1099–1100.

111 On the parameters of the crime see Lipsius 1905, 377–80. Cf. Thonissen 1875, 161–9; MacDowell 1971, 175–91; Berneker 1956, *passim*.

112 Mostly some of the older translators including Jowett. O. Luschnat, *RE* Supp. 12, 1104, is a modern writer overinclined to take a similar view.

113 Cf. perhaps Classen-Steup, *Thukydides*, 3rd edn, 1900, 1.XI.

114 Grundy 1948, 1.30 n. 1, 41.
115 On the amnesty (or amnesties) see A.P. Dorjahn, *Political Forgiveness in Old Athens*, Evanston 1946, 3–6. On the amnesty as the authority for Thucydides' return see Grundy 1948, 1.41; O. Luschnat, *RE* Supp. 12.1103. On the tradition for his murder, Grundy 1948, 1.43–7. As Luschnat, 1105, points out, his history breaks off in mid-sentence.
116 E.g. Classen-Steup, 1.XI–XII; Grundy 1948, 1.30 n. 1, 41; Gomme, 3.584–8; Hansen 1975, Cat. No. 10; MacDowell 1971, 173; R. Warner, Penguin Thucydides, rev. edn 1972, 364.
117 Gomme, 3.584–5.
118 MacDowell 1971, 173.
119 ibid., 255.
120 Not that we have much idea of the charge against him . For some conjectures see MacDowell 1971, ibid.; Sommerstein, op. cit. (n. 86) 192.
121 Thucydides' gold-mining interests in Thrace certainly put him in this category.
122 Classen-Steup, 1.XII.
123 On Thucydides' attitude to Cleon see A.G. Woodhead, *Mnemosyne* 13 (1960), 289–317.

IV FIFTH-CENTURY ATHENS: 'WHOM THE GODS WISH TO DESTROY'

1 Plut. Nic. 11, *Alc.* 13. He was however important enough to be killed by the oligarchs on Samos in 411. Thuc. 8.73.1.
2 Thuc. 6.27–9, 53, 60–1. Other sources will be brought in as appropriate.
3 Lists of names have been compiled by Gomme, 4.276–80 (68 names plus 20 'others'); Hansen 1975, Cat. Nos. 11–60 (50 names); Ostwald 1986, 539–40, 329 (64 names, but he does not entirely reject the traditional number of 300).
4 MacDowell 1962, 73, rejecting double impeachment.
5 On Androcles see Plut. *Alc.* 19; Thuc. 8.65.2; Andoc. 1.27, with MacDowell 1962, 81–2. Note especially Plut. *Alc.* 19.1: 'Androcles the demagogue produced slaves and metics who accused Alcibiades and his friends of mutilating other sacred images and of parodying the Mysteries in a drunken revel.'
6 See the solutions of Gomme, 4.271–6 and MacDowell 1962, 181–5.
7 As to whether a political club was behind the mutilations see MacDowell 1962, 190–3.
8 Cf. MacDowell 1962, 70.
9 Harrison 1971, 147–50; MacDowell 1978, 245–7.
10 Cf. n. 3.
11 On this rule, though not specifically in relation to the Hermae/Mysteries case, see Lipsius 1905, 894–5; Harrison 1971, 150. The rule is inferred from Andoc. 1.22.64.

12 MacDowell 1962, 79, deduces such powers from Andoc. 1.15, 64, though he is not considering the link between impiety and treason. As far as I know that link has not been suspected before. Von Wedel 1971, 146–7, says that the Boule also dealt with the repeal of Scamander's *psēphisma*, which forbade the torture of citizens.

13 Bauman 1974, 43–8, 55–9.

14 The full implications of the priestly jurisdiction and its relation, *inter alia*, to Alcibiades' case can be better understood in the context of the trial of Andocides in 399. See therefore Chapter VI 2.

15 Cf. n. 3.

16 They were also relaxed with respect to citizens and metics: Lipsius, von Wedel as cited in nn. 11, 12. But our present interest is in the slaves.

17 Details in n. 5.

18 MacDowell 1962, 193.

19 H. Gundel, *Kl.P.* 3 (1969), 349; F. Kiechle, *Kl.P.* 1 (1964), 263.

20 Derenne 1930, 45–55. Also K. von Fritz, *RE* 23 (1957), 910–11; Ostwald 1986, 532–3.

21 Ehrenberg, *AJP* 69 (1948), 168–9, arguing plausibly that he dealt more with private law than with constitutional. See also von Fritz, *RE* 23.909–10. He probably updated the great compilation of private law made by Charondas at Catana in the seventh century. Diod. 12.11–19 confuses Charondas with Protagoras, and the mini-digest that he supplies probably reflects the latter's laws rather than the former's.

22 Derenne 1930, 57–70; Ostwald 1986, 275–7 and n. 284.

23 Cf. n. 3.

24 So Derenne 1930, 66–70.

25 The best government that Athens had had in Thucydides' time: 8.97.2.

26 On Phrynichus' deposition see Roberts 1982, 36–40. On depositions followed by charges see Chapter V 2, pp. 82–4. I agree with Durrbach 1956, 72 n. 1, that his crime is obscure, but the reconstruction in the text suffices for our present purpose.

27 Lyc. *Leocr.* 113–5; Schol. Ar. *Lys.* 313. Hansen 1975, Cat. No. 62, argues that the defenders were not Alexicles and Aristarchus, as stated by Lycurgus, but Phrynichus' heirs, who were alarmed by the threat of confiscation.

28 Bauman 1974, 141, 93.

29 Assuming, with Hansen 1975, Cat. No. 62, that the trial was held under the Five Thousand.

30 On which see Bauman 1974, *passim*.

31 The sources, both for the matters outlined in the text so far and for the eventual trial, are Xen. *Hell.* 1.5.16, 1.6.19–38, 1.7.1–35, 2.3.32, 35; Diod. 13.97–100, 13.100–3.2; *AP* 34.1 (brief and inaccurate). For the most part I propose following Xenophon's account. On Andrewes' preference for Diodorus, and on my reasons for not sharing that preference, see n. 42.

32 Hansen 1975, Cat. No. 65.
33 On this *graphē* see Chapter V 3, p. 84.
34 von Wedel 1971, 161.
35 Lipsius 1905, 43 n. 131, 912 n. 43. Ostwald 1986, 438, unconvincingly argues that they were not *denied* a full hearing; as it was only 'an ordinary meeting of the Assembly' they were not entitled to a special ration of speaking-time.
36 But see nn. 31, 42.
37 von Wedel 1971, 163, 165–70.
38 The four groups postulated by G. Nemeth, *Klio* 66 (1984), 51–7, strain the evidence.
39 W. Schwan, *RE* 5A. 2311–2.
40 On the three penalties and the scholiast cf. Rhodes 1981, 361.
41 K.J. Beloch, *Griechische Geschichte*, Strassburg 1914, 2.1.421.
42 Andrewes prefers Diodorus to Xenophon because Xenophon is determined to present the generals as innocent. See Andrewes, *passim*. That the two sides were jockeying for a first strike cannot be denied, but Andrewes is as anxious to present Theramenes as innocent as Xenophon is said to be on behalf of the generals. He cites Theramenes' exculpation in Xen. 2.3.35 but fails to mention Critias' accusation in 2.3.32. Also, his attempt to play down the weakness in Diod. 13.102 by emphasizing the excellence of the rest of the account will not work. Nor does he face up squarely to the fact that Theramenes was rejected at a *dokimasia*. See above, and cf. Roberts, 20, 160. But his most serious weakness is his total unawareness of the importance of the legal issues in the case. This may be because Diodorus is also reticent on that score. But the upshot is that on this most important aspect of all we have no yardstick for any criticism of Xenophon. G. Cawkwell, Introd. to Xenophon's *Hellenica*, Harmondsworth: Penguin 1986, 93, 117, vacillates between supporting Andrewes and defending Xenophon, but does not add anything new to the debate.
43 This interesting point is made by von Wedel 1971, 174–5.

V FOURTH-CENTURY ATHENS: LAW REFORM, SCRUTINY, AND ILLEGALITY

1 Ostwald 1986, 414–20; Sealey 1987, 45.
2 This *nomos* outlawed anyone who subverted the democracy, or held any office after its subversion, or set up a tyranny: Andoc. 1.96. If any proof that this was not the first law concerning *katalysis tou dēmou* is required, it is supplied by Andoc. 1.95 and by the fact that as ancient a norm as the ban on tyranny was restated in Demophantus' law.
3 On the date of the law on the Boule's jurisdiction see Bonner and Smith 1938, 1.201–5, 336–45. On Lysimachus' case see von Wedel 1971, 149–50.
4 Ostwald 1986, 58–60, 400, 422, 449.

5 See *AP* 35.2 with Bonner and Smith 1938, 1.327–32; Rhodes 1981, 440–2; Krentz 1982, 60–2.

6 Cf. Krentz 1982, 62.

7 On Sulla's inroads into the tribunes' jurisdiction see R.A. Bauman, *Athenaeum* 51 (1973), 278 n. 50; *Latomus* 33 (1974), 249–50.

8 Krentz 1982, 60–2, does not address the role of the Areopagus or the Heliaea in this regard. But the Heliaea was not stripped of its jurisdiction any more than the Areopagus was. The *ephesis eis to dikastērion* of *AP* 9.1 refers to it, not to the jury-courts, which were post-Solonic. Cf. Rhodes 1981, 160. *Contra* Hansen 1975, 51–2.

9 Krentz 1982, 60. Cf. Rhodes 1981, 446. The main source for the Agoratus group is Lysias 13.

10 Krentz 1982, 60, 62. Cf. Lys. 13 *passim*; Xen. *Hell.* 2.3.12. The Thirty flouted the normal (if that is the right word) rules of procedure. Lys. 13.36–8.

11 This is a necessary inference from the decree; the Thirty did not propose it merely in order to violate it.

12 Xen. *Hell.* 2.3.51; *AP* 37.1. Cf. Rhodes 1981, 452.

13 A similar charge would be brought against Agoratus in *c* .399. Lys. 13.

14 Xen. *Hell.* 2.3.32, 35, within the context of 24–56, on Theramenes' trial. See also *AP* 37.1.

15 *AP* 35.4. Sulla, who was charged with rewriting the laws as the Thirty had been, and crippled the radical jurisdiction as they had done (n. 7), had every reason to be grateful to Critias when he came to draw up his law of proscription.

16 Terms in *AP* 39.1–6. Discussions: Rhodes 1981, 462–72; Ostwald 1986, 497–509.

17 Despite Rhodes 1981, 468.

18 Such as Theramenes and the generals, or Agoratus and the anti-peace lobby (above). Agoratus was charged before a jury-court in *c*.399; Lys. 13.1.

19 This was more onerous than under Patrocleides' amnesty (above), where adverse *euthynai* not yet converted into a trial qualified for the indemnity. For examples of some who managed to qualify under the present indemnity see Ostwald 1986, 503; and on the one violation, ibid., 510. On the scope of 'consigning to oblivion' see Dorjahn 1946, 24–33.

20 On the difference between these two types of *nomothetae* see Ostwald 1986, 512–19; Sealey 1987, 35–7. The *nomothetae* who inscribed were appointed by the Boule; the 500 *nomothetae* who scrutinized were elected by the demes.

21 Andoc. 1.83–4 with Ostwald 1985, ibid., Sealey 1987, ibid., and MacDowell 1962, 194–9.

22 Bonner and Smith 1938, 1.277–8.

23 E.g. Ostwald 1986, 517–19.

24 A.R.W. Harrison, 'Lawmaking at Athens at the end of the fifth century B.C.', *JHS* 75 (1955), 26–35.

25 This is not contradicted by our example in Chapter III 5, p. 48, of the Areopagus' consideration of the legitimacy of the Thirty. That was in the course of a case of direct murder. That the Areopagus consistently found a way around restrictions is clear. But we are here concerned with its official powers.

26 On his appointments and status see Ostwald 1986, 122, 407–8, 416–18, 511–12. See also the remarks of Jones 1956, 114–15.

27 On the Cleophon case cf. Chapter IV 5, pp. 75–6.

28 So Sealey 1987, 37–41, on which the summary in the text is partly based.

29 So Sealey 1987, 37. A closer parallel than his comparison with the Common Law is the Digest, except that there the disappearance of all material extraneous to the code was mandatory. Justinian *Const. Deo Auctore* 7, *Const. Tanta* 10. On the difficulties of the Athenian rule see Sealey 1987, 39 and 159 n. 12. The difficulties caused by Justinian's ban are notorious. See e.g. H.F. Jolowicz and B. Nicholas, *Hist. Introd. to the Study of Roman Law*, 3rd edn, Cambridge 1972, 500–15.

30 The word *nomos* is used consistently in Andoc. 1.83–4. This made *psēphismata* particularly susceptible to the *graphē paranomōn*, on which see Chapter V 4. *Psēphismata* also emanated from the Boule, but the main need was to inhibit snap votes in the Assembly. Cf. Sinclair 1988, 83.

31 Merely a restatement of the procedure laid down for ostracism, as Sealey 1987, 38, points out. The difficulties which he adumbrates are real enough, especially the reappearance of the Assembly in what seemed to be machinery in which it had no part. On this see Sealey 1987, 40–1.

32 On this see Sealey 1987, 41–5; Sinclair 1988, 83–4.

33 Details in Sealey 1987, 41: laws concerning the Boule, miscellaneous matters, the archons, other officials.

34 R.A. Bauman, *Lawyers in Roman Republican Politics*, Munich 1983, 2, 4, 233, 248, 288, 424–6.

35 Lys. 30.27–8. Lysias is not using a technical appellation. Ostwald 1986, 511–12.

36 See, e.g., R.A. Bauman, *ANRW* II 13, 103–233.

37 Hansen 1987, 55, 97.

38 On these procedures see MacDowell 1978, 167–72; Hansen 1987, 221–2, 208, 214; Roberts 1982, ch. II; Sinclair 1988, 77–9.

39 So Roberts 1982, 20, 192–3, citing M.H. Hansen, *GRBS* 28 (1987), 36–7 and n. 18. I am unable to detect any reference to this matter by Hansen at the place indicated.

40 For an analysis of Timotheus' two cases see Roberts 1982, 40–5, 45–9. See also Hansen 1975, Cat. No. 8 and p. 64 b. 47 ('T. escaped with . . . a symbolic fine'); K. Kinzl, *K1.P.* 5.849. On the first occasion Timotheus' treasurer (*tamias*), Antimachus, was convicted of embezzlement and executed: Roberts 1982, 40–1. But it would be unkind to suggest that Timotheus threw him to the lions.

41 He impeached his colleague Chabrias in 366, Timotheus and two others in 356–5, and Lysicles in 338 after Chaeronea: Roberts 1982, 77, ascribing Chares' actions to self-preservation. Self-promotion is a better guess.

42 H. Volkmann, *K1.P.* 5.846.

43 Roberts 1982, 111–12.

44 Dem. 23.152–67. Cf. K. Wickert, *K1.P.* 3.191–2.

45 Dem. 58.27. Cf. Lipsius 1905, 66 n. 53.

46 Roberts 1982, 24–5, 194 n. 62, suggesting that only a third of the generals who were impeached served their full terms. She cites twenty-four generals who were deposed during their terms, of whom the fourth-century examples are Pamphilus, two unnamed generals of 378, Timotheus (twice), Autocles, Leosthenes, Timomachus, Theotimus, Cephisodotus, Iphicrates, Menestheus. Also probable in the fourth century are Callistratus and Ergophilus.

47 ibid., 194 n. 62.

48 ibid., naming Ergocles, Chabrias, (probably) Agyrrhius, Thrasybulus, Dionysius, Menon, Philon, Hegesileos, Lysicles.

49 Roberts 1982, 24, recognizes this.

50 See Chapter V 3, pp. 84–94.

51 See G. Dobesch, *K1.P.* 3.1164; Roberts 1982, 24.

52 Roberts 1982, ibid. But I am unable to make anything of her citation of 'the attack on Theodorus in 347'.

53 Durrbach 1956, xlix.

54 Fr. 11.2. See Durrbach 1956, 95 and n. 2, endorsing Kiessling's allocation of the fragment to this speech.

55 On this case see Lamb's Introd., Loeb edn of Lysias 586–7. Thrasybulus did not stand trial because he was killed in a riot at Aspendus.

56 Envoys may also not have been required to submit to *dokimasia*: Mosley 1973, 39.

57 For a recent account of the debate see C.L. Morison, *Phoenix* 25 (1971), 12–31. See also G. Busolt, *Griech. Gesch.* 3.1.356 n.; Lipsius 1905, 403; Kirchner, *RE* 10.1617.

58 Plut. *Mor.* 833D–F, 834A–B. On the transmission see Bonner and Smith 1938, 1.321; H.N. Fowler, Loeb edn of Plut. *Moralia*, vol. 10, 351 n. 'c'.

59 Roberts 1982, 109–10, citing Thuc. 8.91.2–3.

60 For the emendation on which this reading is based, see M. Cuvigny, Budé edn of Plut. *Moralia*, vol. 12 ad loc.

61 Though Phrynichus was a member of the peace mission he was not indicted, because he had already been tried posthumously. Cf. Chapter IV 4, p. 68.

62 Hansen 1975, 115.

63 Hyp. *Eux.* 7–8, 29, 39 – *katalysis tou dēmou*, betraying a city or army, being bribed as a rhetor to speak against the best interests of the people. For other possible charges see Rhodes 1979, 107.

64 So Bonner and Smith 1938, 1.302. For a different view see Hansen 1975, 12–20.

65 Mosley 1973, 40–1, says that *parapresbeia* covered wilful misconduct, peculation, bribery, failure to follow instructions, and treason. But he adds that no formal charges of treason were pressed against state envoys – an astonishing statement in the light of Antiphon's case. Dem. 19.278–9 lists disobeying instructions, reporting untruthfully to the Assembly orally or in dispatches, giving false evidence against allies, and taking bribes.

66 G. Dalmeyda, Budé edn of Andocides 3, 81–2; F. Jacoby, Supp. 519 ad *FGrH* 3B 328 F149; Bruce 1966, 274 (ad Argument to Andoc. 3), 278–80; Mosley 1973, 30, 32–3, 36, 40; Roberts 1982, 87–93.

67 On the congress of 386 at Sparta and the Peace see Xen. *Hell.* 5.1.32, 5.1. 25–31; Diod. 14.110; Polyaen, 2.24. The Peace declared all states in Asia to be subject to Persia, all states in Greece to be autonomous, except that Athens was to keep Lemnos, Imbros, and Scyros.

68 Bruce 1966, 276, 279–81.

69 On this remedy see Hansen 1987, 55, 154 n. 360, 99, 175 n. 639. Another remedy, *eisangelia eis ton dēmon*, was available against a rhetor who supported an unconstitutional proposal moved by another: ibid., 55.

70 For partial lists see n. 65.

71 A. Neumann, *Kl.P.* 5.986–7.

72 E.g. G. Dalmeyda, Budé Andocides 3, 82–3.

73 On which see in general Mosley 1973, 30–8.

74 Viz., 415 and 400–399. See Chapter IV 2 and VI 1–2.

75 Xen. *Hell.* 7.1.33–40; Plut. *Pel.* 30–1; Dem. 19.137.

76 Aesch. 2.13–14, explaining that Philocrates had chosen Demosthenes in preference to himself because he was ill.

77 On the decree see Diod. 16.60.2: Phocian fugitives and those who had taken part in robbing the Delphic shrine were to be accursed and subject to arrest by the first comer. Aesch. 2.114–17 may pinpoint Aeschines as the inspirer of the decree. Phocian impiety may have been used by Philocrates to secure the passage of his anti-Phocian *psēphisma*. Charges of *asebeia* always had a profound effect on the Athenians.

78 G. Mathieu ad Dem. 19.211–12.

79 V. Martin and G. de Budé, Budé edn of Aeschines, 2nd edn 1952, 14.

80 ibid., 14–15.

81 ibid. Demosthenes is known to have written the defence: Ryder, *DemAes* 36–7.

82 This is the felicitous rendering of Dem. 18.134 by Saunders, *DemAes* ad loc.

83 See Chapter V 4, p. 94.

84 On the whole question see V. Martin and G. de Budé, Budé Aeschines, vol. 1, 106–8; Mathieu 1956, 19 n. 4.

85 *Hypoth.* I 3, II 11–13.
86 The upper limit is favoured by Ryder, *DemAes* 37, the lower by Mathieu 1956, 14 n. 3.
87 They comprise five of the thirty-nine cases listed by Hansen 1974, 28–41. On the report that Aristophon was attacked by *graphē paranomōn* seventy-five times see Cloché 1960, 81; Sinclair 1988, 153. On Antiphon in general see D. Whitehead, *CP* 81 (1986), 313–19. Cato the Censor was said to have been prosecuted forty-four times: Pliny *NH* 7.100.
88 Hansen 1987, 215. As to what Hansen understands by 'rhetors', see *GRBS* 24 (1983), 151–80. See also Connor 1971, 116–17.
89 Hansen 1987, 215. Cf. Hansen 1974, 44–8; MacDowell 1978, 50; Sinclair 1988, 154. The best evidence for the postulated distinction is statistical. Hansen 1974, 46–7, notes that there are thirty-nine extant examples of the *paranomōn* compared with six of the *mē epitēdeion*, corresponding to the handful of fourth-century *nomoi* (laws passed in that century by *nomothetae*) as against the hundreds of fourth-century *psēphismata* (passed by the Boule or the Ecclesia). As to how a proposal was held to be 'inexpedient' or 'unsuitable', there is no satisfactory answer: cf. Sealey, 44. *Mē epitēdeion* is so obviously discretionary that one must have doubts as to whether it could be coupled with the objective criterion of conflict with an extant law.
90 This will be used as a convenient abbreviation for *graphē paranomōn*.
91 Hansen 1974, 49. Very often the *hypōmosia* was all that was needed to force the withdrawal of the proposal: Dem. 18.103.
92 Barkan 1935, 86–95; MacDowell 1978, 64–6.
93 MacDowell 1978, 50; Sinclair 1988, 154–5. Eudemus was put to death in 382–1 for an unsuitable law: Dem. 22.69, 25.87, 24.138.
94 R. Sealey, *CJ* 77 (1982), 298, doubts whether this means the actual jury or the album from which juries were empanelled. MacDowell 1971, 77, thinks the profanation issue was so traumatic that only the largest possible jury was considered adequate.
95 Sealey 1987, 161 n. 47.
96 H.J. Wolff, cited with approval by Sealey 1987, ibid.
97 The relevance of this is suggested by the discussion in von Wedel 1971, 146–7.
98 See Chapter IV 2, pp. 62–7.
99 von Wedel 1971, 147.
100 As von Wedel 1971, ibid., does when he infers that the proposal was not seen as illegal because every proposal which became the subject of a duly enacted *psēphisma* was lawful.
101 R. Sealey, *CJ* 77, 300, refers to the assurance to the president of the Assembly in 415 that he ran no risk of prosecution if he resubmitted a decree of the Ecclesia: Thuc. 6.14. Sealey

deduces from this that the *GP* may have originated at an earlier date, though after 427, because the Mytilenian debate does not mention any danger in resubmitting. Ryder, *DemAes* 46–7, thinks the *GP* originated when Ephialtes deprived the Areopagus of its function as guardian of the laws. But on the argument in the text, 415 is the date of origin.

102 On the others, Demosthenes of Aphidna in *c.* 414, Thrasybulus in *c.* 403–1, and Theozotides in *c.* 403–1, see Hansen 1974, 28, 30, 45–6. Cf. MacDowell 1978, 50.

103 Sealey 1987, 49–50.

104 Honours: Hansen 1974, Nos. 7–9, 12, 14, 23, 26, 28, 30–2, 34, 36, 39. Foreign relations: Nos. 10, 11, 17, 21, 22, 24. Finances: Nos. 13, 18, 33, 35. Citizenship: Nos. 15, 16, 27. Impiety: Nos. 29, 38. *Nomothetai*: No. 25. Uncertain: Nos. 6, 19, 20, 37. Two-thirds of all fourth-century decrees preserved epigraphically relate to honours or citizenship: Hansen 1974, 62.

105 I do not propose debating the genuineness of documents in the orators as a whole. That the system lent itself to fraud cannot be denied, though the substitution of written depositions for oral evidence in *c.* 378–7 (Harrison 1971, 134–5) was an improvement. Ryder, *DemAes* 13–15 is pessimistic, but does not notice that reform; the omission of all documents from *DemAes* is unfortunate. There are admittedly errors, such as the dating to the archonship of Chaerondas in Dem. 18.54–5, since the archon in 337–6 was Phrynichus. But can we be sure that the *GP* of c.338 on a previous crown awarded to Demosthenes (Hansen 1974, 36) has not confused the tradition? It appears to have confused H. Gärtner, *K1.P.* 1.191, for he has the charge of 336–30 arise out of a proposal made in 340.

106 Richardson 1889, 75 n. 7.

107 He was disfranchised inasmuch as he was barred from bringing future cases of the same type, and if he defaulted on the fine he suffered total disfranchisement. References in n. 92.

108 He may have spent some time with Alexander at Ephesus: Plut. *Mor.* 840D.

109 Syrianus *ap.* Richardson 1889, 74 n. 49.

110 Dem. 18.13–15, 222, 251. On the *GP* brought by Diondas in *c.* 338 see Hansen 1974, No. 26, p. 36.

111 C.A. Vince, Loeb edn of Demosthenes, 2.3–4; Ryder, *DemAes* 48–9.

112 Ryder, ibid.

113 Ryder, ibid., realizes this.

114 Arrian, 1.10; Diod. 17.15; Plut. *Dem*, 23.3–5. On the judicial functions of the League see Chapter VII 6, pp. 139–51.

115 Diod. 17.15.2–4. The Assembly passed a *psēphisma* in terms of Demades' proposal, a document that Diodorus describes as subtly worded.

116 If Demades only went because he was bribed, as Plutarch says, it strengthens the likelihood of Aeschines having sided with

Phocion. Except for Chaeronea, the charges related to breaching the Common Peace, which was essentially League business. Cf. Chapter VII 6, pp. 139–51. On Chaeronea see below on Leocrates' case.

117 On Lycurgus generally see Durrbach 1956, vii-lii; J.O. Burtt, Loeb edn of Minor Attic Orators, vol. 2, 1954–62, 2–6. On his prosecutions see Durrbach 1956, xvi, xli-xlix. It is said that he was made responsible for policing the city and arresting malefactors, and purged the city so completely that some Sophists said he was dipping his pen in blood, not ink. Plut. *Mor.* 841E. Durrbach 1956, xvi n. 2, takes this to mean a sort of political and moral censure of citizens who avoided their civic duties. But how was blood shed if not by capital condemnations? He joined forces with Demosthenes to prosecute Aristogiton, a friend of Macedon and notorious sycophant whose dossier included an unsuccessful *GP* against Hyperides' citizenship/amnesty decree in 338-7 and seven *graphai* plus two *euthynai* against Demosthenes. Lycurgus was *synēgoros* for Polyeuctus in the *GP* attacking the honours proposed for Demades in 336-5. Durrbach 1956, xlvi-xlviii; Lofberg 1917, 78–83; Hansen 1974, 36–7, 39.

118 Cf. Lyc. *Leocr.* 122-3 on the man who was stoned at Salamis for merely speaking treason against the city.

119 Despite Durrbach 1956, 27.

120 See Durrbach 1956, 33 with notes. See also p. 102.

121 *Adikēma.* Not 'son forfait' or 'his offence', despite Durrbach 1956 and J.O. Burtt (Loeb edn) ad loc. The difference is important.

122 This refers to emergency powers conferred on the Areopagus at the time and only valid for the duration of the emergency. MacDowell 1978, 191; Carawan 1985, 129–30. Cf. Durrbach 1956, 50 n. 1.

123 Cf. n. 122. Hansen 1975, Cat. No. 113, assigns Autolycus' trial to a *dikastērion*, but as he agrees that it dates to 338, the Areopagus under its emergency powers is more likely.

124 Cf. n. 122.

125 The Greek implies physical running away, not legal exile.

126 Aeschines calls it 'a certain misfortune which I hate to recall'. As a Macedonian lackey he could not have described Chaeronea as a disaster.

127 Cf. Saunders, *DemAes* 233 n. 94. V. Martin and G. de Budé, Budé edn of Aeschines 2, 82 n. 1, think it was an official mission.

128 On Lycophron as a horsebreeder see J.O. Burtt, Loeb edn of Minor Attic Orators, vol. 2, 371.

129 Lycurgus frs. 9.1–3; Hyperides frs. of *Apologia hyper Lykophronos.*

130 Dem. 18.180, 19.337; Plut. *Mor.* 840A.

131 So Durrbach 1956, 26, assigning another decree, evacuating the Boule to Piraeus, to Hyperides. Hansen 1974, No. 27, pp. 36–7, ascribes everything to Hyperides.

VI FOURTH-CENTURY ATHENS: *ASEBEIA*, THE WILLING WORK-HORSE

1 But see note 49.
2 See Chapters IV 2 and V 3.
3 Or 'not cultivating', on which see Rudhardt 1960, 91–2. The distinction may be important: not cultivating is perceivable, not believing has to be inferred.
4 For an account of the controversy see Derenne 1930, 139–47.
5 This point is well made by Ostwald 1986, 534–5.
6 See n. 49.
7 The quasi-legislative function, defining the crime by describing it in the indictment, applies primarily to *eisangelia* in one of its modes, namely offences for which no law existed. Cf. Meier-Schömann 1824, 260–71; MacDowell 1978, 184. The view of Lipsius 1905, 185 n. 26, is unclear. Rhodes 1979 does not clarify *eisangelia* as much as one might have hoped. Allen 1980, 22–32, argues in effect for quasi-legislative indictments, but he relies rather heavily on modern terminology. Nevertheless his analysis of Athenian legality is important.
8 Lipsius 1905, 363 n. 24.
9 Derenne 1930, 143–7.
10 He argues that Aspasia's case combined two jurisdictions because she was charged with both impiety and prostitution. But she was not charged with prostitution; because of her low morality she polluted temples by her presence.
11 So Allen 1980, 17–18.
12 M. Croiset, Budé edn of Plato, vol. 1, 6th edn, 1953, 139, thinks Xenophon's *Apology* marks the first stage in the formation of the legend. Xenophon is partially rehabilitated by L.E. Navia, in E. Kelly (ed.), *New Essays on Socrates*, New York 1984, 47–65.
13 The tradition enshrined in Libanius and Maximus of Tyre was derived from Plato *Gorg.* 486A–B, 522 B, and has no historical value: Allen 1980, 4. See also Croiset, op. cit. (n. 12), citing Xen. *Memor.* 4.8.4, *Apol.* 3.4.
14 Derenne 1930, 73, 79; Croiset, op. cit. (n. 12) 131–8; Allen 1980, 33–6.
15 Cf. Navia, cited in n. 12.
16 Despite Allen 1980, 22–32.
17 Despite Plato *Apol.* 25D, *Euthyph.* 2B, Meletus was not young. He may have been about fifty at the time of the trial: Ostwald 1986, 543. Nor was he an ignoramus. See below.
18 Derenne 1930, 170–1.
19 T.C. Brickhouse and N.D. Smith, in E. Kelly (ed.) *New Essays on Socrates*, New York 1984, 43 n. 4.
20 Derenne 1930, 178. Allen 1980, 133 n. 8 lends it some credence.
21 Derenne 1930, 123–6.
22 Ostwald 1986, 495.

23 Ostwald 1986, 166, 168–9 n. 88, 495 and n. 141 against
   MacDowell 1962, 208–10. The latter equates Leon's apprehender
   with Andocides' accuser, but not with Socrates' accuser. Our
   notice of Socrates' allusion to the Leon arrest closes the gap.
24 On 400–399 as the date of Andocides' trial see MacDowell 1962,
   204–5.
25 Jones 1956, 99–100. See also Ostwald 1986, *passim*.
26 Lys. 6.10. The passage is noted without comment by Lipsius
   1905, 359; it is discussed by Ostwald 1986, 166, 530–1, but not
   on the lines pursued here. To Rudhardt 1960, 89, its main
   interest is its attestation of written laws of impiety. Our main
   interest at this point is in the unwritten laws. See also n. 49,
   p. 197.
27 Plut. *Alc.* 22.3. Text in translation in Chapter IV 2, p. 65.
28 Ostwald 1986, 167, realizes this.
29 On the punishments see Plut. *Alc.* 22.4 One assumes that a
   vote on sentence counted as a *psēphisma*. In Alcibiades' case
   there may have been a special need for an enabling statute in
   the form of a *psēphisma* because of the inclusion of curses,
   which may have been an innovation in the secular jurisdictional
   sphere. Ostwald, 168, observes that if Alcibiades was tried by
   the Assembly its verdict was indistinguishable from a vote. A
   similar position obtained at Rome. See J.L. Strachan-Davidson
   and Ch. Brecht, cited by R.A. Bauman, *ANRW* II 13, 108 n. 11.
30 MacDowell 1962, 10–11.
31 R.A. Bauman, *Lawyers in Roman Republican Politics*, Munich 1983,
   2, 48 n. 203, 72.
32 Non-priestly *exēgētes* drawn from the noble families (Eupatrids)
   as a whole were known. Jones 1956, 99; MacDowell 1978,
   192–3. But they are far from prominent.
33 Jones 1956, 100.
34 MacDowell 1962, 82; Ostwald 1986, 166, 530.
35 The Sophist Polycrates who wrote an *Accusation of Socrates* in *c.*
   393 and had it spoken by Anytus – on which see Derenne 1930,
   180–1, Allen 1980, 18, 34 – does not threaten the role here
   postulated for Meletus. Allen 1980, 14, does not expressly call
   him a jurist when he describes the indictment as distinguished
   by its lawyerly cunning, but the implication is there.
36 For his data see Derenne 1930, 130–1.
37 Derenne 1930, 126.
38 ibid., 128.
39 ibid.
40 The label is not always favoured by scholars. Thus G.E.M. de
   Ste Croix, *The Class Struggle in the Ancient Greek World*, London
   1983, 71–2, concedes that 'middle class' is the usual rendering
   of *hoi mesoi*, whom Aristotle considered the best element in a
   city's government, but he refuses to use it. Also, he does not
   identify two groups within the 'Haves', namely, the old
   aristocracy and the upwardly mobile; his only division is into

the upper classes (the propertied) and the lower classes (the non-propertied). Even Solon did better than that. Readers who object to 'middle class' are requested to substitute *hoi mesoi* when reading what follows.

41 The exposition offered here is suggested by the analysis of Derenne 1930, 132-9. But he does not see it as a concerted move by a number of groups in coalition.

42 Derenne 1930, 135.

43 Cleon's classic statement of the middle-class attitude to clever people (Thuc. 3.37) could have been written by Anytus.

44 Derenne 1930, 135.

45 Cf. Perhaps M. Croiset, Budé edn of Plato's *Apology*, 124. Cf. also Lycurgus' description of Leocrates' cowardice as a threat to the democracy: Lyc. *Leocr.* 147.

46 See e.g. Allen 1980, 22-32.

47 But see below on the possible political background to Andocides' case.

48 Other pupils of Socrates like Charmides, also a member of the Thirty, and perhaps Alcibiades, can be tarred with the same brush as Critias. Cf. Derenne 1930, 137; Allen 1980, 18-19. But Critias was the main cause of complaint: Aesch. 1.173.

49 Ostwald 1986, 536, dates the introduction of the *graphē asebeias* to 403-2. This depends on the first trial for *asebeia* after 415 being that of Archippus at the instance of Andocides in 403: Lys. 6.11-12. But MacDowell 1978, 199-200, thinks the *graphē asebeias* was also the normal process for impiety in the fifth century; *eisangelia* will have been used for serious cases of impiety, but minor infractions could not be allowed to take up the time of the Boule and the Ecclesia. But no fifth-century uses of the *graphē asebeias* are known. On the theory of a comprehensive *asebeia* law (before 403-2) see Derenne 1930, 217-36; Rudhardt 1960, 91 and *passim*. Ostwald 1986, 536 doubts whether there was ever a comprehensive statutory formulation. I do not share his doubts, although I also do not agree with Derenne and Rudhardt that the crime was always charged under a *nomos*. In order to establish that, one has to do more than close one's eyes to the statement attributed to Pericles (n. 26 above). Although I posit 400-399 as the date of a comprehensive statute, I do not entirely exclude the possibility that a law of that year supplemented an earlier law dating to 403-2. But prior to 403-2 anything other than Diopeithes' *psēphisma* is an act of faith. Whether that *psēphisma* survived independently after 403-399 is a moot point; it may have been absorbed into the comprehensive ordinance.

50 Harrison 1971, 134; Allen 1980, 26.

51 MacDowell 1962, 3-4. See also p. 109.

52 ibid., 3-6.

53 ibid., 11-15. 'Banal' is my adjective, not MacDowell's.

54 ibid., 174.

55 Derenne 1930, 123–6.
56 On the definition of *asebeia* in Arist. *On Virtues and Vices* 7.2 see Chapter VI 5, pp. 126–7.
57 Cf.Bonner and Smith 1938, 1.259; H. Gärtner, *Kl.P.* 5.358.
58 Sources: Dem. 59.117; Galen *Protreptikos* 10; Athen. 590E. The *terminus post quem* for the case is 335, when Alexander destroyed Thebes; the *terminus ante quem* is 322, when Hyperides was put to death.
59 Plut. *Mor.* 849E; Diog. Laert. 4.7; Athen. 583B, listing the going rates.
60 Lipsius 1905, 359 n. 2 prefers Euthias as the accuser. But Anaximenes probably wrote Euthias' speech. On Anaximenes' political stance see K. Stiewe, *Kl.P.* 1.340.
61 Joseph. *C. Apion* 2.267; Dem. 18.259–60, 19.199, 249, 281, on which see Rudhardt 1960, 92–3.
62 D.O. Edzard, *Kl.P.* 4. 133–4.
63 Lipsius 1905, 365, citing Dem. 19.281, Plato 909B , 933D.
64 Dem. 25.79–80; Harpocr. s.v. Theoris.
65 MacDowell 1978, 197.
66 See Chapter II 4, p. 25.
67 Meier–Schömann 1824, 312 n. 59.
68 I here follow Derenne 1930, 186–7. The sequence in the text would not stand up if Tarn 1950, 2.370–3, correctly makes the return of the exiles the sole reason for which Alexander wanted divine honours. But Derenne's sequence is more cogent. The essence of Tarn's theory can however be preserved by making the pre-Olympic request for honours a kite which was flown with a view to the imminent exiles issue. But Hammond 1981, 253, denies that the honours had any political purpose.
69 Despite dismissals of Aelian's assertion that Alexander was made a thirteenth god (Habicht 1970, 29 and n. 4), I see no good reason why that should not be how it was done. Aelian had no precedents on which to invent a thirteenth godhead, but he did have a report of Demades' trial which we do not have.
70 Derenne 1930, 188. Cf. Habicht 1970, 219–20.
71 Plut. *Phoc.* 26.2. Three times according to Diod. 18.18, twice according to Suidas s.v. Demades.
72 Hansen 1974, 41.
73 Derenne 1930, 187–8, avoids the Harpalus case, perhaps wisely. Thalheim, *RE* 4.2704, refers to it and to the *asebeia* case but does not try to link the two. Recent works refer to Harpalus but avoid the *asebeia*, e.g. Hammond 1981, 254.
74 Demophilus is the accuser in Athen. 696A–B and Favorinus *ap.* Diog. Laert. 5.5. Eurymedon the Eleusinian Hierophant is Diogenes' own choice, but Athenaeus makes him an associate. On the date see Derenne 1930, 194–7.
75 The hymn is recorded in Diog. Laert. 5.7–8, Athen. 696B–D. Cf. Derenne 1930, 192.

76 Eusebius *Praep. Evangelica* 15.2.8.

77 Cf. n. 74.

78 Diog. Laert. 5.5, 10; Ael. *V.H.* 3.36. Cf. Derenne 1930, 193; H. Dörrie, *Kl.P.* 1.583; A. Edel, *Aristotle and his philosophy*, Chapel Hill 1982, 26.

79 Despite Derenne 1930, 197-8.

80 Derenne 1930, 190-1.

81 Some postulate a wider range, over 319-15. See O. Regenbogen, *RE* Supp. 7 (1940), 1360; W. Pötscher, *Kl.P.* 5.720. But Derenne 1930, 201, argues well for 317-315.

82 On Demetrius see especially Ferguson 1911a, ch. 2; it has not been superseded. See also O. Hiltbrunner, *Kl.P.* 1.1468-9.

83 Ferguson 1911a, 40, 43, 60. More fully developed in Ferguson 1911b.

84 It was of special interest to Theophrastus as a metic. He was born at Eresos on Lesbos under the name of Tyrtamus in *c.* 370. Aristotle gave him the name of Theophrastus to mark his divine gift of words: Diog. Laert. 5.38. On his status cf. Ferguson 1911a, 60.

85 Syncellus *sub* 316-15; Ael. *V.H.* 3.17.

86 Suidas s.v. Demades says that he put an end to the *dikastēria* and the rhetorical contests. The reference is to Demades' disfranchisement of citizens who possessed less than 2,000 drachmae: Diod. 18.18.4-5.

87 His poor showing before the Areopagus is in some sense a confirmation of his juristic credentials. The Roman jurists were mostly ineffective in court, and often hostile to rhetorical excesses. Bauman, *Lawyers in Roman Republican Politics*, Munich 1983, 341-51, 315-16; *Lawyers in Roman Transitional Politics*, Munich 1985, 15-24.

88 On this aspect of Theophrastus' work see Ferguson 1911a, 43; 1911b, 270-1. See also Szegedy-Maszak 1981, *passim*.

89 Cf. Ferguson 1911b, 269-70.

90 On Theophrastus' use of the comparative method see Szegedy-Maszak 1981, 1-13.

91 On Solon's law see the Roman jurist Gaius, *Dig.*47.22.4. The official character of Theophrastus' school was due to Demetrius, who secured official permission for the association headed by Theophrastus to purchase a garden in which to erect buildings for academic purposes and a shrine of the Muses, thus making the circle of students both a religious club and a legally endowed institution. Its lifelong head disposed of its property by will to his successor. Thus Ferguson 1911a, 60-1, summarizing findings of Wilamowitz.

92 Ferguson 1911a, 106-7.

93 In any case as a metic Theophrastus could not have brought the action himself.

94 Ferguson 1911a, 106-7.

95 See fragment F2 in Szegedy-Maszak 1981, 19-22: Caecilius (first

century BC) made *eisangelia* the process for new and unwritten offences. But Theophrastus said in *Nomoi* Book IV that *eisangelia* was used for specific, statutory crimes – *katalysis tou dēmou*, various acts of *prodosia*, and being bribed to offer bad advice. Caecilius the rhetorician was not restrained by any respect for legal norms; Theophrastus the jurist was. Szegedy-Maszak 1981, 20–2, thinks Theophrastus cited the actual text of the *eisangelia* law, and reconciles the differences between his version and that of Hyperides, 3.7–9. But does one have to choose between Caecilius and Theophrastus, as Szegedy-Maszak, following Hansen 1975, 12–20, rather than MacDowell 1978, 183–5, seeks to do? It seems to me that the statute was as stated by Theophrastus and Hyperides. But by Caecilius' day it had become so overloaded with interpretations that it seemed to cover anything and everything. Without going into the vexed question of whether the Nomophylakes instituted by Demetrius had originated under Ephialtes (Bonner and Smith 1938, 1.262–3, Rhodes 1981, 315), it is fair to say that Demetrius' officials were intended to inhibit fanciful extensions of the *nomoi* and were thus one of the measures that would have been urged on Demetrius by Theophrastus.

96 Stobaeus *Serm.* 481, 439, *Flor.* 2.31.31.
97 On Demetrius' sumptuary laws and creation of Gynaikonomoi (Regulators of Women) see Ferguson 1911a, 41–7, 1911b, 268–9. Theophrastus' sentiments are made clear by his statement that women should be good economists, not politicians. Stob. *Serm.* 481.
98 See Chapter VI 3, p. 117.
99 On his strait-laced reaction to a remark of Theodorus see below.
100 Pötscher, *Kl.P.* 5.720.
101 Cf. Liddell and Scott, sv. *anasyromai*.
102 Derenne 1930, 205–6
103 On his lack of belief see Derenne 1930, 202–4.
104 ibid., 213.
105 On Theophrastus' authorship cf. the remarks of H. Rackham, Loeb edn of Aristotle, *Ath. Pol. et al.*, rev. edn 1952, 485: 'The descriptive treatment of the virtues and vices . . . links the work with the *Characters* of Theophrastus, and seems to have been customary in the Peripatetic School from his time onward.'

VII ALEXANDER IN ASIA

1 R. Taubenschlag, *The law of Greco–Roman Egypt in the light of the papyri: 332 BC–640 AD*, 2nd edn, Warsaw 1955, repr. Milan 1972, 473–5, 477. His earlier work, *Das Strafrecht im Rechte der Papyri*, Leipzig 1916, repr. Aalen 1972, prints papyrological

texts not reproduced in the later work but is otherwise identical as far as treason is concerned.

2   In the sphere of treason nothing significant is added to Taubenschlag by such recent works as H.J. Wolff, *Das Justizwesen der Ptolemäer*, Munich 1962; E. Seidl, *Ptolemäische Rechtsgeschichte*, 2nd edn, 1962; or J. Modrzejewski, *Zeitschr. Savigny-Stiftung f. Rechtsgesch.*, Rom. Abt., 80 (1963), 42–82. The dearth of information was noted long ago by Bouché-Leclercq 1903, 4.190–5. On treason under the Seleucids see E. Bikerman, *Institutions des Séleucides*, Paris 1938, 207–10.

3   Derenne 1930, 264–6.

4   Habicht 1970, 29–36 argues, in opposition to Tarn 1950, 2.371, that Athens' recognition of the new god included a cult – temple, altar and statue. The description of Hephaestion's hero status as *theos paredros* (Diod. 17.115.6, Lucian *Cal. non. tem. cred.* 17) is seen as a juristic metaphor pointing to the higher godhead of Alexander himself. Habicht's detection of legal language is most interesting, for we then have a new god created by statute (cf. Demades' *psēphisma* – VI 4), defined in legal terms and defended by legal process. That the sycophants failed, as far as we know, to capitalize on this can only be due to the brevity of Alexander's tenure of his Athenian godhead.

5   On this see Hammond and Griffith 1979, 152. See also below.

6   E.g. Arrian 3.26.1,2,4; 4.14.2; Plut. *Alex.* 49.4; Diod. 17.79.1,2, 80.1; Strabo 15.2.10. Cf. Curt. 6.7.6, 8.6.12.

7   Curt. 6.7.24; 6.9.4, 17; 8.6.23; 8.8.4.

8   For the sort of thing that might have been expected see Bauman 1974, 1–10, on *asebeia* in the Greek sources for the Principate.

9   See especially Chapter VII 5, p. 138, on Cleitus. Also VI 6 on Callisthenes.

10 On the controversy see Tarn 1950, 2.347–59; Préaux 1978, 1.244–5; D. Kienast, 'Alexander, Zeus und Ammon', in *ZAG* 1.309–34.

11 Koenen 1983, 149–50.

12 See Chapter VI I 6 at n. 62.

13 Sources: Arrian 3.26.1–3; Diod. 17.79.1–80.2; Plut. *Alex.* 48–9; Curt. 6.7–11; Justin 12.5.3; Strabo 15.2.10.

14 Arrian's attestation of death by being shot down with javelins is preferable to that here attested by Curtius. Cf. Hammond 1981, 181.

15 Much the same was said about Tiberius: Bauman 1974, 116. But perhaps Plutarch should be given the benefit of the doubt.

16 Berve 1926, 30–1; Hammond 1981, 41.

17 That Curtius has confused this Amyntas with Amyntas III, father of Philip II, who was worshipped as a god (Hammond 1981, 248) is possible but does not have to be assumed.

18 Arrian's attestation of the execution of Amyntas, in *Succ. Alex.* 22, does not even note a trial, let alone a charge of *asebeia*. Despite Berve 1926, 394, 395, and Carney 1975, 114, I am quite

unable to extract from Arrian *Anab.* 3.26.1 a statement to the effect that 'Philotas . . . mocked and resented Alexander's claim of divine parentage'. Philotas' specific criticisms are given by Curt. 6.9.18.

19 E.g. by Berve 1926, 393–7; Badian 1960 *passim*; Schachermeyr 1973, 266–75; Bosworth 1980, 359–63.

20 Hammond 1981, 182–3. See also Tarn 1950, 1.62–5; Hamilton 1969, 134–5.

21 In addition to Philotas, Parmenio, and Dimnus we hear of Demetrius, Peucolaus, Nicanor, Aphobetus, Iolaus, Theoxenus, Archepolis, Amyntas and his brothers: Curt. 6.7.15. Demetrius was executed at a later stage than Philotas: Hammond 1981, 182. On Amyntas and his brothers see below.

22 Cf. Hammond 1981, 182–3.

23 Arrian 3.27.1–3; Curt. 7.1.10–2.10.

24 Harrison 1971, 147–50; MacDowell 1978, 245–7; L. Schumacher, *Servus Index*, Wiesbaden 1982, *passim*.

25 Harrison 1971, ibid.; MacDowell 1978, ibid.

26 E.g. H. Berve, *RE* 18 (1949), 1564–5; Tarn 1950, 2.270–2; Badian 1960, *passim*; Bosworth 1980, 362–3.

27 Cf. Chapter II 4.

28 Curt. 6.11.20 describes the suspension as *remittere edixit*. This probably means no more than an *ad hoc* relaxation, but even if it meant repeal, the result would be the same, because the '*lex*' was probably no more than a custom (Tarn 1950, 2.270), and if the king's undefined powers included power to suspend or abolish the custom (ibid., 271 n. 2) they also included power to reinstate it.

29 Robinson 1956, 334, thinks Parmenio had been arrested for disobeying an order to march into Hyrcania and had been superseded by the three officers. That Parmenio's command would have been split up into three is likely enough, given the division of the Companions' regiment into two after the fall of Philotas (Arrian 3.27.4), but if Parmenio had been superseded some time before, what was he still doing on the premises? The solution in the text makes better sense.

30 Arrian 1.25. Cf. Curt. 7.1.5–9; Diod. 17.32.1–2; Justin 11.7.1–2.

31 Macedonian custom appears to have made a defence speech compulsory.

32 Curt. 7.1.8–9; Diod. 17.80.2

33 Hammond 1981, 184.

34 According to Diod. 17.32.1–2, the warning about the Lyncestian came not from the Persian intermediary via Parmenio, but from Alexander's mother. C.B. Welles, Loeb edn of Diodorus, 8.206 n. 1, finds this credible, but Hammond 1981, 88, does not.

35 Plut. *Alex.* 50.6, 51.3; Arrian 4.8.4.

36 The similarity with Vespasian's complaint about Helvidius Priscus (Suet. *Vesp.* 15) should not be allowed to affect Arrian's

credibility. We cannot always reject the earlier because of the later.

37 That the pronouncement of *iure interfectum* was preceded by a trial is certain. How else could the Army have reached a verdict? These conclusions may have been glimpsed by Goukowsky 1978, 1.46, but he does not exploit the idea.

38 On Callisthenes see W. Kroll, *RE* 10.1674–84; O. Regenbogen, *RE* 20.1411, 1414; W. Spoerri, *Kl.P.* 3.85–6; Hammond 1981, 198–9; Pédech 1984, 15–18.

39 Diog. Laert. 5.44; Cic. *Tusc.* 3.21, 5.25.

40 Arrian 4.9.7–8; Plut. *Alex.* 52.3–4.

41 On which see Goodenough 1928, *passim*; Tarn 1950, 2.366; Aalders, *Palingenesia* 4 (1969), 315–29; Jones 1956, 71; Préaux 1978, 1.271; Walbank, *CAH*^{2} 7.76–7.

42 Arrian 4.11. Cf. Curt. 8.5.5–19.

43 Cf. Chapter VII 5, p. 139, on Arrian 4.8.7–8.

44 Cf. Chapter VII 2, p. 129.

45 Sources: Plut. *Alex.* 55.2–5; Arrian 4.12.7–14.4; Curt. 8.6–8; Justin 12.7.1; Diog. Laert. 5.5. The silly story in Arrian 4.12.1 about Callisthenes' refusal to render *proskynēsis*, causing him to lose the right to kiss the king, does not merit any consideration.

46 Schachermeyr 1973, 393.

47 Despite Tarn 1950, 2.301. Hamilton 1969, 155, lix–lx, gives a balanced assessment of the Alexander letters.

48 Sources on the constitution of the League: Tod, *GHI* 177; Dem. 17, *On the treaty with Alexander*. Discussions: Larsen 1966, 47–65; Hammond and Griffith 1979, 623–46; Heisserer 1980, xxiii–xxvii, 9.

49 See the references in n. 4. On the undertaking see Heisserer's translation of Tod, *GHI* 177. On whether the document reflects the original constitution or a renewal by Alexander see ibid., 13–24.

50 Cf. Chapter VII 5, p. 138. Although the Macedonians' ruling in Cleitus' case was not binding on the *synedrion*, it was a persuasive precedent.

51 Hammond and Griffith 1979, 625–6, 634–9.

52 The theory of Goukowsky, 1.49–50, that the letter was written as a warning to the regent about his association with Aristotle, may identify a subsidiary purpose of the letter, but not its main purpose.

53 Despite Hammond 1981, 198; Hamilton 1969, 155. Without the interpretation in the text, 'I will punish those who sent him to me' (Plut. *Alex.* 55.4) is meaningless.

54 Cf. Berve 1926, 228–31. See also Larsen 1966, 52, 210 n. 11; Hammond and Griffith 1979, 624–40 *passim*.

55 It is fair to say, however, that this is by no means the only example of terse citation of Ptolemy by Arrian.

56 Despite Hammond 1981, 198, who thinks Ptolemy was not particularly interested in what happened to a Greek.

57 Cf. at n. 41.

58 See also the references in n. 41

59 Cf. Berve 1926, 72–4, though he infers from Aristotle's comment about Callisthenes being a good speaker but lacking common sense (Plut. *Alex*. 54.1–2) that Aristotle did not react to his death with overt hostility. Goukowksy 1978, 1.111–14 is even more sceptical. But a hostile Peripatetic tradition is widely accepted. See Robinson 1956, 326; Schachermeyr 1973, 159; Hammond 1981, 199.

60 Schachermeyr 1973, 390–3.

61 On Antipater's links with Aristotle and coolness towards Alexander see Berve 1926, 49–51; Schachermeyr 1973, 517 and n. 621.

62 On the Army/Assembly's jurisdiction in general see Hammond and Griffith 1979, 160–2. Hedicke's supplement as shown in the text is rejected by Hammond, *GRBS* 19 (1978), 341 n. 27, though he agrees that the king only acted as a prosecutor. Bosworth 1980, 361, points out that the jurisdiction was still in place under Philip V. Curtius' further statement, that in peacetime jurisdiction rested with the people rather than the Army, is rejected by Hammond and Griffith 1979, 160 n. 1, 161 and n. 1. But see Briant 1973, 286–302, 338–45 and *passim*. In any event we are not dealing with peacetime. But see Chapter VIII 3, p. 162.

63 Hammond and Griffith 1979, 158 n. 2.

64 See e.g. Bauman 1974, 159, 195–6, 180–1.

65 *Mor*. 178A, 178F (Nos. 23, 24), 179A, 179C–D.

66 Ib. 178B (No. 15). Not noticed by Hammond and Griffith 1979, 393–4 and n. 6.

67 Plut. *Mor*. 181F; *Alex*. 41.1: 'It is the fate of kings to be maligned for doing good.'

68 Berve 1926, 1.212.

69 Hammond 1981, 189–90.

70 Briant 1973, 155.

71 Athen. 12.539D–E. This and Arrian 4.7.3 make up Berve's evidence.

72 The experimental nature of the penalties under the 'liberated' jurisdictions of the senate and the emperor is well known. See e.g. Th. Mommsen, *Römisches Strafrecht*, repr. Graz 1955, 925–8 on being thrown to the lions. Was Diog. Laert. 5.5. aware of the need to find an extraordinary penalty for Callisthenes when he had him suffer that punishment?

73 On the controversy see R.A. Bauman, *ANRW* II 13 (1980), 154 n. 3.

74 A new theory as to Alexander's motives in the Callisthenes case has been propounded by D. Golan, *Athenaeum* 1988, 99–120. Alexander will have seen Callisthenes' work as a historian as an obstruction to the creation of the new heroic image that Alexander wanted to project. This is quite possible, and fits in

well with one part of the legal basis of the charges as we have posited them, namely denigration of Alexander's pretensions to divinity.

VIII FROM PERDICCAS TO POLIORCETES

1 He is sometimes referred to in modern works as 'Vizier'. He is also seen as the senior cavalry officer. The chiliarch, literally the commander of a thousand, was the Macedonian version of the important commander of the Persian king's bodyguard. Alexander first gave the title to Hephaestion, thus underlining its special importance, and after Alexander's death it was given to Perdiccas. R. Geer, Loeb Diodorus, vol. 9, 123 n. 4 thinks Alexander appointed Perdiccas, but see Arrian 7.14.10. Dr. J.L. O'Neil compares the chiliarch with the Roman praetorian prefect.
2 On what follows cf. Briant 1973, 240–56.
3 Cf. Briant 1973, 249.
4 ibid. *Perdiccam ad mortis periculum adductum*, Curt. 10.8.5, can mean either 'exposed to mortal danger' or 'exposed to a capital charge'. Justin 13.3.1 makes the infantry indignant at being excluded from the decision-making process. This is prior to the salutation of Arrhidaeus as king, but the same indignation will have been expressed later when they were excluded from the trial process initiated by Meleager in the king's name.
5 Cf. Chapter VII 6 on the mutineers at Opis.
6 *De jure* Perdiccas was regent jointly with Craterus, but *de facto* he was sole regent. R. Geer, Loeb, Diodorus, 9.15 n. 2, also dating Meleager's lieutenancy under Perdiccas to this time. See also Briant 1973, 121 n. 2. On the Asian satrapies see n. 9.
7 Diod. 18.4.7. In 18.2.3 he has Meleager commissioned by a *synedrion* of Friends, Bodyguards, and Companions to get the phalanx to obey, but instead he has himself chosen as their leader. Cf. Justin 13.3.2.
8 Briant 1973, 253.
9 More accurately Upper Phrygia, Lycia and Pamphilia. But Western Asia Minor locates his general position in the region. The other satraps, apart from Perdiccas, were Ptolemy (Egypt), Lysimachus (Thrace), Eumenes (Cappadocia and Paphlagonia) and – for a short time – Leonnatus (Hellespontine Phrygia). Macedonia itself was under Antipater and Craterus. Briant 1973, 141–3, thinks that Perdiccas deliberately devised a satrapy for Antigonus that would weaken his position.
10 Briant 1973, 145–51, though he underestimates the importance of Antigonus' refusal.
11 That Diodorus reflects the anti-Perdiccas posture of Hieronymus of Cardia is generally recognized. See Wehrli 1968, 22, 23; Briant 1973, 153.

12 Briant 1973, 153–7.
13 This is said to follow from Polyaenus' *oneidisasa*, which is said to equal *katēgorein*: Briant 1973, 261 and n. 9.
14 Briant 1973, 261–3.
15 Cf. Hammond and Griffith 1979, 154: 'The women of the royal family played no part in . . . public life.' But see Goukowsky 1978, 1.99, on the official functions performed by Eurydice. However, her functions, as also those of Olympias, are not known to have included accusing.
16 Berve 1926, 2.229.
17 She had a martial spirit, fought in the Illyrian wars and killed the enemy queen. She brought her daughter up the same way. Athen. 13.560–1; Polyaen. 8.60.
18 There is no reason to think that she had such a force with her at the confrontation with Alcetas. Polyaenus portrays her as a defenceless woman.
19 As even Briant is obliged to do despite his belief that it was only a partial Macedonian body.
20 On the coalition see Will 1979, 36–7.
21 References in Seibert 1969, 118 n. 41. Only Bouché-Leclercq 1903, 1.23, entered a caveat. See below.
22 Schwahn 1930, 263.
23 Bouché-Leclercq 1903, 1.23.
24 H. Volkmann, *RE* 23 (1959), 1610–11.
25 Seibert 1969, 119.
26 M.J. Fontana, 'Le lotte per la successione di Alessandro Magno dal 323 al 315', *Atti Acc. Sc. Lett. Art. Palermo* 18 (1957–8), 103–337. To mention only one glaring weakness, are we to suppose that Ptolemy assisted the defeat of his negotiations by appearing at the trial in order to be acquitted? Did Perdiccas think he would appear?
27 Seibert 1969, 118–20; Briant 1973, 264–8.
28 Seibert 1969, 118, 119. Briant 1973, 264, locates it after Perdiccas' arrival in Egypt.
29 Seibert 1969, 120.
30 ibid. Cf. Bouché-Leclercq 1903, 1.22.
31 Perdiccas was fighting a propaganda war on all fronts. On his use of Alexander in that regard see Goukowsky, 1978, 1.88–92.
32 Cf. Goukowsky 1978, 1.81–4.
33 Cf. Goukowsky 1978, 1.89, on the royal army's hatred of Ptolemy as a result of the theft; and ibid., 91–2, on other aspects of the theft. Seibert 1969, 110–11, 103 n. 19, tends to play down the significance of the episode; he thinks that Ptolemy gave the body proper Macedonian burial. Dr J.L. O'Neil has expressed the view that Ptolemy's claim to Egypt was not based on possession of the body but on the fact that it was spear-won land. Quite so, but it was possession of Alexander's charisma that Ptolemy wanted. In any case it is not just a question of deciding whether the body's lodgement at

Memphis instead of Siwa was permissible. The traditional burial-place of the Macedonian kings was Aegeae (Hammond and Griffith 1979, 12–13, and *passim*), and to suggest that Perdiccas only insisted on that location in order to advance his claim to the throne would beg the question.

34 Goukowsky 1978, 1.82, 83.

35 Seibert 1969, 112–14.

36 Cf. Goukowsky 1978, 1.91–2.

37 On this see Seibert 1969, 122–6; Briant 1973, 268–72.

38 Briant 1973, 264–8.

39 See Chapter VIII 4, at n. 53.

40 Sources: Arrian *Succ.* 14–15; Diod. 18.48.2–4; Plut. *Dem.* 31.3–4, *Phoc.* 30.4–6; Athen. 13.591–2. The text is the best solution to a confused tradition. Plutarch has Cassander kill Demades' son on the spot and order Demades' execution. But Diodorus has Antipater (probably a mistake for Cassander, since Antipater was in his last illness) hand them over 'to those responsible for punishments'. This seems to mean the Athenian Eleven, hence extradition, rather than a Macedonian equivalent.

41 Larsen 1966, 52–71, thinks the decree resurrected the League of Corinth. *Contra* Will, 50–1, perhaps rightly.

42 Plut. *Phoc.* 33.2–3; Diod. 18.65.6 (though anticipating the actual trial).

43 Cf. Chapter VII 6 on Alexander's *synedrion*.

44 Plut. *Phoc.* 33.5–34.1–3; Diod. 18.66.1–3; Nepos *Phoc.* 3.2.

45 As to what he had really done, see Beloch 1922, 4.1.100–1; Ferguson 1911a, 21.

46 Plut. *Phoc.* 34–8; Diod. 18.66.4–67.6; Nepos *Phoc.* 4.

47 On what follows see Beloch 1922, 4.1.107–9; Strasburger, *RE* 18.179–82; Will 1979, 51–2. Sources in Strasburger and Will (incl. Pausanias 1.25.6).

48 There can be no question of an appeal to, or retrial by, the same tribunal.

49 Briant 1973, 298–9. Beloch 1922, 4.1.109 n. 1, and Granier 1931, 87–91 and 90 n. 155, do not differentiate the two tribunals, thus leaving the whole matter up in the air.

50 W.W. Tarn, *JHS* 51 (1931), 307. *Contra* Granier 1931, 91; Briant 1973, 298.

51 Diod. 19.61.1: *parepidēmontōn*. The exact meaning is uncertain, but 'civils' (Briant 1973, 300) brings out the contrast with the soldiers clearly enough. Briant sees them as a floating population around the army, 'dans le bagage' (= 'camp-followers'). See also R.H. Simpson, *Hist.* 8 (1959), 389; K. Rosen, *Act. Class.* 10 (1967), 79.

52 He had been appointed *stratēgos* of Asia by Antipater. But Polyperchon had given a rival appointment to Eumenes. Will 1979, 52–3.

53 E.g. by Will 1979, 55: 'jugé et condamné'. Cf. Briant 1973, 301, but see ibid., n. 6.

54 Sources in Klotz, *RE* 10 (1917), 223.
55 The similarity between the decrees of 321 and 315 is noted by Briant 1973, 301. Cf. Appian *Syr*. 53, *Mith*. 8; Arrian *Succ*. 39. But Briant does not notice the one important difference between the two decrees. See below.
56 Cf. R.A. Bauman, 'The *hostis* declarations of 88 and 87 BC', *Athenaeum* 51 (1973), 270–93.
57 On the mixed assembly convened by Antigonus at Tyre see Briant 1973, 301. But some problems remain. One would not expect an assembly combining a largely mercenary army (Wehrli 1968, 43) with camp-followers to have had much of a Macedonian flavour. But of course Macedonia was no longer a country of simple soldiers.
58 Diod. 19.61.3: 'When the crowd joined in his indignation he wrote a decree.' Is this how the Army/Assembly always expressed its verdict? It would accord with a widespread practice. See J. Colin, *Les villes libres de l'Orient gréco-romain et l'envoi au supplice par acclamations populaires*, Brussels 1965.
59 On which see Will 1979, 61–5.
60 Schoch, *RE* Supp. 4.731 no. 2.
61 Will 1979, 74–5.
62 Diod. 20.45.5, 46.1–3; Plut. *Demet*. 10.1. They also have him restore the traditional constitution – *patrios politeia*. This identifies him with the democratic forces.
63 See especially Habicht 1970, 44–58.
64 Dion. Hal. *De Dinarch*, 3. Cf. *FGrH* 328 F66. The charge was *katalysis tou dēmou* . On Poliorcetes' democratic stance cf. n. 62.
65 Death sentences were only imposed on those who had fled; those who stood trial were acquitted. Dion. Hal. *De Dinarch*. 3.
66 On this league see Will 1979, 77–9, arguing that it was not a mere revival of the old league.
67 Ferguson 1911a, 121.
68 On Stratocles see Ferguson 1911a, 101–2; Fiehn, *RE* 28.269–71; Berve 1926, 2.364. He first became known when he headed the ten official accusers in the Harpalus affair. Plutarch is critical of him, but his fulsome flattery stood him in good stead. He was still serving his master loyally in 303–2 when he put through a decree permitting Poliorcetes to be admitted to the Eleusinian Mysteries without any preliminary initiation: Plut. *Demet*. 26.2. He needed that to round off his status as *nomos empsychos*. That Stratocles organized the trials of Demetrius of Phalerum and his friends, and that he devised the penal differential (n. 65) is probable.
69 Plut. *Demet*. 12.1 has some honours proposed by men other than Stratocles but does not name them. Habicht 1970, 51, thinks it was Dromocleides.
70 See Chapter VI 4, p. 68.
71 Fergson 1911a, 126 n. 1, 276–7, thinks it may have been as late as *c*. 200, when Athens had to take up a position on the confrontation between Macedon and Rome. Préaux 1978,

1.246–7, takes Plut. *Demet.* 46.1 to imply abolition in 289–8 when Athens revolted. But it is possible that the decrees had a chequered career.

72 Ferguson 1911a, 123.

73 Cf. Chapter VII 6, p. 147.

74 See Chapter VI 4, p. 119.

75 See n. 71. I do not see how a man (or a god) who had been declared tantamount to an enemy could have remained in full possession of his honours. At the very least the operation of the honours must have been suspended.

76 Habicht 1970, 50–5.

77 So Ferguson 1911a, 143.

78 See Chapter V 3, p. 89.

79 Cf. Habicht 1970, 215 and n. 75.

80 Cf. perhaps Ferguson 1912, especially 31–7, though he makes the first phase (Alexander himself) more decisive than is done here. For a useful review of the texts see Walbank, CAH^2 7.75–100.

81 Specialists in the period tend to avoid this question. The only reference that I have been able to find is by Kaerst, *RE* 4 (1901), 2784. He says that Poliorcetes did not alter the constitutions of Greek cities or interfere in their internal structure; their principal obligation was to pay a sort of annual tribute. Cf. Diog. Laert. 2.140. One would need to know much more about Poliorcetes' Greek League to deal with the problem properly.

SELECT BIBLIOGRAPHY

Works not frequently cited and, with a few exceptions, ancient sources and articles in standard reference works are sufficiently identified in the notes and in the abbreviations and are not listed here.

Allen, R.E. (1980) *Socrates and Legal Obligation*, Minneapolis.
Andrewes, A. (1974) 'The Arginusai Trial', *Phoenix* 28, 112–22.
Badian, E. (1960) 'The death of Parmenio', *Transactions of the American Philological Association*, 91, 324–38.
Balogh, E. (1943) *Political Refugees in Ancient Greece*, Johannesburg.
Barkan, I.(1935) *Capital Punishment in Ancient Athens*, Diss., Chicago, repr. New York 1979.
Bauman, R.A. (1967) *The Crimen Maiestatis in the Roman Republic and Augustan Principate*, Johannesburg, repr. 1970.
—— (1968) 'A Message for Amphipolis', *Acta Classica* 11, 170–81.
—— (1974) *Impietas in Principem*, Munich 1974.
—— (1986a) 'Comparative Law in Ancient Times', in *Law and Australian Legal Thinking in the 1980s: A collection of the Australian contributions to the 12th International Congress of Comparative Law*, Sydney/Melbourne, 99–114.
—— (1986b) '*Odi et Amo*: Some Remarks on Roman Attitudes to Greek Law', *Ancient Society* 16, 8–12.
—— (1986c) 'Rome and the Greeks: Apropos of a recent work', *Acta Classica* 29, 85–97.
Beloch, K.J. (1922) *Griechische Geschichte*, vols. 3 and 4, 2nd edn, Berlin 1922–7.
Berneker, E. (1956) 'Hochverrat und Landesverrat im griechischen Recht', *EOS* 48, 105–37.
Berneker, E., ed. (1968) *Zur griechischen Rechtsgeschichte*, Darmstadt.
Berve, H. (1926) *Das Alexanderreich auf prosopographischer Grundlage*, repr. New York 1973.
Bonner, R.J. (1927) *Lawyers and Litigants in Ancient Athens*, repr. New York 1969.
Bonner, R.J., and Smith, G. (1938) *The Administration of Justice from Homer to Aristole*, 2 vols, repr. New York 1970.

210

Bosworth, A.B. (1980) *A historical commentary on Arrian's History of Alexander*, vol. 1, Oxford.

Bouché-Leclercq, A. (1903) *Histoire des Lagides*, 4 vols, Paris 1903-7.

Briant, P. (1973) *Antigone le Borgne*, Paris.

Bruce, I.A.F. (1966) 'Athenian Embassies in the Early Fourth Century BC', *Historia* 15, 272-81.

Burn, A.R. (1960) *Pericles and Athens*, London.

—— (1962) *Persia and the Greeks*, London.

Busolt, G., and Swoboda, H. (1926) *Griechische Staatskunde*, 3rd edn, Part Two, Munich.

Calhoun, G.M. (1927) *The Growth of Criminal Law in Ancient Greece*, repr. Greenwood 1977.

—— (1944) *Introduction to Greek Legal Science*, Oxford.

Carawan, E.M. (1985) 'Apophasis and Eisangelia: The role of the Areopagus in Athenian political trials', *Greek, Roman & Byzantine Studies* 26, 115-40.

—— (1987) 'Eisangelia and Euthyna: The Trials of Miltiades, Theimstocles and Cimon', ibid., 28, 167-208.

Carney, E.D. (1975) *Alexander the Great and the Macedonian Aristocracy*, Diss., Duke University.

Cawkwell, G.L. (1970) 'The fall of Themistocles', in *Auckland Classical Essays*, Auckland, 39-58.

Clinton, K. (1982) 'The nature of the late fifth-century revision of the Athenian law code', in *Studies in Attic Epigraphy, History and Topography*, Princeton, 27-37.

Cloché, P. (1960) 'Les hommes politiques et la justice populaire dans l'Athènes du IVe siècle', *Historia* 9, 80-95.

Connor, W.R. (1971) *The New Politicians of Fifth Century Athens*, Princeton.

Croiset, M. (1909) *Aristophanes and the Political Parties at Athens*, tr. J. Loeb, London, repr. New York 1973.

Derenne, E. (1930) *Les procès d'impiété intentés aux philosophes à Athènes au Vme et au IVme siècles avant J.-C.'*, repr. New York 1976.

Dorjahn, A.P. (1946) *Political Forgiveness in Old Athens: The Amnesty of 403 BC*, Evanston.

Dover, K.J. (1976) 'The freedom of the intellectual in Greek society', *Talanta* 7, 24-54.

Durrbach, F. (1956) *Lycurgue contre Léocrate*, 2nd edn, Paris: Budé.

Ehrenberg, V. (1973) *From Solon to Socrates*, 2nd edn, London.

Ferguson, W.S. (1911a) *Hellenistic Athens*, London.

—— (1911b) 'The laws of Demetrius of Phalerum and their Guardians', *Klio* 11, 265-77.

—— (1912) 'Legalized absolutism en route from Greece to Rome', *American Historical Review* 18 (1912-13), 29-47.

Frost, F.J. (1964) 'Pericles, Thucydides, Son of Melesias, and Athenian Politics before the War', in *PSZ* 271-89 (= *Historia* 13, 1964, 385-99).

—— (1980) *Plutarch's Themistocles*, Princeton.
Garner, R. (1987) *Law and Society in Classical Athens*, London: Croom Helm.
Goodenough, E.R. (1928) 'The political philosophy of Hellenistic kingship', *Yale Classical Studies* 1, 55–102.
Goukowsky, P. (1978) *Essai sur les origines du mythe d'Alexandre*, 2 vols, Nancy 1978–81.
Granier, F. (1931) *Die makedonische Heeresversammlung*, Munich.
Grundy, G.B. (1948) *Thucydides and the history of his age*, vol. 1, 2nd edn, Oxford.
Habicht, Ch. (1970) *Gottmenschentum und griechische Städte*, 2nd edn, Munich.
Hamilton, J.R. (1969) *Plutarch: Alexander. A Commentary*, Oxford.
Hammond, N.G.L. (1981) *Alexander the Great*, London.
—— (1986) *A History of Greece to 322 BC*, 3rd edn, Oxford.
Hammond, N.G.L. and Griffith, G.T. (1979) *A History of Macedonia*, vol. 2, Oxford.
Hammond, N.G.L. and Walbank, F.W. (1988) *A History of Macedonia*, vol. 3, Oxford.
Hansen, M.H. (1974) *The Sovereignty of the People's Court in Athens*, Odense.
—— (1975) *Eisangelia*, Odense.
—— (1987) *The Athenian Assembly in the Age of Demosthenes*, Blackwell.
Harrison, A.R.W. (1971) *The Law of Athens: Procedure*, Oxford.
Heckel, W. (1977) 'The Conspiracy against Philotas', *Phoenix* 31, 9–21.
Heisserer, A.J. (1980) *Alexander the Great and the Greeks: The epigraphic evidence*, Norman.
Hignett, C.H. (1952) *A History of the Athenian Constitution*, Oxford, repr. 1962.
Jones, J.W. (1956) *The Law and Legal Theory of the Greeks*, Oxford.
Kahrstedt, U. (1934) 'Themistokles', *RE* 5A, 1693–5.
Kienast, D. (1953) 'Der innenpolitische Kampf in Athen von der Rückkehr des Thukydides bis zu Perikles' Tod', *Gymnasium* 60, 265–83.
Koenen, L. (1983) 'Die Adaptation ägyptischer Königsideologie am Ptolemaerhof', in 'Egypt in the Hellenistic World', *Studia Hellenistica* 27, 143–90.
Krentz, P. (1982) *The Thirty at Athens*, Cornell.
Larsen, J.A.O. (1966) *Representative Government in Greek and Roman History*, Berkeley.
Lendle, O. (1955) 'Philochorus über die Prozess des Phidias', *Hermes* 83, 284–303.
Lipsius, J.H. (1905) *Das attische Recht und Rechtsverfahren*, 1905–15, repr. Hildesheim 1966.
Lofberg, J.O. (1917) *Sycophancy in Athens*, Diss., Chicago.
Luban, D. (1987) 'Some Greek Trials: Order and Justice in Homer, Hesiod, Aeschylus and Plato', *Tennessee Law Review* 54, 280–325.

MacDowell, D.M. (1962) *Andokides: On the Mysteries*, Oxford.
—— (1971) *Aristophanes: Wasps*, Oxford.
—— (1978) *The Law in Classical Athens*, London.
—— (1986) *Spartan Law*, Edinburgh.
Mansfeld, J. (1979) 'The chronology of Anaxagoras' Athenian period and the date of his trial', *Mnemosyne* 32, 39–69, 33 (1980), 17–95.
Mathieu, G. (1956) *Démosthène: Plaidoyers Politiques*, vol. 3, 2nd edn, Paris: Budé.
Meier, M.H.E. and Schömann, G.F. (1824) *Der attische Process*, repr. New York 1979.
Mosley, D.J. (1973) 'Envoys and diplomacy in Ancient Greece', *Historia Einzelschr.* 22.
O'Neil, J.L. (1988) 'The fourth century revival of the Council of the Areopagus', *Classicum* 14, 3–7.
Ostwald, M. (1986) *From Popular Sovereignty to the Sovereignty of Law*, Berkeley.
Pédech, P. (1984) *Historiens Compagnons d'Alexandre*, Paris.
Piccirilli, L. (1987) *Temistocle Aristide Cimone Tucidide di Melesia fra politica e propaganda*, Genoa.
Podlecki, A.J. (1975) *The Life of Themistocles*, Montreal.
Préaux, C. (1978) *Le Monde Hellénistique*, 2 vols, Paris.
Quass, F. (1971) *Nomos und Psephisma*, Munich.
Rhodes, P.J. (1979) 'Eisangelia in Athens', *Journal of Hellenic Studies* 99, 102–14.
—— (1981) *A Commentary on the Aristotelian Athenaion Politeia*, Oxford.
Richardson, R.B. (1889) *Aeschines against Ctesiphon*, Boston, repr. Arno 1979.
Roberts, J.T. (1982) *Accountability in Athenian Government*, Madison.
Robertson, H.G. (1924) *The Administration of Justice in the Athenian Empire*, Toronto.
Robinson, C.A. (1956) 'The extraordinary ideas of Alexander the Great', *American Historical Review* 62 (1956–7), 326–44.
Rudhardt, J. (1960) 'La définition du délit d'impiété d'après la législation attique', *Museum Helveticum*, 17, 87–105.
Schachermeyr, F. (1973) *Alexander der Grosse*, Vienna.
Schwahn, W. (1930) 'Die Nachfolge Alexanders des Grossen', *Klio* 23 (1930), 211–38, 24 (1931), 306–32.
Sealey, R. (1987) *The Athenian Republic: Democracy or the Rule of Law?*, Pennsylvania.
Seibert, J. (1969) *Untersuchungen zur Geschichte Ptolemaios' I*, Munich.
Sinclair, R.K. (1988) *Democracy and Participation in Athens*, Cambridge.
Sordi, M, ed. (1981) *Religione e Politica nel Mondo Antico*, Milan.
Starkie, W.J.M. (1909) *The Acharnians of Aristophanes*, London, repr. New York 1979.
Stone, I.F. (1988) *The Trial of Socrates*, Boston.
Swoboda, H. (1893) 'Ueber den Process des Perikles', *Hermes 28*, 536–78.
Szegedy-Maszak, A. (1981) *The Nomoi of Theophrastus*, New York.

213

Tarn, W.W. (1950) *Alexander the Great*, 2 vols, Cambridge.

Thonissen, J.-J. (1875) *Le droit pénal de la République Athénienne*, Brussels/Paris.

von Wedel, W. (1971) 'Die politischen Prozesse im Athen des fünften Jahrhunderts', *Bulletino dell'Istituto di Diritto Romano*, 3rd ser., 13, 107–88.

Wehrli, C. (1968) *Antigone et Demetrios*, Geneva.

Will, E. (1979) *Histoire politique du monde hellénistique (323–30 av. J.-C)*, 2nd edn, vol. 1, Paris.

INDEX

215

ta theia 181 n.38
Teisamenus 79–80
Theano 65
Themistocles 2, 12–13, 15–16, 18,
  21, 26, 47, 50, 69, 81;
  fictitious first trial of 24;
  ostracism of 22–3, 26; trial of,
  22–8, 51
Theocrines 83
Theodorus, trial of 125–6
Theogenes, trial of 116
Theophrastus 9–10, 23, 39, 65,
  81, 122–4, 140, 169, 175 n.27,
  199 n.84; character of 124–5,
  200 nn. 97, 105; legal science
  of 9–10, 35; Nomoi of 9–10,
  122, 175 n.29, 199 n.95; trial
  of 10, 122–3
Theoris, trial of 117
Theramenes 69–70, 73–5; trial of
  79
thesmia 9
thesmothetae 4–5, 9, 13, 77
Thessalus 64–5
Timarchus 83
'things not good for Greece' 23,
  25, 51, 118
Thirty 48, 67, 78, 80, 86, 108,
  114; abolition of dikastēria by
  78; executions by 79;
  restoration of Areopagus'
  powers by 48, 78–80; trials
  under 78–9
Thrasybulus 68–9, 74, 84, 190
  n.55
Thrasyllus 69, 74; see also
  Arginusae generals, trial of
Three Thousand 79
Thucydides (historian), trial of
  50, 57–60, 82
Thucydides (son of Melesias) 32,
  35–6, 40–1; not tried 60;
  ostracized 36
Thurii, 64, 67
Timagoras, trial of 89, 169
Timarchus (accuser) 91
Timarchus (inspector) 83
Timocreon, trial of 24–5
Timomachus 83

Timotheus, trial of 82
torture 91, 95, 122, 132–3; 141–3,
  161, 186 n.12
treason, 2–3, 5–6, 34, 64, 96,
  101, 116, 128, 130, 146, 155,
  163, 164, 165, 194 n.118; links
  with impiety of 61, 64–5, 110,
  113, 126, 130, 149, 155, 168,
  186, 186 n.12
Trials see Aeschines; Aeschylus;
  Alcibiades; Alexander the
  Lyncestian; Amyntas (son of
  Andromenes); Amyntas (son
  of Perdiccas II); Anaxagoras;
  Andocides; Antigonus
  Monophthalmus; Antiphon
  (orator); Anytus;
  Archeptolemus; Archias;
  Archippus; Arginusae
  generals; Aristides;
  Aristophanes; Aristotle;
  Aspasia; Autolycus; Bessus;
  Bouleutai; Callias (son of
  Phaenippus); Callisthenes;
  Cassander; Cephisodotus;
  Cimon; Cleitus; Cleomedon;
  Cleophon; Cratinus;
  Ctesiphon; Cynnane; Delos
  and Athens; Demades;
  Demetrius of Phalerum;
  Demochares; Demosthenes;
  Diagoras; Epicrates; Ergocles;
  Euboulides; Eumenes;
  Euripides; Eurymedon;
  Hagonides; Harpalus;
  Hyperides; Ismenias; Laches;
  Leocrates; Leodamas;
  Leogoras; Lycurgus; Lysicles;
  Lysimachus; Melanopus;
  Meleager; Meletus; Melians;
  Miltiades; Mytilenians;
  Nicomachus (law-inscriber);
  Ninos; Olympias; Onomacles;
  Orestes; Parmenio; Perdiccas;
  Pericles; Pheidias; Philocrates
  (diplomat); Philocrates
  (purser); Philon (bandit);
  Philotas; Phocion; Phryne;
  Phrynichus (playwright);

Phrynichus (politician);
Polemon; Polyperchon;
Protagoras; Ptolemy I;
Pyrilampes; Pythodorus;
Royal Pages;
Socrates;Sophocles (general);
Sophocles' law; Sophocles
(playwright); Speusippus;
Stilpo; Themistocles;
Theocrines; Theodorus;

Theogenes; Theophrastus;
Theoris; Theramenes; Thirty;
Thucydides (historian);
Timagoras; Timarchus
(inspector); Timocreon;
Timomachus; Timotheus
Trials *in absentia* 22–3, 26, 39, 59,
64, 87, 91, 135–6, 156, 161

Xanthippus 17–18, 20, 177 n.19